Keeping it in the Family

Keeping it in the Family

Social networks and employment chance

Margaret Grieco

TAVISTOCK PUBLICATIONS
London and New York

First published in 1987 by
Tavistock Publications
11 New Fetter Lane, London EC4P 4EE

Published in the USA by
Tavistock Publications
in association with Methuen, Inc.
29 West 35th Street, New York NY 10001

Printed in Great Britain at the University Press, Cambridge

British Library Cataloguing in Publication Data
Grieco, Margaret
    Keeping it in the family: social
    networks and employment chance.
    1. Recruiting of employees –
    Social aspects – Great Britain
    I. Title
    306'.36   HF5549.5.R44

ISBN 0-422-60820-3

This book is dedicated to all those men who have walked the roads for work, who have helped others to find it and who are poorly rewarded in a society which finds four million unemployed acceptable. To my father, Hugh Hossack, and his toe rags.

Contents

Acknowledgements

I am grateful to the following for helpful comments on earlier drafts of this manuscript: Colin Bell, John Child, Dian Hosking, Ravi Kanbur, Reinhard Kreckel, Ray Loveridge, Peter McCaffrey, Kenneth Macdonald, Stephen Mugford, Clare Wells, J.C. Mitchell (my supervisor), and an unknown referee. For continuous support throughout this endeavour, I thank Professor A.H. Halsey. For enabling the transformation of my original thesis manuscript into a book, I give particular thanks to Caroline Lane and hope her faith finds sufficient reward in my execution of the task. I would also like to thank participants in seminars at Aston, Cambridge, LSE, Oxford, Warwick, and the University of the South Pacific for discussions on the ideas in this book. For moral and graphical support throughout the exercise, I am deeply indebted to Arvind and Malini Deshpande. Special thanks go to the librarians and library staff of Nuffield College, who have provided unceasing help throughout my interminable reworkings of this material. Thanks, too, to Amstrad for a timely provision of the technology which made the prospect of this ultimate rewrite endurable. This stage itself could not, however, have been reached without the skilful typing abilities of Ann Widdop and Pamela Hepworth on earlier versions of the manuscript; to them my sincerest thanks. Thanks also to Michaela Boyce for diligent and skilful proof-reading. Lastly, but most importantly, I would like to thank the workers in Corby, Peterhead, Aberdeen, and Basildon, without whose help and co-operation the interviews reported in this book could not have been conducted.

Transport Studies Unit
University of Oxford
February 1987

1
Kinship and economic life

Introduction

The theme of this book is the role of kin networks in the social organization of employment. Its object is to explore the various ways in which family relationships are relevant to the employment chances of the individual. Its major argument is that the economic chances of the individual are strongly affected by his or her membership of a particular kinship group.

In other words, against the widespread belief that modern labour markets operate on the basis of a 'universalistic-achievement orientation', the hypothesis is upheld that 'particularistic' and 'ascriptive' mechanisms continue to play an essential part in the allocation of labour power. It is argued that kinship networks operate in modern western society as both employment information systems and an employment sponsorship systems. The argument is derived from both a theoretical and an empirical base. The focus on kinship within this book is primarily in respect of its special network properties; the concern with economic life is primarily in terms of employment relations.

The rest of this chapter critically reviews the existing literature and suggests that there is good reason to suppose that kinship remains of relevance to occupational choice and functioning in modern industrial society.

Family and employment: a critical review of the literature

The central theme of this section is that the information and network mechanisms involved in employee search and in employer search mean that the family, in particular the working-class family, has the wherewithal to maintain itself in modern industrial societies and, moreover, in the employment context. The Parsonian orthodoxy is that with modernization and industrialization – and the accompanying rise of universalistic, bureaucratic hiring criteria – the role of the extended family would decline in the employment context, and indeed, the family would take on an isolated, nuclear form.[1]

My arguments run counter to this orthodoxy. Information networks are important in employment search; kin networks represent the most effective channels of information transfer and they provide employers with possibilities of social control over individual workers.[2] For these reasons, and particularly in working-class contexts, kin networks will indeed be present and be used in the employment context. Moreover, while networks determine the pattern of information transfer and employment/migration aid, these in turn strengthen ties in the network. It is not surprising, then, to find the working-class family active in the workplace, yet such a possibility is largely denied by the existing literature.

> The main trends in family life may be tentatively summarised as a decline in the close knit extended kinship network, and in the supportive function of kin, resulting in the privatisation of family life, but the persistence of loose-knit affective kinship ties as a source of identity.
>
> (Cotgrove 1978: 71)

> one of the characteristics of large scale societies is the large number of single-stranded relationships in them. The relative weakness of institutional integration in these societies is directly connected with the paucity of multi-plex relationships for there are few circumstances in which people in large scale industrial communities meet one another constantly in a variety of social settings. Instead their activities in one sphere of life are comparatively isolated from their activities in some other sphere. In social network terms the constituent links of partial networks are largely independent of one another and do not communicate.
>
> (Mitchell 1969: 48)

The two quotes above provide brief, albeit stylized, statements of the orthodoxy on kinship and friendship relations in modern industrial society – the first from a standard text in mainstream industrial sociology and the second from a standard reference in social-network analysis. The argument is that a concomitant of the later stages of industrialization and modernization, with the increasing complexity of organization that follows in their wake, is the erosion of kin linkages. In particular, the sphere of employment comes to be isolated from the sphere of family, which in turn shrinks to that of the isolated nuclear family.

The modern literature is dominated by the work of Parsons (1960, 1964) and his associates. The central thesis is that in modern industrial society the family has lost many of its traditional functions, currently taking an isolated and nuclear form. Parsons and Bales provide a statement of the basic argument as follows:

> Our suggestion is . . . that what has recently been happening to the American

family constitutes part of one of these stages in a process of differentiation. This process has involved a further step in the reduction of importance in our society of kinship units other than the nuclear family. It has also resulted in the transfer of a variety of functions from the nuclear family to other structures of the society, notably the occupationally organised sectors of it. This means that the family has become a more specialised agency than before, probably more specialised than it has been in any previously known society. . . . Over much of the world and of history a very large proportion of the world's ordinary work is and has been performed in the context of kinship units. Occupational organisation in the modern sense is the sociological antithesis of this.

(Parsons and Bales 1956: 9, 12)

The erosion of kin linkages is thus seen as functional given the perceived needs of complex industrial society. Parsons and his associates saw the extended family as inhibiting that geographical mobility necessary to the efficient working of a technologically developed society. Efficiency in the use of human resources paralleled efficiency in the use of physical resources. The efficient allocation of human resources required the minimization of the importance of the family, reserving to it only the roles of 'socialisation of the child and stabilisation of the adult personality'. Thus for Parsons the family must exist within the domestic sphere alone, producing those characteristics of use to industrial society.

British scholars in the 1950s and 1960s echoed Parsons's analysis.[3] Anderson, for example, while conceding that during the early stages of industrialization the family could have had an important role, argues for a declining role in employment in later stages:

In sum, then, in industrialising England men continued to be able and indeed possibly became more able to perform functions for their kin which were to these kin a considerable economic advantage. They could moreover do this at a minimum cost to themselves except sometimes in the rather short run. The twentieth century by contrast reduced the control of kin over jobs.

(Anderson 1971b: 90)

Turner continues the argument as follows:

In small scale societies with comparatively simple material cultures, kinship can easily supply the dominant organising principle for social life. Allocation of social positions can be made on the basis of an individual's position in the kinship system. But the likelihood of a reasonable fit between the patterning of kinship and economic, political, religious or leisure activities decreases with the development of a more complex society. . . . When highly complex and differentiated social structures have developed kinship is only likely to provide the basic structural principle underpinning social relationships for members of certain special groups such as the British royal family, or a large family firm.

(Turner 1971: 122)

The message is thus that those families which are isolated or structurally separated from the industrial context possess familial completeness by virtue of this isolation. Or to put it differently, those families which are subject to employment relations lose the strength of kin ties.

At the theoretical level, underlying the above hypothesis is the assumption that families in the employment context are unable to enforce their own boundaries. Other authors explicitly make the statement that kin do not have the ability to select kin as workmates – kinship is seen as irrelevant to occupational choice and location.[4] The market operates efficiently, allocating individuals to occupational locations on the basis of achievement and not ascription, with the result that family members are separated from one another in the sphere of economic activity.

Turner's sociological argument (Turner 1971) strongly parallels Mitchell's social-networks argument (Mitchell 1969). Complex societies lead to the development of 'single-stranded' relationships, with little overlap between different spheres of existence. However, in social-network terms, even if the bulk of relationships were single stranded, this could not of itself be taken as evidence of the erosion of community; provided that multi-stranded relationships still held place as an organizing principle in certain crucial spheres of social interaction, community may still persist.[5] In this book I suggest that the latter is indeed the case. Primary and secondary evidence is put forward on the persistence and extensiveness of multi-stranded relationships in the linkage between kinship, friendship, and employment. A conventional division within the current orthodoxy in both industrial sociology and social-network theory is that between kinship and friendship on the one hand and work on the other. My evidence challenges such a division and examines the ways in which employers' recruitment practices may serve to generate precisely those sets of social linkages which are generally labelled 'community', and so runs counter to the current position prevailing in the literature.

Evidence on kin-connected recruitment channels

A major source of evidence on kin-connected recruitment channels are studies of migrant labour and patterns of job placement. This evidence is surveyed in Chapter 4. The task of this section is to present evidence on the role of 'family and friends' in employment allocation in the context of non-migrant, local labour markets. Much of the existing evidence does not distinguish between 'family' and 'friends' and I will initially consider these two categories as one. However, there are some case studies which do give direct information on the role of family and kin, and these will also be commented on – in addition, my own case study evidence also strengthens the claim that kin contacts are important in the employment context.

An early source of evidence on the use by employers and employees of kin and friendship contacts is that provided by the classical

American labour-market studies (Reynolds 1951; Kerr 1954; Myers and Shultz 1951; Parnes 1954; Lester 1954; Rees 1966; Sheppard and Belitsky 1966). These studies find the predominance of 'informal' mechanisms such as personal contacts through family and friends, or by 'direct application' to an employer, as opposed to 'formal' methods such as advertisements or employment agencies. To quote Rees:

> We may divide information networks in the labour market into two groups: formal and informal. The formal networks include the state employment services, private fee-charging employment agencies, newspaper advertisements, Union hiring halls, and school or college placement bureaus. The informal sources include referrals from employees, other employers, and miscellaneous sources and walk ins or hiring at the gate. ... In the four white-collar occupations under study, informal sources account for about half of all hires; in the eight blue-collar occupations, informal services account for more than four-fifths of all hires.
>
> (Rees 1966: 559)

The other studies produce findings in a similar vein. Granovetter summarizes these findings as follows:

> The blue collar studies carried out from 1930s to the present in American cities of widely varying size, economic base, and market conditions, have been remarkably similar in their conclusions. All showed that formal mechanisms of job allocation rarely accounted for more than 20 per cent of placements. By contrast, 60–90 per cent of jobs were found informally, principally through friends and relatives but also by direct application.
>
> (Granovetter 1974: 5)

Studies of white-collar workers in America confirm these findings (Shapero, Howell, and Tombaugh 1965; Brown 1967; Caplow and McGee 1958), but it is also interesting to observe that studies which have compared white-collar and blue-collar job placements (e.g. Rees 1966) find that the use of 'friends and relatives' is largest amongst semi-skilled and unskilled manual workers. These findings are paralleled for the UK.

It is interesting to note that a number of UK studies in the 1950s and 1960s pointed to the presence of kin in the workplace in non-migrant contexts (Scott *et al.* 1956; Wedderburn 1965; Young and Wilmott 1957; Kahn 1964; Tunstall 1969). Wedderburn, aware both of Scott *et al.*'s[6] research in the steel industry in the 1950s and of the American labour-market literature referenced above and encountering a strong pattern of occupational inheritance in her study of redundancy in the railway industry, has this to say:

> It seems possible that kinship ties are more important than has been fully recognised in any long established plant or works. One reason for this is the part which 'speaking for' relatives plays in the process of recruitment.
>
> (Wedderburn 1965: 50)

Indeed, in the 1960s it was primarily studies of redundancy which highlighted the role of the family in job search and job finding (Kahn 1964; Wedderburn 1964, 1965). Wedderburn reports that not only had kinship been an important determinant in the procuring of the now 'redundant' job but it was also an important channel for procuring replacement employment:

> There was a great emphasis upon the personal approach of asking around at possible places of employment and among the immediate circle of acquaintances. 58 per cent made enquiries on the 'offchance' as they put it, and 64 per cent asked friends and acquaintances if they knew of jobs going, or were 'spoken for' by their friends. Taking together the categories of being spoken for and asking friends and relatives, no less than 46 per cent found their jobs in this way.
>   (Wedderburn 1965: 146)

Researching job-search methods in the context of redundancy threw up the accompanying question of past job-search strategies and techniques. It was a concern with these questions which served to draw attention to the presence of kin in the workplace. Thus enquiry into the economic structure of the family in industrial society did not emanate from sociologists of the family, rather it occurred as an accident of research into labour mobility and the repercussions of redundancy. To date, the implications of such findings for mainstream sociology, both of industry and of the family, and for social-network theory, have not been taken up.

A more recent crop of UK labour-market studies have investigated recruitment channels directly. The General Household Survey for 1971 asked respondents about which channel they used in finding out about their present job. Among unskilled manual workers, 'friends and relatives' accounted for 50 per cent of the sample while 'direct application' accounted for 20 per cent. The remaining 30 per cent were distributed between 'advertisement', 'Job Centre', 'private employment agency', and 'other channels'. As in the American evidence, the use of the two informal channels declined when non-manual workers were concerned – only 45 per cent fell in the combined categories of 'friends and relatives' and 'direct applications'.

The General Household Survey findings relate to employees finding out about their current jobs. There are, however, other studies which investigate employer recruitment practices directly.[7] Dunnell and Head (1973) and Courtenay and Hedges (1977) find between 40 and 50 per cent use by employers of the informal recruiting channels for manual workers. Similarly, W. Brown reports that for the employers he studied the frequency of use of 'friends and relatives' and 'direct application' was above 50 per cent for unskilled, semi-skilled and skilled recruitment (W. Brown 1981). Most employers had also used Job Centres, but as Beardsworth and his colleagues point out, employers may feel obliged to notify such official channels without actually taking on anyone sent through them (Beardsworth *et al.* 1981). W. Brown also provides some interesting evidence on the effect of firm size on recruitment channels, at least for skilled workers:

> The choice of recruitment channels appears to be very much influenced by workforce size. . . . Noticeboards appear to increase in utility with increased size of establishment. The greater use of informal methods of recruiting in larger factories may reflect the larger 'grapevine' offered by the workforce.[8]
>
> (W. Brown 1981: 193)

Thus contrary to the argument that greater bureaucratization in larger organizations would lead to more universalistic, formal channels of recruitment, W. Brown's evidence suggests that size strengthens the particularistic, informal channels – with the result that more use is made of them.

In interpreting the above survey evidence, we clearly have to be careful of the different categories used. To what extent does direct application, turning up at the gates, constitute the use of informal channels? Manwaring's study of recruitment in Birmingham, London and Wales is helpful here:

> the remarks of personnel managers especially in the Birmingham and South Wales areas suggest that those who call at the gate often do so because they know of a job coming up. Personnel managers confirm that friends and relatives are often the first to get into the 'queue' of applicants. . . . We would expect most of those calling in on spec to have heard of the job through present employees, so that this channel can be included with friends/ relatives.
>
> (Manwaring 1982: 9)

A recent piece of newspaper reporting further illustrates the nature of the 'direct application' category:[9]

> The desperation for work and a willingness not simply to accept the grim lot was shown earlier this year when 15 temporary vacancies were advertised *internally* by a firm in the Black Country. Less than 24 hours later *word of mouth* had led to more than 500 applicants turning up on the company's doorstep.
>
> (*Guardian*, 17 May 1983: 3)

Direct applications are thus strongly related to contact with the existing workforce. Making this adjustment to the categorization, Manwaring's evidence is striking: 'Friends/relatives was the most frequently cited channel in the current Birmingham study for non-skilled manual workers, 90 per cent of employers mentioning this channel' (Manwaring 1982: 10).

Recent evidence for the UK thus confirms the role of friends and relatives in job finding and job placement (further evidence is presented by Jenkins *et al.* 1983; Wood 1982b; Marsden 1982). These studies do not draw a distinction between friends on the one hand and relatives on the other. However, a number of studies have further identified family as the key component in job acquisition, even in local labour markets. Among the early studies are those of Wedderburn (1965) for the railway industry discussed above and Kahn (1964) for the car industry. Thus in the latter study the interview evidence was collated as follows:

> Typical replies were: 'well, a chap spoke for me'; 'most of the family were there'. . . . All levels of kinship were involved. Thus, 'my father had been there 25 years'; 'mother worked there at the time, and she thought she'd get me a job there'; 'my sister was in service with one of the directors and said she could get me a job' – and there was even a grandfather who secured the crucial interview.
>
> (Kahn 1964: 49)

Another study for the UK which emphasizes kin presence in the workplace is by Hill on dockworkers:

> Among the people I interviewed, direct father–son inheritance accounted for 67 per cent of the men and 75 per cent of the foremen. Other categories of relatives, such as brothers, fathers and brothers-in-law, also included large numbers of dock workers. More distant kin[10] were frequently employed in the docks, though here there is no information on precise proportions. Only 10 per cent of men and 8 per cent foremen could not name one relative who worked in the docks.
>
> (Hill 1976: 174)

Lest it be thought that the pattern identified by Hill is peculiar to the particular manual occupation he studied, Hedges and Beynon provide more recent evidence from the steel industry. A shift manager on the blast furnaces is quoted as saying:

> We had as many as eight or nine Barwells working here; you go back 40 or 50 years, if you was a Fletcher you'd be alright when you'd growed up, you'd get a job here; it was a sort of generation move up. All my relations worked at the crane foundry. My brother is gaffer there now, there was about 14 Darby's worked there. I used to work there myself but being as how my brother was gaffer he used to expect more out of me than the others. . . . My daughter worked here in the office. That was the fourth generation.
>
> (Hedges and Beynon 1982: 10)

Following on from Kahn's evidence on the car industry in Birmingham (Kahn 1964), Hedges and Beynon's evidence on the steel industry in the West Midlands in general (Hedges and Beynon 1982), and Hill's evidence on dockers in London (Hill 1976), Marsden's recent work provides a case for arguing that the overlap between family and employment extends to other regions in the UK as well: 'In the north-east there were families who had never moved to look for work and whose social lives were a set of closely interlocking networks of relatives who were workmates and workmates who were neighbours' (Marsden 1982: 14).

In conclusion, the evidence presented indicates that the overlap between work relationships and non-work relationships is of some significance in a modern industrial society. Further support for the argument is to be found in the work of Lee and Wrench (1981), Mogey (1956), and Buchan (1978). Further evidence from my own case-study material is presented in the next chapter.

2
Two case studies

Introduction

This chapter presents material from two case studies which demonstrates the overlap between kinship and employment networks in
modern industrial society. The cases presented are from different
geographical regions and from different industrial sectors. The first, an
examination of recruitment practices in the Aberdeen fish-processing
industry, places considerable emphasis on the rationales offered by
employers in their explanation of the harnessing of social networks in
the hiring of labour. The importance of social networks in training new
labour is seen to be a factor of some considerable importance and draws
our attention to the overly narrow analysis of workforce skills operating
in conventional industrial sociology. This first case study is of a sector,
fish processing, and a skill, fish filleting, in which female labour
predominates. It serves to emphasize that occupational inheritance is
not confined to the male gender.

The second case, an analysis of the communal employment history of
a working-class East London kinship network, focuses more firmly
upon labour's own account of its involvement in employment sponsorship practices. In analysing the field evidence I make use of the term
'employment net'. I define 'employment net' as the total number of
individuals linked directly and indirectly by kinship and/or friendship
ties and shared place of work. The two case studies are supplemented
by a third, that of migrant labour to Corby steel works, presented in
Chapter 4, which makes use of the same tool. It is to the first and second
of these case studies that I now turn, with general background
information on research methods being provided in the Appendix.

Employment, information networks, and the Aberdeen fish-processing industry

In a 1977 survey of the Aberdeen fish-processing sector – in which 100 out of a total of 203 firms identified were contacted – it was established that employers in this sector made extensive use of their existing workforces in recruiting additional supplies of labour when and as the need arose.[1] A further in-depth sample of ten of these enterprises confirmed the importance of social networks in employee recruitment in this sector. This in-depth study was composed of eight small fish-houses (permanent labour force size between three and twelve) and two larger concerns (one of which had a permanent labour force of seventy and the other of 100) (Table 2.1). Nine of the ten companies depended primarily upon female part-time labour, periodically supplemented by casual female labour; only one company (C) had a completely full-time workforce.

Recruitment of additional employees through the existing labour force was a recurrent practice in an industry with highly fluctuating labour demands. Advertising for labour occurred principally as a last resort with only 20 per cent of the enterprises concerned making any use of advertising whatsoever. Similarly, employers expressed a reluctance to use the state labour exchange; labour recruited through this channel typically did not possess the necessary skills and consequently only portering labour was recruited through this channel.[2] As one small-firm employer said:

> Although a lot of the work is casual, it's highly skilled. If you put somebody not trained on it, they spoil the fish and you don't have time to teach them or even watch them when you have a rush on and you're in the middle of it all. They slow you down. . . . But if you take on somebody's sister or daughter, like Helen here, you know she's had a bittie practice first even if she's only starting at it. And somebody'll keep an eye on her and give her a hand out when she needs it. It's much more efficient, you ken.
>
> (Employer E, Table 2.1)

Other small-firm employers echoed these sentiments:

> Advertising is just a waste of time, all you get is bad labour. It's never trained and when you do train it, they just move on to somewhere else. It's just a waste of time. If I need more hands, I just get the girls to put the word around, that usually works out all right. I only take skilled workers and usually only married women. The youngsters play about too much. I'll only start steady girls, it's better that way. We're too small to do anything else.
>
> (Employer H, Table 2.1)

> We only employ six girls on a permanent basis, and two of those are part-time. We've never needed to advertise, when we need more help the girls always know of somebody suitable. At least so far, with the oil it's bound to get more difficult. They're all related, the skills run in families. They all live up in Torry,[3] so they're nice and close to us here. It's a convenient

Table 2.1 *Female labour and employer recruitment practices: the Aberdeen fishing sector*

Employer	Labour force size	Formal recruitment channels		Informal recruitment channels		Trained recruits only	Training given on job	
		Advertising	Employment exchange	Workforce recommendation only	Workforce recommendation and direct applications		Company	Contact
A	70	No	No	No	Yes	No	No	Yes
B	100	No	No	No	Yes	No	Yes	Yes
C	12	Yes	No	No	Yes	No	Yes	Yes
D	11	No	No	Yes	No	Yes	No	No
E	8	No	No	Yes	No	No	No	Yes
F	6	No	No	Yes	No	Yes	No	No
G	6	No	No	Yes	No	No	No	Yes
H	5	No	No	Yes	No	Yes	No	No
I	3	No	No	Yes	No	Yes	No	No
J	3	Family business: categories not applicable						
Total	224	1	0	6	3	4	2	5

set-up, both for us and for them. It's really something of a family business, I suppose.

(Employer F, Table 2.1)

So far, I have only discussed the sentiments of small employers on the matter. But what was true of the smaller concerns was also true of the larger ones. Although intuitively it might be expected (see Granovetter 1974) that the use of the social network of the existing workforce as the major recruitment channel would be confined to the smaller establishments, this was not the case. Increase in size, at least in this industry and sample, is not accompanied by a greater use of more formal channels.

We don't take untrained girls here. Once you've trained them, they only move on to the small companies. We can't compete with their wages at the height of the season. They're not tied like us, the bigger concerns. They take on casual labour at will and pay it top whack. We take on some but not as much; we usually buy in fillets when the competition is too strong. No, we're much better off with the trained girls, most of our staff is married; women in their forties and early fifties. We've got one woman who's past retiring age still working here – and a bloody good worker she is as well. I couldn't tell you exactly what the connections between them all are but there's a lot of family there. And it's a good bet, if one of them asks you to start somebody she'll stay – and what's more she'll be a good worker too. We don't train anybody, but we turn a blind eye if somebody brings in a youngster and trains them up, provided the work doesn't suffer that is. Yes, it's a pretty good bet that if they know people here before they arrive they'll stay. It's been steady here for about three or four years. Of course you always get some 'floaters' but mainly they're stop gaps anyway. People we take on when we get a sudden increase in business and who arrive at the door on the off chance. But even then they come back to us, some of them every year. But they always go again. We're more tolerant with the women than the men. We wouldn't let a man come and go as he liked. Generally, we put the word round that we've got a big order and we need more staff and that's sufficient. Also most of our women are part-timers so when there's a big order, they switch over to full time and that helps out quite a bit. Our men are full time, anyway, so there's not the same flexibility there. . . . Most of our girls come from families which have been in the fish for years, a lot of them live in Torry and from our point of view that's quite a bonus. Further out and their time-keeping becomes less reliable.[4]

(Employer A, Table 2.1)

The other large employer told more or less the same story:

Most of the training in this industry is given by 'sitting with Nellie'. Older, experienced workers train new recruits standing by them and showing them where they go wrong. There are lots of tricks of the trade that could never be included in a training manual; you have to be shown by somebody who knows exactly what they are doing. The girls train one another, but they won't just train anybody. They'll train their own but ask them to train a stranger, and you run up against a brick wall fast enough. Of course, they go through the motions but that is it. That's your lot. For a start, it slows them down to teach somebody and affects their earnings. Keeping an eye on somebody else's work means slowing down on your own. If they bring someone here to work, they'll carry their load for them until they can stand on their own two feet. Everything proceeds as normal. If I put somebody on the floor myself, then spoil rates are up and work rates are down. And nothing I can do about it. It isn't worth advertising, you only get untrained girls that way. Normally we get our workers one of two ways, either somebody here asks us to start one of their family or we get trained staff applying here when the fish house they usually work for has been unlucky with orders. We prefer workers who know people here, it makes everybody's life easier. And we've got good workers here. See that row of machines standing there, they're the newest in German filleting technology, they cost the earth and we're not using a single one. Why not? Because those machines are slower and spoil more fish than our girls do. Isn't that something? We've got a good steady workforce. Of course like everybody else we get our share of 'wasters' but really we can't complain.

(Employer B, Table 2.1)

Of the ten firms, only one of the smaller firms made use of advertising. Four years previous to our research it had expanded, in terms of its size, dramatically from four part-timers to twelve full-timers. The existing workforce was unable to provide the necessary access to the much-needed labour. Through advertising the firm obtained two trained (and connected) workers and three untrained. The two trained new recruits then introduced three new trained workers to the firm.

Since that date the firm has never re-advertised. Advertising was used as a way of identifying and harnessing another network, rather than as a way of recruiting separate individuals, given that the network of the existing workforce was insufficient to supply the labour demands of the expanded establishment. At no time did this employer intend replacing the use of informal channels of recruitment by the use of high-cost formal channels such as advertising. Rather his intention was to increase the network span of his workforce so as to make certain of a ready supply of labour in the future:

One thing that struck me about advertising was that it produced fewer responses than I would have expected. I put the advert in once a week for three weeks and only got thirty replies. Of those, fifteen were obvious non-starters. We got down to ten reasonable applications in the end. Of the ten only five had direct experience of the kind of work we do. Two of them were sisters – who got the jobs in the end – and were good little workers. I gave them all a try for a morning to see what they were like but three of them ruined the fish. You're much better off training a worker to your own way than taking somebody who has already learnt bad practice somewhere else, so I decided to train up three of the girls who had no experience. I picked up the phone on them first and was told they were all right – it was just bad luck that saw them unemployed. After Jean and Betty had been with me a couple of weeks, I asked if they knew anybody like themselves. That was it, I've never advertised since.

(Employer C, Table 2.1)

Finally, before moving on to the employees' accounts of the relationship between family and work, I look at one last benefit conferred on the employer by harnessing the network of the existing labour force as a source of labour supply:

> We're a very small business – only three girls – and very new. We've only been open three years. So we all have to rely on one another rather a lot. For instance, if one of the girls is sick, they always arrange for somebody to cover for her. If they didn't I don't know what I'd do. I suppose I'd have to take on somebody new every time somebody was sick and sack the sick person. That doesn't seem right does it.
>
> (Employer I, Table 2.1)

The extent to which part-time and casual[5] employment dominate the industry, at least with regard to female labour, provides part of the explanation of the ability of absentee fishworkers to field replacements at their place of work; the strength of network ties within this sector provides the remaining part.

All the employers interviewed indicated that they had a preference for recruiting labour connected to their existing labour force; six of the ten employers would only recruit labour so connected. Furthermore, all employers stressed the extent to which fish gutting and filleting was a family skill.[6] No employer attempted to describe in detail the exact relationships holding between the different members of his workforce but all had what might be termed a good general feel for the strength and character of the connections in existence. We asked three of these employers, A, C, and I, for permission to interview their workforces on the structure of these connections: all three agreed.

We interviewed these workers outside their place of employment, mainly in their own homes. We interviewed the whole of the workforce of C and I, ten workers from workforce A (randomly selected, one in seven) and five fellow fishworkers connected to the latter but who worked elsewhere. Thus we interviewed a total of thirty workers in this sector, and it is to the fishworkers' own evidence on the role of network ties in employment search that I now turn.

Commencing with workforce I – an establishment which had only been open for three years – all three workers were related to one another: two sisters and the daughter of one. Mother and daughter had worked together in the job immediately previous to their present employment, while all three had worked together on a number of occasions in the past. There were four more relatives, derived from their secondary kin, with whom they had regularly worked over the previous fifteen years, and it is from this pool of kin they field replacement workers in case of illness (Fig. 2.1). Put in slightly different terms, the employees' obligations to the employer and network-members' obligations to one another are sufficiently strong to permit employers an indirect call on kin labour. Proxies are in use. This issue is taken up again later in a more theoretical section of the book; here I note the web of work relations which support such practices.

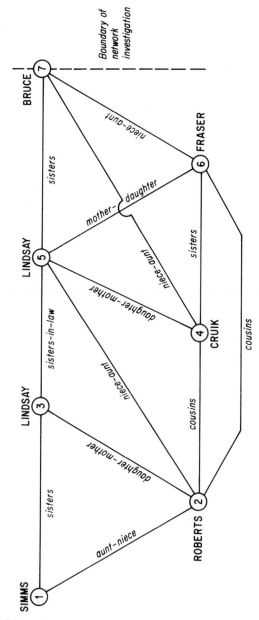

Figure 2.1 Workforce I employment net
- 1, 2, 3 presently working in enterprise I.
- 4, 5, 6 presently working in enterprise K.
- 3, 2 last job in enterprise L with 7.
- 7 presently working in enterprise L.
- 1 last job in enterprise K with 4, 5, 6.

Workforce C, depicted in Figure 2.2, is larger than that of I, with twelve full-time workers. It was this employer whose labour demands outstripped the capacity of his labour force's network to supply much-needed new recruits and who as a consequence had to advertise for new workers. Three members of this workforce had no contacts in the workplace prior to their engagement, have no extra-work connections holding between them, and have brought no new recruits into the workplace. They are, in recruitment terms, isolates.[7]

The original four members of the workforce had been with the company for ten years prior to its expansion and are all related to one another; two sisters and one daughter of each. Their brothers have married out of the fishing community, as have they themselves. They have no immediate in-laws working in the fishing industry, hence their inability to secure the necessary new supplies of labour. The other five members of the workforce are also connected to one another though not to the original workforce. Four of this group are related and one is a friend. Two of this group, sisters, were found through advertising; the other three were subsequently recruited by these two. This latter network is well connected into the fishing community, overlapping in terms of shared employment and kin connection with an additional ten fishworkers. Effectively, this employer has replaced a contracting employment network with a healthier, more vigorous one.

Turning now to Figure 2.3 and workforce A, one of the larger concerns (workforce size: seventy), our random sample of ten provided access to five distinct employment nets and one isolate.[8] Here the whole of the greater part of the employment net tended to be inside the one establishment. Clearly, scale is of major importance here, for although the smaller establishments to some extent rely on the existence of large nets for stand-by labour, they cannot accommodate these nets in employment on a permanent basis. Larger establishments are, however, able to do so.

Greater size appears to result in all of a net's employment eggs being put in the same basket. (This is an issue which I will consider at some length in Chapter 7, focusing on kin-connected employment in Corby steel works where a major redundancy occurred.) We note that of the five nets identified, only two have members outside of workforce A. In addition to interviewing the ten members of workforce A, we interviewed five workers connected to these latter two nets in order to ascertain what the inducements to enter workforce A were and what were the drawbacks.

The patterns of linkage holding between the various parts of the workforce support the employers' general perceptions of the close ties within the worker sub-groups. This pattern of female occupational inheritance within the fish-processing sector strongly resembles the male pattern of occupational inheritance within the docking industry (Hill 1976). Our sample only revealed one isolate – a worker who had arrived in the industry 'by accident':

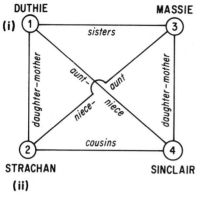

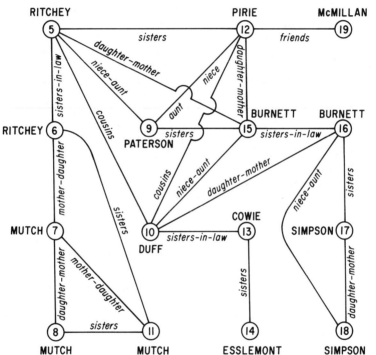

Figure 2.2 Workforce C employment nets
- 1, 2, 3, 4 worked at C for 10 years.
- 20, 21, 22 are isolates; worked at C for 4 years.
- 5, 6, 9, 12, 19 worked at C for 4 years.
- 5, 12 recruited 6, 9, 19.
- 5, 6, 7, 8, 10, 11 previously worked together at Enterprise M.
- 7, 8, 10, 11, 15, 16 currently work at Enterprise M.
- 9, 12, 17, 18, 19 previously worked together at Enterprise N.
- 17, 18 currently work at Enterprise N.
- 10, 13, 14 previously worked together at Enterprise O.
- 13, 14 currently work at Enterprise O.

(i)

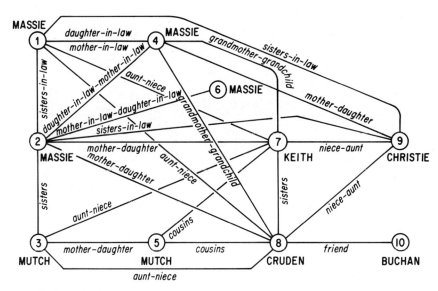

Employment net:

Workforce A = 10

Figure 2.3 Workforce A employment nets (i) to (vi)
- 1, 2, 3, 4, 5, 6, 7, 8, 9, 10 all work in Enterprise A.
- 1, 2, 3 were interviewed as part of sample. These three are directly connected by primary and secondary kin relationships to 4, 5, 6, 7, 8, 9 and indirectly, through 8, by friendship ties to 10.
- With the exception of 5, all members of the net are reported to have helped at least one other member find employment at some stage in the past.
- With the exception of 5, all members of the net have worked together at at least one other establishment at some point in the past.
- The sequence of entry to A was as follows: 4; 1, 2, 3, 9; 5, 7; 6, 8; 10.
- All are part-time workers.

I'm the only one from my family in the fish. I got into it by accident really. My daughter wouldn't touch it with a barge pole. Far too smelly. It's fine for me though, it's been good and steady here. That's more important to me. Yes, I used to work in a canning factory and we were being laid off and one of the girls said 'What about trying . . . with me'. We'd always got on together. So she did the speaking for both of us and we got started here. She showed me all the ins and outs. I've been here ever since, she moved on but I see her now and again. I wouldn't have got the job if it hadn't been for her.

(Aberdeen fishworker)

There are more primary kin relationships than secondary kin relationships contained in the five employment nets identified, but this

(ii)

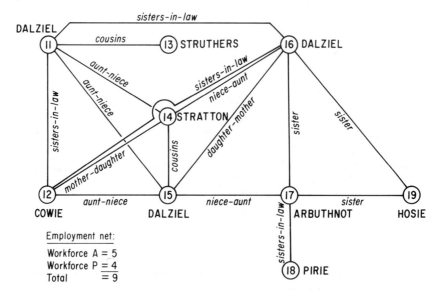

Employment net:

Workforce A = 5
Workforce P = 4
Total   = 9

- 11, 12, 13, 14, 15 all work in Enterprise A.
- 16, 17, 18, 19 all work in Enterprise P.
- 11, 12 were interviewed as part of Workforce A sample, 16, 17, were interviewed as part of additional sample of 5.
- 11 and 12 were connected by primary kin relationships to 13, 14, 15.
- All members of the total net are reported to have helped at least one other member of the net find employment at some stage in the past.
- With the exception of 18, all members of the net have worked together at two other establishments with another member of the net in the past.
- The sequence of entry to A was as follows: 14, 12; 11; 15, 13.
- 11, 12, 13, 14, 15 are all part time.
- 16, 17, 18, 19 are all full time.

is due in part to the large number of inter-generational relationships included. In-law links are clearly of substantial import in the social organization of work within this sector. Yet when asked to name relatives within the enterprise and within the industry, these workers typically excluded in-laws from their lists. On the whole, it was not until they were prompted with a specific question on the topic that they included in-laws in their accounts of kin presence in the workplace. It seems likely that many studies may have under-represented kin presence in the workplace by failing to ask a specific question on in-laws.[9]

(iii)

⑳ COULL: *No recruitment connection to other members of the workforce; workmate connections only to other enterprises. Interviewed as part of workforce A sample.*

(iv)

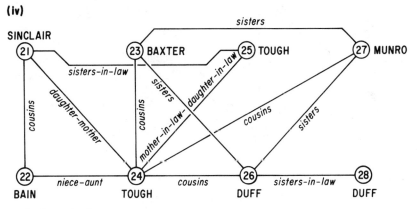

Employment net:
Workforce A = 8

- 21, 22, 23, 24, 25, 26, 27, 28 all work in Enterprise A.
- Only 24 was interviewed.
- 21, 22 have never worked elsewhere.
- 24 is connected by primary kin relationships to 21, 22, 23, 26, 27; by secondary kin relationships to 25; and indirectly, through 26, to 28.
- The sequence of entry to A was as follows: 26, 27; 23, 24, 28; 21, 25; 22.
- 26 and 27 are reported as having spoken for 24; 24 spoke for 21, 22, 25.
- 23, 24, 26, 27, 28 are part-time workers.
- 21, 22, 25 are full-time workers.

The considerable presence of in-law relationships within this industry is partly attributable to high rates of in-marriage within this particular occupational community. Fourteen of our workforce A interviewees (sample = fifteen) considered themselves as having married within the fish and described it as a customary practice:

> I used to work with his sister before we even knew one another. She and me were pals. Then after we were married, I just carried on working alongside her. I reckon we worked our way round every fish house in Aberdeen, at one time or another. Aye, and we work together still.
>
> (Aberdeen fishworker)

Within this occupational community, friendship/workmate relationships frequently converted into kinship relations. It is an aspect of occupational community which has received no attention in the literature to date.[10] Thus in-law relationships between 1 and 9, 11 and 12, and 12 and 16 were all preceded by friendship/workmate contacts.

(v)

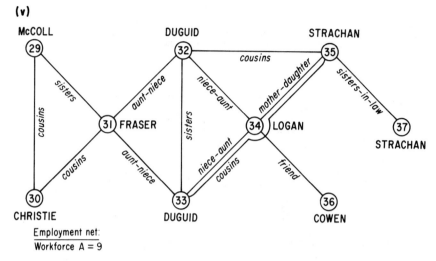

Employment net:
Workforce A = 9

- 29, 30, 31, 32, 33, 34, 35, 36, 37 all work in Enterprise A.
- 32 and 34 were interviewed.
- 29, 30, 31 entered A together and separately from 34, 35, 36 and 37.
- 31 and 34 spoke for 32 and 33.
- 32, 33 and 35 are full-time workers, all other members of the net are part time.

Only two current non-kin linkages show up in our workforce A sample; 8 and 10, and 34 and 36. The former of these is a friendship linkage between a young married woman and a single girl, the latter a long-standing relationship stretching over 20 years and a number of workplaces.

Asked what explained the clustering of kin in specific workplaces, our respondents answered that enterprise A was a good payer for part-time workers, the conditions were better and employment steadier than in the smaller establishments. It was a good place to work, and management looked favourably on bringing family in provided they were good workers:

> We're all good workers in our family, he knows that. We're not shy of a bit extra work, not like some. We'll always stay on and help out if it gets busy. That's when you really see the money. I wouldn't like to do it all the time but now and again you can make a bob or two. An awful help that is.
> (Aberdeen fishworker)

The five workers connected to workforce A but employed elsewhere (16, 17, 41, 42, 43) preferred full-time to part-time work. Full-time employment was scarce at A and this more than any other factor explained the division of the nets between workplaces. Nobody mentioned scale as a direct benefit of working at A; rather the emphasis was on the steady character of the employment provided there.

In summary, kin presence in the workplace is strong within this

(vi)

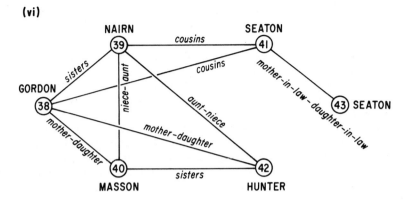

Employment net:

Workforce A = 2
Workforce Q = 4
Total   = 6

- 38, 40 work in Enterprise A.
- 39, 41, 42, 43 work in Enterprise Q.
- 38, 41, 42, 43 were interviewed.
- 42 had previously worked in Enterprise A.
- 38, 40 had previously worked in Enterprise Q.
- The sequence of entry to A was as follows: 42; 38; 40.
- The sequence of entry to Q was as follows: 41, 43; 38, 40; 39, 42.
- 38, 40 are part time.
- 39, 41, 42, 43 are full time.

sector. Patterns of direct occupational inheritance and more indirect routes of introduction to the workplace are to be found, with overlaps frequently occurring between the two. Expanding the definition of kin so as to include in-law relationships permits the identification of the larger, more elaborate structures which are involved in the social organization of work in this sector. The involvement of kin in training relationships is strongly pronounced, a circumstance which serves to explain the degree of influence exercised by the workforce over the selection of new recruits. The role of kin in the provision of occupational training is given more explicit consideration in the next chapter, where the relationship of employer training strategies to kin presence in the workplace is explored in greater detail.

Using the network: job-search methods and the East End working-class family, 1944–84

In the previous section, I focused upon an industry where worker attachment is high; indeed most of those interviewed (twenty-six out of thirty) had no experience of any other industry. In this next section, by contrast, I am going to focus upon one particular family network – the

Sheldrakes – which has been employed in a large number of different occupations over the last forty years.[11] The network derives originally from the East End of London – Canning Town, Custom House, and Stepney – and presently has substantial sub-nets in Edenbridge, Kent; Petersfield, Hampshire; Basildon New Town, Essex; and within the East End itself. I focus specifically upon the patterns of job search prior to the sub-net arrival in Basildon and upon the subsequent patterns of job search in Basildon.

This section serves two purposes in terms of the overall structure of the book. First, by examining a socio-occupational group in which men and women frequently work alongside one another in the same workplace, it furnishes a contrast, on the one hand, to the all-female employment structure of fish processing discussed in the previous section and, on the other, to the all-male employment situation of steel discussed in Chapter 4. Second, by examining the operations of job search in a multi-employer, multi-industry New Town, it offers a contrast to the situation encountered in the one-industry, one-employer site of Corby New Town. At the same time, by examining job-search methods within this network, it becomes apparent that kin presence in the workplace is pervasive and not merely a feature of one-employer labour markets, though such circumstances clearly serve to accentuate the pattern. Nor is it confined to the highly skill-specific sectors of the economy, for the East End and Basildon employment nets (Fig. 2.4) show the same family groups passing through a number of industrial sectors.

These nets taken together provide us with an understanding of the importance of tacit skills in labour mobility. In the next chapter, I discuss Manwaring's concept of tacit skills more fully (Manwaring 1982). Here I note that, according to our informants, employers (i) to (x) in Figure 2.4 all preferred recruiting on a family basis, even where the family was new to that particular industry. This recruitment strategy required, however, that the first entrant (the spearhead) to the new workplace be regarded as competent and industrious. The adaptability and suitability of subsequent connected entrants are estimated from the performance of this spearhead or pathmaker. Effectively, there was a tacit dimension to employers' recruitment practices.

As can be seen from the nets (i) to (xi) in Figure 2.4 and from the summary table of shared workplace overlaps between the nets (Table 2.2), the interlocks between industries, extended kin, and different generations are strong.[12] Nine different industrial and service sectors are linked by their common use of this pool of labour; kin presence and employment aid extends to cousins and in-laws as frequently as it does to members of the nuclear family, indicating that occupational inheritance need not always be accomplished through direct father to son and mother to daughter routes.[13] Finally, two generations are frequently found working together, indicating the strength of family ties even for the younger generation.

Figure 2.4 Sheldrake employment net

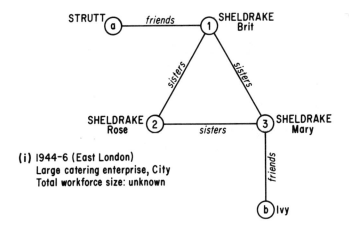

(i) 1944–6 (East London)
Large catering enterprise, City
Total workforce size: unknown

- 1, 3, a, b are all waitresses.
- 2 is a cashier.
- 2, 3, a, b are single.
- 1 is married.
- Sequence of entry 1, 2, 3, a, b.
- Sequence of exit 2, 3, 1, unknown.

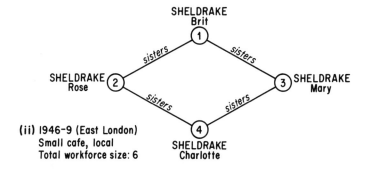

(ii) 1946–9 (East London)
Small cafe, local
Total workforce size: 6

- 2, 3, 4 are waitresses.
- 1 is a cook.
- Sequence of entry 2, 3, 1, 4.
- Sequence of exit 2, 3, 4, 1.
- 2 and 3 depart on marriage, 3 migrates to Scotland.
- 3, 4 are married.

This data would seem to challenge the assumption that the East End family has lost its hold over its members in the modern period; its control over jobs appears as strong as ever (see Young and Wilmott 1957

1940s to early 1950s: Sheldrake/White
Tate & Lyle sugar factory, Silvertown.

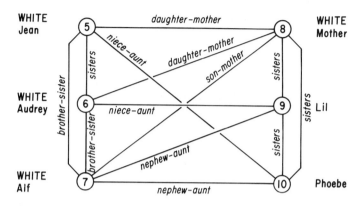

• 9 and 10 were first to enter, followed by 8.

(iv) Late 1950s to early 1960s: Sheldrake/White
Lesney's toy manufacturer's, Hackney

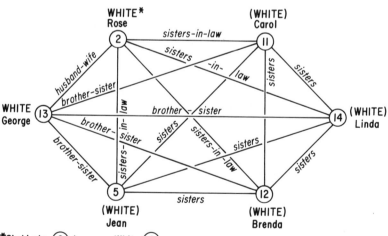

*Sheldrake ② becomes White ②

• 5 was first to enter. 2 and 3 were introduced by 5.
• 13 was first to leave.

(v) Late 1950s to mid-1960s: Sheldrake/White
General Cleaning Company, East London based → Basildon

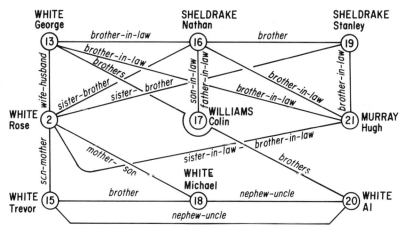

- 13 is the first to enter and the last to leave.
- The company transfers its office to Basildon New Town and 2 and 13 move with it.
- 21 is already employed in Basildon but in a different company (see vii) before 2 and 13 arrive there.
- Subsequently, 17 migrates to Basildon with his wife, the daughter of 16, and is followed by his wife's sister and her husband.
- 15 and 18 move to Basildon with their parents, and work for GCC in the New Town base.
- 21 is husband of Sheldrake 3, who is now Murray 3.
- 21 and 3 have migrated from Scotland to East London due to unemployment.

for an account of an earlier period).[14] The evidence on the basis of this data is that employment favours are still primarily exchanged within the boundaries of kin. Furthermore, these linkages between kin in the workplace serve an important social purpose as information routes to kin outside the workplace and vice versa.

Thus Mary Murray, with employer (viii), would often send a message to her daughter, Val Marks, through her son-in-law, Barry Marks – Val and Barry living some distance away. Similarly, packages and presents were often sent by the same route. Messages also came from Val Marks to Barry Marks through Mary Murray. The latter as a technician had easy access to the phone within her working space; she was also free to move around the factory at her own discretion. Messages, which were not critical enough for the relevant person to be called to the factory office to take the call, were passed directly to Mary Murray, who then relayed them to the shop floor without involving the bureaucracy. Thus any member of kin wanting to get a message to the factory floor during working hours went through Mary Murray.

(vi) Mid–1960s: Sheldrake/Murray
      Standard Telephone & Cables Ltd, Woolwich → Basildon

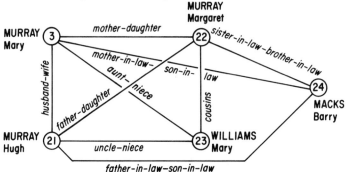

- 3 was first to enter. The company transferred offices to Basildon and 3 moved with it. All other members worked within the Basildon location, all have different types of job.
- 3 gets jobs for 21, 24; 21 gets job for 23. 23 is wife to 17 (see v) and daughter to 16.
- 22 gets job through agency whose owner was previously personnel officer at STC and who knows work history and orientation of other family members.

Linkages between the kin group and in-laws serve to strengthen the links between the kin group as a whole and the member whose marriage partner and relatives are being serviced. In-law inclusion in the employment net is in the first instance a consequence of strong ties between his/her partner and the other members of the net; it is thus an indirect exchange amongst strong ties.[15] Although some of these in-law/kin relationships have converted into independent strong ties, this is not by any means true of all of these relationships:

> If he weren't my son-in-law I wouldn't lift a finger to help him. If she ever left him I'd cut him completely adrift. I'm helping her really; he thinks I'm helping him but I'm not. I wouldn't give him the time of day if I could help it.
> (Female tobacco worker, Basildon)

Unlike the fish-processing employment nets studied, no workmate relationships have been converted into kinship relationships. Whereas within the fish-processing sector we could identify an occupational community with marriage occurring between members of this community, in the East End/Basildon net we have identified a community of kin, based on shifting but shared workplace where marriage provides entry, sometimes full and sometimes limited, to the community of kin.

A particularly interesting feature of this set of employment nets is

(vii) 1950s to early 1960s: Sheldrake/White/Roberts
West Ham Power Station

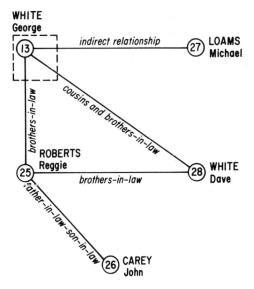

WHITE
George

- 25 is husband of 1.
- 28 is husband of her sister Sally.
- 27 is a close friend of 16, 2, 3.
- 13 introduces 25, 26, and 27 to employer.
- In the late 1960s, 25 and 26 along with one other brother-in-law migrate to Petersfield, Hampshire.
- 27 dies.
- 27 occupies status of social kin and lives within the family with 16.
- 13 (----) subcontracted from General Cleaners to Power Station. Offered permanent job which he refuses, but offers to bring in other labour like himself.

that they contain all-female, all-male, and mixed groups of family workers. In the all-male groups brother-in-law relations figure very strongly, whilst in the all-female groups sibling relations are of the most import. Whilst it would be reckless to argue that this pattern is typical of East End employment patterns, it is consistent with the matri-local account of East End society provided by Young and Wilmott (1957). The identification of the importance of in-law relationships in male access to employment alerts us to the hazards of assuming that it is only the behaviour of males which is important in determining the allocation of male-employment opportunities. In later sections the role of women as employment information brokers will be considered; for the present,

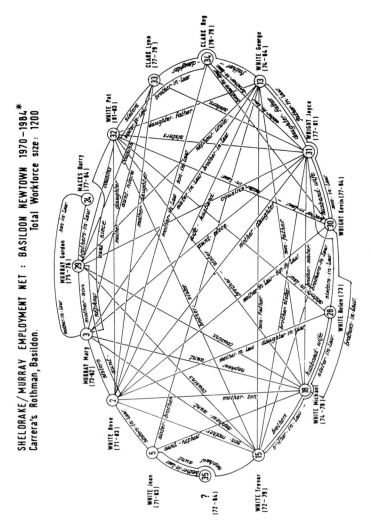

SHELDRAKE/MURRAY EMPLOYMENT NET : BASILDON NEWTOWN 1970–1984*
Carrera's Rothman, Basildon.   Total Workforce size : 1200

* January 1984 Carreras Rothman announced their decision to close their Basildon plant down completely.
? Name not known.

- 2 and 5 entered together applying at the gates with no direct contact inside the workforce at the point of engagement.
- 2 made the arrangements for 15; 28; 18; 33, 24, 34, 30, 31; 32 to enter.
- 3 and 13 made direct applications, but their family connections were known to the employer.
- 3 made the arrangements for 29 to enter.
- 5 made the arrangements for 35.
- 30, 31, 3 are clerical and technical staff; 18, 24, 34 are skilled maintenance staff; 28 and 32 are canteen workers; 13 is a forklift truck driver; 2, 5, 35, 15, 29, 33 make cigarettes.

(ix) 1960s: Sheldrake/Macks
Marconi's Engineering, Basildon

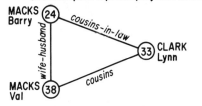

WHITE
Michael

MACKS
Barry

(36) MACKS
Fred

son-father

son-father

(18) ——— (24)
cousins-in-law

brothers

(37) MACKS
Dan

- 36 entered first.

(x) 1970s: Sheldrake/Macks
Small computer tape company near Basildon

MACKS (24)
Barry

cousins-in-law

(33) CLARK
Lynn

wife-husband

cousins

MACKS (38)
Val

- 38 entered first and made the arrangements for 33 and 24.
- 24 is casual labour and works in this job in addition to Carreras Rothman.

we note that the patterns observed in our data suggest that matri-local influence may extend to the sphere of employment.

Mixed family work-groups have received some attention in studies of the cotton industry during the Industrial Revolution and the nineteenth century. I know of no modern study of this phenomenon, with the exception of the work of Whipp (1983),[16] yet my data would suggest it is worthy of attention. Some part of this lack of attention is no doubt due to the mythology that men go out to work whilst women stay at home. Tilly and Scott have taken issue with this perception and argue that for working-class women, work has always been the normality (Tilly and Scott 1978). Certainly, within the nets studied it is the general expectation that women will work, although during child-bearing and -rearing years employment takes either a part-time or a casual seasonal form. Even here the family is the major procurer of employment; thus part-time jobs – 28 in (viii), 32 in (viii), 33 in (x) – were all obtained in order to permit members to combine earning with child-rearing. For both men and women, their individual and family standing as workers is a matter of some importance: 'We're all workers in this family and always have been. We've earned every penny we've ever had. . . . That's the main thing if somebody's a good worker, they'll always get by somehow' (male tobacco worker, Basildon). 'We've always had a good name as workers. None of us have ever shirked work. Oh, I'm not saying we've never given anybody any trouble, we have, but not as far as work's concerned' (female tobacco worker, Basildon).[17] 'Even with

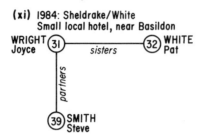

(xi) 1984: Sheldrake/White
Small local hotel, near Basildon

Direct overlaps between employment nets (i) to (xi)

	i	ii	iii	iv	v	vi	vii	viii	ix	x	xi
i		3	0	1	1	1	0	2	0	0	0
ii	3		0	1	1	1	0	2	0	0	0
iii	0	0		1	1	0	0	1	0	0	0
iv	1	1	1		.2	0	1	3	0	0	0
v	1	1	1	2		1	1	4	1	0	0
vi	1	1	0	0	1		1	2	1	1	0
vii	0	0	0	1	1	1		1	0	0	0
viii	2	2	1	3	4	2	1		2	2	2
ix	0	0	0	0	1	1	0	2		1	0
x	0	0	0	0	0	1	0	2	1		0
xi	0	0	0	0	0	0	0	2	0	0	
Total no. of direct links:	8	8	3	9	12	8	4	21	5	4	2
No. of nets to which directly linked:	5	5	3	6	8	7	4	10	4	3	1

- 30 and 31 marriage broke down.
- 39 and 31 landlord/landlady of pub.
- 32 is barmaid.

this redundancy, it pays to have worked hard. It gets known. George just got a phone call, somebody who'd worked for him back in London, offered him a cleaning contract. It's because they know he's a worker. He won't be long without a job' (female tobacco worker, Basildon).

Being known as good workers was seen as a form of insurance as well as a matter of morality. Because of their concern with their reputation as workers, this kin group would only introduce 'good workers' to their employer. Yet they reported no conflict between their obligations to kin and their need to maintain their reputational standing. There was no evidence of kin ever being refused help, although it is possible that there is a reluctance to volunteer such information. Within these nets, then, it was the case that both men and women were defined as workers; furthermore, there was a general pressure to perform to a high standard. Intuitively, one might have expected that labour which was so mobile would perform to lower standards, but it would seem to be the case that precisely because of such mobility reputation is an issue of critical concern.

The concern with reputation and the exchange of employment favours primarily within the framework of kin are consistent, for the latter provides a denser set of relationships than those provided by friendship or acquaintanceship and this in its turn provides for a denser set of controls. In addition, employer preference is for strong and identifiable ties within the workforce; some of the benefits to the employer can be seen from the previous discussion of workers' reputations. It is therefore in the interest of the individual kin network to field a sizeable and identifiable catchment of labour. I take these issues up in the following chapter. Here, I note that within this particular network the concern with reputation resulted in the recruitment of strongly tied individuals, though these strong ties were of both a direct and an indirect character.

Finally, within these employment nets family labour, whilst homogeneous in disposition and attitudes, occupies on occasion different rank and skill categories. For instance, the earlier discussion of Mary Murray's access to a telephone and her freedom to move within the factory is a reflection of differential status between her and the other family members working in (viii). The former and the latter have access to different information sets, in the first instance, yet they are strongly tied, as evidenced by, for example, their use of Mary Murray to relay messages. In a later section I take issue with Granovetter's argument that strongly tied individuals necessarily share information (and influence) sets, in the first instance. It is noted that within this set of nets there is evidence to the contrary.

I shall return to the East End/Basildon data elsewhere in the book, in the context of other issues, but taking together the evidence on the fish-processing industry, the nine sectors covered by the East End data, and the secondary material, the overall conclusions must be that there is widespread use of friends and relatives by employers and employees in hiring and in securing employment.

Moreover, the documentation of direct kin presence in the workplace, and of use of kin networks in employment placement, is substantive enough to call for a theoretical investigation of the causes and consequences of such overlap. The next section takes up these theoretical arguments.

3

Social networks: how they work and why they are used

Introduction: discounting the evidence

In the previous two chapters widespread evidence was marshalled on (a) kin presence in the workplace and (b) the use of kinship and friendship ties in the transmission of employment information and in the securing of employment. In this chapter, I consider in more detail the rationale behind the use of kinship and friendship networks in employment, both by employers and by employees. Before proceeding to this analysis of why social networks are used in the search for labour and for employment, I would like to draw attention to a paradox. Despite considerable evidence to the contrary, in studies during the 1950s, 1960s, and 1970s the relationships between the employment sphere on the one hand and the family/friendship sphere on the other were seen as weak in general – each of the successive studies being represented, and in some cases representing themselves, as exceptions to the rule.

A leading case of the latter is Hill's study of dockworkers (Hill 1976). In this study Hill recognized that the mode of recruitment and social organization of work in this sector diverged radically from the modernist, meritocratic model identified in the conventional literature.

> The most obvious sources of these informal structures were to be found in the ascriptive, specific and personal ties with foremen which existed before the employment relationship, rather than in the achievement (performance)-oriented and diffuse ties which sociologists regard as characteristic of the modern contractual institutions of employment which are typically found in developed societies.
>
> (Hill 1976: 23)

Yet Hill pronounces upon the practices he observes as 'anachronistic'. Such was the hold of orthodoxy that Hill believed he had discovered but an exception (Hill 1976). Brooks and Singh made a similar discovery, this time in the foundry industry, amongst a recently arrived ethnic population (Brooks and Singh 1979). Here ascriptive factors played a similar part in the recruitment process and forms of work organization. Faced with orthodoxy, they too decided that they had discovered an exception, and argued that such practices were confined to ethnic migrant labour.

Hill thus makes a claim on exceptionality – the persisting importance of personal contact in securing employment in the docking industry is to be explained by its historical reliance on casual labour (which ended in 1967) (Hill 1976).[1] In the two preceding chapters, however, both primary and secondary evidence was presented showing that the particularism identified by Hill in the docks, and by Brooks and Singh among ethnic migrants in the foundries, is indeed widespread in other industrial sectors and social groupings – they are not exceptions to the rule.

The strength of the orthodoxy is revealed again when Hill turns to the question of occupational community outside work:

> The large proportion of docking kin is relevant to the discussion of the occupational community outside work. . . . [An] aspect of occupational community, in some definitions at least, is the overlapping of kinship ties at work and outside. Such overlapping was apparent among the people interviewed here, because so many had relatives in the docks, particularly fathers. This situation must have helped the transmission of occupational values and norms, particularly in the past when docking communities appear to have been more closely knit. . . . But it has not necessarily led to the sorts of sociability which constitute a community among kin. . . . Evidence suggested that frequent contact with parents was normal for most of the sample but that interaction with other relatives was less common. Indeed, there was evidence of a privatised family life among dock workers and foremen. At the same time, few relatives appeared to be workmates inside the docks, despite being members of the same occupation. One can conclude that, in this respect, as others, dock workers and foremen are members of an occupational community to a greater extent than are many other workers in different occupations, but not to the extent that might have been anticipated.
>
> (Hill 1976: 175–6)

I suggest that the complex patterns of job assistance found among workers in different industries, different regions, and of different ethnic backgrounds, and evidenced from both primary and secondary sources, can be taken as evidence of the extent of occupational community in modern industrial society. On these grounds alone I would take issue with Hill on the interpretation of his data.

However, issue can be taken with Hill on his assessment of what precise level of contact constitutes a community among kin. In the week of Hill's 1976 survey, 80 per cent of the dockers sampled had seen some relatives other than parents or parents-in-law, in their own home or in their relatives' home. I would regard this as a somewhat high contact rate but, more importantly, not only did 73 per cent of interviewees see their own parents once a week, 69 per cent saw their parents-in-law once a week as well. The latter figure is the key to recognizing that interlinkages between families provided through the husband–wife bonding represent a community of kin wider than any single nuclear and 'privatized' family. My own data shows the complexity of the community of kin that can be constructed through the female link. But, as with many community studies of the period, women were not interviewed by Hill (1976).

Hill's (1976) total neglect of the female connection is indicative. In network terms the assumption is that on marriage a daughter is segregated from her own kin network. Yet marriage may mean exactly the opposite – it may indeed more strongly link a daughter to the male world of her own family of origin, for she provides the bridge between her husband and her male kin. More importantly, her role may well be that of broker or recruitment agent for the male employment net. My fieldwork evidence clearly shows up these patterns. The data collected both on the East London workers and on Scots workers in Corby demonstrate that females link the employment chances of their spouses to the male kin of their family of origin and vice versa. Mobilizing resources for employment search occurs through both kinship lines.

Regarding female and male nets as connected alters our understanding of the completeness of Hill's analysis – in common with most of this literature, where the role of female nets in a male-employment context is not investigated. The few scattered studies which do investigate this link, directly or indirectly, tend to support our position (Mogey 1956; Brooks and Singh 1979).

Attending to the concept of proxy, it is important to recognize that wives may play a major part in servicing and managing the links between their husband and his kin. Wives may stand proxy for their husbands in the social visiting of the male-side relatives. In order to establish the strength of occupational community, the combined sociability patterns of both male and female must be taken into account. This may be a particularly important consideration in those situations where the pattern is one of male-only employment; differences in male/female time budgets are likely to produce situations where sociability requirements are met by the female.

Where complex patterns of job assistance exist, there is good reason for close examination of the mechanisms by which information is passed and group membership defined. The implication of my analysis is that there is a teamwork dimension to this process which has gone under-recorded due to an over-simplistic concentration on the wage-earner as the relevant unit of analysis. This is unlikely to be a suitable unit of analysis for any investigation of the extent of community.

Rationale for use of kin networks

The particularism and ascription in hiring and job search evidenced requires investigation at the theoretical level since, at the very least, it runs counter to Parsons's view of the process of modernization as leading to emphasis on universalism in general, and in industrial recruitment procedures in particular. Why should employers use family and friends of the existing workforce as opposed to advertising vacancies generally? Why should individual workers, in their turn, rely on family and friends in finding out about job opportunities? In answering these questions, I start with Rees's distinction between the extensive and intensive margin in search:

> The search for information in any labour market has both an extensive and an intensive margin. A buyer can search at the extensive margin by getting a quotation from more than one seller. He can search at the intensive margin by getting additional information on an offer already received. Where the goods and services sold are highly standardised, the extensive margin is the more important. Where there is great variation in quality, the intensive margin moves to the fore-front.
>
> (Rees 1966: 50)

Rees goes on to argue that the labour market is one where there is a commodity with great variations in quality, and search at the intensive margin, by both employers and employees, would be prevalent. Commencing with employers, three reasons may be put forward as to why the recruitment of labour through the informal networks of the existing labour force is such a widespread practice. First, employee referral provides the cheapest method of obtaining labour. Second, employee referrals provide an efficient screening mechanism. Third, recruitment through employees acts as a form of control since the new worker is constrained by the interests and reputation of his sponsor. I will elaborate on each of these in turn.

The cost-effectiveness of employee referral as a method of recruitment goes beyond the obvious point that the costs of advertising are avoided. The costs of processing applications are also important. Rees argues that the employer's task is not to generate a large number of applications, but few applications of sufficient quality to justify further investigation (Rees 1966). As one of Lee and Wrench's interviewees said:

> I advertised once in the Birmingham Evening Mail. We were deluged with applications so I never did it again. . . . We haven't advertised this year. The news gets round by word of mouth. So far this year we have had eighty applications for six jobs. Another two hundred would come in if I advertised.
>
> (Lee and Wrench 1981: 9)

Similarly, Manwaring notes that for his case study 'personnel managers often prefer to use as few recruitment channels as they can to save on time and money' (Manwaring 1982: 9–10).

While the large responses to general advertisements may be a recent phenomenon because of the present recession, the overall point that employee referrals may be the cheapest way of acquiring a new worker still stands. Related to this is the second reason why employers may prefer to recruit friends and relatives of the existing workforce: this channel provides an efficient screening mechanism which will produce new workers with characteristics similar to the existing workforce. Again my own case-study evidence speaks to this directly, but Hill's evidence is also suggestive:

> Each side [managers and employees] nominated half of the new recruits, which guaranteed this proportion at least would be the close relatives of existing dock workers. In practice, managers observed conventional priorities, so that the sons and other relatives of dock workers have normally had preference in the employer allocation as well. . . . The highly personal and ascriptive ethos of the docks is clearly shown in this convention: the idea that certain families produce 'good' employees and that a worker already employed will vouch for his kin. There was also the fact that, in the absence of proper training schemes, existing workers had to train new recruits and that kinsmen were more likely to be willing to do this than strangers.
>
> (Hill 1976: 32)

The practice of preference being given to family members is also documented by Lee and Wrench, who identified an engineering firm which used the phrase 'lads of dads' to indicate its hiring policy, the rationale, of employers in general, for this policy being that 'sons of employees had a better awareness of the industry' (Lee and Wrench 1981). From a network point of view the existence of a set of kin and friends at the workplace not only provides a training or familiarizing agency but also provides a norm-enforcing device. The ability to enforce norms and the maintenance of work-group reputations are thus linked by the employer's recruitment practice of preferential hiring.

The concept of 'training' and 'awareness of the industry' in unskilled manual occupations may seem paradoxical, but Manwaring provides a formalization in terms of what he calls tacit skills:[2]

> Efficient performance requires that new recruits will be able to learn the specific (tacit) skills required in formally unskilled jobs, to apply those skills at sufficiently intensive and sustained rate to meet production targets and to fit into the work group within which these skills are learnt and applied. . . . The likelihood that a candidate can meet the ideal is not randomly distributed according to individuals' personality attributes, but is shaped by mutual obligations within particular social networks.
>
> (Manwaring 1982: 15, 18)

This argument has not been taken to its logical conclusion, that it is the family grouping within which mutual obligations are likely to be the strongest, and therefore the most attractive to prospective employers. This is partly because Manwaring's data cannot distinguish between family and friends. But, as we have seen, in studies where such a distinction is made the role of the family comes out strongly. Socialization to work is a feature not only of mining communities (Pitt 1979), but also of industrial work in general, as one of the interviewees of Hedges and Beynon makes clear:

> I started here when I was fourteen. Straight from school. . . . I used to come and bring my father's tea on Sunday afternoon and I used to ride up and down the plant on the stripper with him. I'd seen furnaces tapped because as a lad aged 10 or 11 I used to walk along the landing to go the swimming baths. I think it may have been during those periods that I got to like the atmosphere of the place, these big men with blue glasses and towels. It could be that I was influenced without being aware of it.
>
> (Hedges and Beynon 1982: 11)

The role of the family comes out most strongly in the third reason as to why employers use kin networks in recruitment. As Lee and Wrench note, 'it was also useful when a lad needed disciplining' (Lee and Wrench 1981). The argument here is that recruitment through existing employees acts as a form of control since responsibilities and obligations hold between workers so recruited: for if the sponsored antagonizes the employer, the reputation of the sponsor himself will be damaged; thus, the new worker is constrained by the interests and reputation of his sponsor.[3] Previously, we quoted one of Hedges and Beynon's (1982) respondents complaining that 'being as how my brother was gaffer he used to expect more out of me than the others'. Moreover, hiring of employee-referred applicants is used as a reward for loyalty and good work on the part of existing workers. As Hill commented, 'The managers whom I interviewed said that . . . they could reward foremen and loyal workers by putting forward their relatives as the employer's own nominees' (Hill 1976: 32).

Employers recruit friends and relatives of existing workers precisely because of the control that mutual obligations between friends and family provide. This understanding has implications for the position that relationships in complex industrial society are single-stranded rather than overlapping across a number of spheres of existence and these will be examined in more detail later. For now, however, it can be noted that there are significant advantages to employers in using family and friend networks for recruiting, and I move on to argue that the same holds for employees in their search and applications for jobs.

Note that such network development within the workplace also contains the potential for the control of employers' behaviour as the mistreatment of a network member can have the consequence of a mass exodus. Clearly, kinship solidariness, in this respect, contains more problems for a small employer than for a large employer. It should also be remembered, however, that from the perspective of the work group, the exchange between itself and the present employer may not be perceived as discrete as the preservation of good reputation may be important in the obtaining of other contracts of employment.

There are a number of advantages conferred on a worker in the competition for employment by the presence of a family member or friend in the location of potential employment. Family members and friends gain information on vacancies in their place of employment and transmit such information in advance of the information being made generally available. Clearly, the fact that large companies often advertise vacancies on internal notice boards before releasing such information for general circulation (Manwaring 1982) provides one basis upon which advance information can be transmitted.[4] In addition, information is obtained on imminent vacancies as a consequence of informal information or grapevine processes within the workplace. Network candidates possess, therefore, a time advantage.

The use of personal contacts provides information at the intensive margin. The searcher can find out details of the job other than the obvious characteristics such as the wage. Moreover, he is more likely to trust such information when it comes from a family member or close friend. Also, the snags and disadvantages of a particular job are rarely indicated by employers seeking labour; a contact in the workforce is more able and inclined to point out the problems. This is particularly important in job search over distance, and will be taken up in the next chapter.

Apart from information about the job, and perhaps about the interview procedures, family and friends in the workplace can transmit the tacit skills in anticipation of the interview. Even for jobs which are formally unskilled, an applicant familiar with the specifics of production in that particular plant is likely once again to be at an advantage over other candidates. Such training and pre-work socialization, however, is more likely to be a feature of family connections rather than simply friendships. For, as my own primary evidence shows, family connections are often a critical component of employers' training strategies. Both workers and employers perceive family reputation[5] – a summary measure of pre-work socialization – as a relevant and reliable indicator of individual employability. Mann, talking of the recruitment practices of a Birmingham employer, states that being 'of a good family' was a firm selection criterion (Mann 1973).

In conclusion, it should be noted that while in the previous chapters evidence was provided of widespread kin presence at work, and of the use by employers and employees of family and friends as recruiting and job search channels, in this section I have been investigating the mechanisms that might lead to such an observed pattern. I have argued that there are indeed sound reasons why employers might use kin/friendship networks for recruiting, and why employees might use these same networks for job search. This theoretically viable and empirically evidenced overlap between the sphere of work and the sphere of kin and friendship relations has major consequence for social-network theory and for mainstream sociology.

On the one hand, it opens up the possibility that relations in modern complex societies may indeed be multi-stranded, at least in so far as relationships at work interact and overlap with relationships with family and friends – the role of employment relations as a trace on social networks outside of this sphere is thus a possible area of investigation. On the other hand, it runs strongly counter to the position in mainstream sociology that the requirements of employment in modern industrial society necessarily lead to an erosion of kin linkages. On the contrary, my evidence and theory suggest that it is precisely the employment context which serves to widen and intensify kin linkages, inasmuch as the workplace affords the major routine location for the greatest number of kin.

Implications for social-network analysis

The major contribution to the study of the importance of networks in the obtaining of employment information is the frequently cited work of Granovetter (1974). Although he makes no direct attempt to work through the networks of his respondents (his data is unreciprocated in that he asked respondents about contacts but did not follow up and ask these contacts about where the respondent was placed in their network), his work is often cited as establishing the role of networks in employment search. The bulk of my own evidence is indeed reciprocated data, and I provide a detailed account in Chapter 4. Here I take up the theoretical argument on networks and information transfer, in particular the emphasis by Granovetter on weak ties in the transmission of information.

Granovetter's central contention is that information transfer is facilitated by weak ties and not strong ties (Granovetter 1973, 1974):

> We must, therefore, begin to ask specific questions about under what circumstances people are *motivated* to give job information to their friends, and whether some of one's contacts are more 'strategically' placed to provide information than others. These two questions interact. A natural *a priori* idea might be, for instance, that those for whom one has strong ties would be more motivated to help with job information. There is, however, a structural tendency for those to whom one is only *weakly* tied, to have better access to job information one does not already have. . . .[6] Those to whom one is closest are likely to have the greatest overlap in contact with those one already knows, so that the information to which they are privy is likely to be the same as that which one already has.

> (Granovetter 1974: 52)

The role for weak ties is generated because they are argued to act as bridges between strongly internally connected groups. Granovetter appeals to balance theory in order to justify this claim: if A is strongly connected to C and A is strongly connected to B, then minimizing of psychological strain (see Heider 1958; Newcomb 1961) would require B to be strongly connected to C, with information being sealed inside such strong nets (Granovetter 1973). (See Anderson 1979 for a critique of this position.) With weak ties, balance is less crucial.

Related to this is the argument that strong ties are to be found amongst persons who are similarly placed, that is to say status equals. Finally, since strong ties among actors are seen, *a priori*, as involving more frequent contact and more time spent by actors with each other, it is unlikely that such ties can be the bridge between dissimilar information structures. In later sections I demonstrate empirically that status equals, strongly tied, may indeed have direct access to different sets of opportunities and information, in the first instance.

First, Granovetter confuses status equality with identical situation. Granovetter's 'forbidden triad' precludes strongly linked individuals having different sets of contacts and thus different sets of information resources (Granovetter 1973). But geographical separation of kin and friends is an obvious case where individuals can be strongly linked, be status equals and yet have access to widely differing information sets in the first instance.

Similarly, low frequency of physical contact cannot be taken as evidence of either weakness of ties or low information transfer. These aspects of geographical separation and migrant labour will be taken up in the next chapter, but the general point being made should now be clear. Status equals with strong ties may have different needs and different access to resources.

The only thorough-going analyses of such a dynamic are located in the peasant and development studies literature, with its focus upon the return of remittances from migrant family members to sedentary kin (Banerjee 1982; Collier and Green 1978). However, within the mainstream literature, the sociology of the family has also produced fragmented but consistent evidence on differential needs and abilities to provide aid (Young and Wilmott 1957; Sussman and Burchinall 1971; Bell 1968; Laumann 1966) as between status equals.[7]

Kin networks provide one example of situations where individuals of unequal resources but equal statuses may be strongly linked to one another. Furthermore, kin networks can also host strong linkages between individuals of unequal status, for the evidence is that kin linkages are preserved even where social mobility occurs (Goldthorpe, Llewellyn, and Payne 1980). Thus status equality (a) does not necessarily entail identical circumstances and (b) is not a necessary requirement for a strong tie.

Granovetter's strongly linked individuals tell all, share all, and do all with their friends – thus within a strongly linked group secrets cannot be kept. The assumption is that within a network of strong ties all members will receive the same information and with the same degree of accuracy.

Implicit in this position are two arguments. First, individuals within the same strong net will not possess information outside that net except by bridging links. Second, and more importantly, receiving information through this net would not place the individual in the necessary position to take advantage of the information, the members of his net being in competition with him for this vacancy. Hence the role of weak ties in the transmission of information.

When advocating this role for weak ties, however, Granovetter assumes that information is transmitted perfectly. He also fails to appreciate the barriers which can be erected deliberately to impede the flow of information even within strong nets; for instance, within certain communities wives often have poor information on the size of their partner's wage packets.[8]

In the previous two sections I have evidenced the use by employers of informal channels of recruitment – attracting family and friends of the existing workforce. I have also argued that one reason for this is the control that can be exercised on the new recruit via the mutual obligations that existed between him and the existing worker who introduced him. It is unclear how a weak tie, in the sense used by Granovetter, could prove useful to the employer in this context. Why should employers permit influence to be exercised in favour of individuals who are but weakly tied to the existing workforce? The organizational accommodation of such influence has to do with the link between sponsorship and control; sponsorship implies an acquaintance with the client prior to entry to the workplace, such relationships possessing a network dimension which has embedded within it certain sanctions and relations of control (see Jacobson 1978).

Consider now an existing member of a workforce not only transmitting job information to a contact but also using influence to place the contact in a job. The exercise of influence is not a costless event, for should a new recruit prove unsatisfactory the sponsor will endanger his own reputation. Furthermore, the active recruitment of unsatisfactory applicants to one's own place of work may generate an increased workload for the sponsor himself. Consequently, to the extent that influence is required to be used, then the weak-tie account must decline in plausibility.

My argument is that just as employers are involved in the use of information networks, employees are similarly involved in such processes of segregation and manipulation – sometimes with the employer as an explicit part of the recruitment process and sometimes off their own bat. Even within strong nets individuals are also capable of segregating and manipulating information and the strength of ties holding between pairs or sets of pairs are subject to variation – thus the strength of tie will affect the choice of first informant on the occasion of an employment vacancy.

Thus it is not even necessary to argue that information does not eventually reach a common pool of information in a strong net, but only that the sequence in which information is received reflects a preference ordering, thereby altering the competitive characteristic which Granovetter assumes always to hold. My own case-study evidence supports the argument that in reality such processes of sequencing exist; for respondents in both sets of primary material – fish-processing workers and the East End kinship/worker net – indicated that they frequently relayed messages about job opportunities in such a way as to benefit their preferred candidates within their kinship group.

I am thus stressing that individuals have preferences and make choices about whom they will inform and on whose behalf they will exercise influence. This is true even within strong nets, and it is difficult to see how or why influence could be exercised on behalf of a weak tie. Granovetter's work, focusing as it does on weak ties, furthermore fails to pay any attention to the norm of *reciprocity*. There is no discussion of the use of employment favours as a deliberate attempt to strengthen a tie or, even if the attempt was not deliberate, the consequence of an employment favour for the strength of a tie *ex post*.

There is no evidence in Granovetter on the strength of the tie *after* the passage of employment information, nor whether the current information is being provided in return for a favour in the past. Granovetter (1974) did not interview the link between his respondents and their employment, that is their contacts. Two consequences follow from this.

First, Granovetter is attempting to measure the strength of a tie independently of the perception of one-half of the dyad – he does not therefore allow for the possibility that a relationship which is construed as weak by one party can be construed as strong by another. Although this possibility would not be admitted by balance theory, my own data does show some evidence of differences in perception as to the strength of ties within dyads – the strongest evidence, however, is that provided by Laumann.[9] Second, Granovetter's failure to interview the other half of the dyads involved prevents him from considering how often the individual guided into employment was indeed the first preference of the contact. This would have shed more light on the strength of the tie.

My worries about Granovetter's use of the notion of weak ties (Granovetter 1973, 1974) may perhaps be crystallized by asking the question: how is the strength of a tie to be defined? Granovetter provides an attempt at definition as follows:

> Most intuitive notions of the 'strength' of an inter-personal tie should be satisfied by the following definition: the strength of a tie is a . . . combination of the amount of time, the emotional intensity, the intimacy (mutual confiding), and the reciprocal services which characterise the tie.
> (Granovetter 1973: 1361)

I have argued for the last of these as the basis of the strength of a tie. The strength of tie seems to lie in reciprocity and exchange involved in it – the mutual obligations that hold and the sanctions that can be applied if these obligations are not met (Bailey 1971; Ekeh 1974). It should be noted that a particular act of exchange does not of itself signify a strong direct tie between the parties exchanging, for the exchanging may be predicated upon the strength of the tie between each exchange partner and a third individual. That is to say, a discussion of strength of tie must accommodate both direct and indirect ties.

Although Granovetter (1974) recognizes the importance of the last three aspects of the strength of a tie, in practice he uses *frequency of contact* as the measure of tie strength:

> I have used the following categories for frequency of contact: 'often' – at least twice a week; 'occasionally' – more than once a year but less than twice a week; 'rarely' – once a year or less. Of those in the interview sample who found their job through contacts, 16.7 per cent reported that they were seeing their contact 'often', 55.6 per cent 'occasionally', while 27.8 per cent saw him 'rarely'. . . . The skew is to the weak side of the continuum. Moreover, those who found their job through weaker ties reported much more often that their contacts 'put in a good word' for them, as well as telling them about the job. *All* of those who saw their contact 'rarely'; 89.7 per cent of those who saw him occasionally; and 66.7 per cent of those who saw him often indicated that he did so.
>
> (Granovetter 1974: 53)

This is the central piece of evidence in Granovetter's contention on the strength of weak ties: 'This is a clear indication of the primacy of structures over motivation; close friends might indeed have been more *disposed* than acquaintances to use influence, but were simply less often in a position to do so' (Granovetter 1974: 54).

This evidence would on surface seem to support Granovetter's contention on the role of weak ties.[10] But considerable evidence for the opposite argument has been produced in the previous two sections (including my own case-study data) to show that for blue-collar workers the use of influence by existing workers who are social contacts is an important factor, indeed that employers encourage this practice. Thus Sheppard and Belitsky's study of Erie (Sheppard and Belitsky 1966) found that not only was friendship and kinship referral the most effective technique of job finding but, significantly, that respondents' evaluations considerably underrated it:

> While friends and relatives is the most effective source according to the effectiveness index, it ranks third in the workers' subjective evaluations. In other words, 44 per cent of all male blue collar workers actually got their jobs using this approach but only 16 per cent said this was the best way in their opinion to get jobs.
>
> (Sheppard and Belitsky 1966: 97)

Marsden's evidence for the UK is also suggestive:

> In times of shortage, it was not enough for the less skilled to be willing and to search hard. Employers did not need to advertise jobs, and the workless were dependent on their friends in work to help them with information, and with that information there came also the personal influence which might help them to get the job.
>
> (Marsden 1982: 64)

Granovetter himself concedes at some points that his professional, technical, and managerial sample cannot shed light on blue-collar patterns, but at other points – as in the above quote – he seems to be arguing for the general applicability of his findings.

It should be noted that when respondents were asked how their contact knew about the job, a substantial proportion of those finding employment through past work contacts (one-fifth of 68.7 per cent)[11] responded that the contact was the new employer himself! These are all cases where the employer has changed companies and provided information (and presumably influence) in connection with a job in the new company.

Quite apart from the fact that such personal one-to-one search by individual employers is unlikely to be efficient in large-scale blue-collar enterprises, there is the theoretical point that since these former employers are hiring individuals who were past employees, past work performance is therefore known.

The return to an employer on aiding in the securing of opportunity for a respondent is different from that involved in any return to persons with less direct control over employment resources. The 'weakness' or otherwise of the tie in social terms is not relevant – the transaction is purely an economic one. The employer offers job information and secures the job in anticipation of good performance – the offer would not have been made otherwise. The weakness or otherwise of the tie in this more directly economic transaction is not of great importance.

There remains the question of why a weak tie, in a social sense, should provide information and indeed use influence to secure employment. In order to develop my argument here, I refer to the work of Sahlins, who argues as follows:

> Yet the connection between material flow and social relations is reciprocal. A specific social relation may constrain a given movement of goods, but a specific transaction – by the same token – suggests a particular social relation. *If friends make gifts, gifts make friends.*
>
> (Sahlins 1965: 139)

Sahlins's analysis was directed towards non-industrial societies (Sahlins 1965), but by exchanging the term 'information flow' for 'material flow' we can immediately see its relevance for our critique of Granovetter. For clearly one possible motivation for providing aid is precisely that of a desire to strengthen the tie. Thus the expectation of creating a stronger tie may precisely underlie the behaviour of weak ties in employment information transmission, *even* if we were to accept Granovetter's characterization of the ties between his respondents and informants based on frequency of contact. Since motivation is never directly addressed, the balance between motivation and structure cannot be properly evaluated from his data set.

Let us now consider more directly some aspects of reciprocity which do not receive attention in Granovetter's theory. This is not surprising given the existing state of the literature:

The economic anthropology of reciprocity, however, is not at the same stage. One reason, perhaps, is a popular tendency to view reciprocity as balance, as unconditional one for one exchange. Considered as a material transfer, reciprocity is often not that at all. Indeed it is precisely through scrutiny of departures from balanced exchange that one glimpses the interplay between reciprocity, social relations and material circumstances.

(Sahlins 1965: 144)

A useful distinction for the purpose of our analysis is that of balanced and generalized reciprocity. The former refers to a direct exchange where there is more or less precise reckoning of the two flows. Sahlins develops the concept of 'generalized reciprocity' as follows:

Reckoning of debts outstanding cannot be overt and is typically left out of account. This is not to say that handing things in such form, even to 'loved ones', generates no counter-obligation. But the counter is not stipulated by time, quantity, or quality: the expectation of reciprocity is indefinite. ... Receiving goods lays on a diffuse obligation to reciprocate when necessary to the donor and/or possible for the recipient.

(Sahlins 1965: 147)

Applying this approach to Granovetter's data and analysis, we can ask what the moral as opposed to mechanical basis of information exchange is. Why should individuals pass information to and exercise influence on behalf of those to whom they are weakly tied? The answer must be that either a past obligation is being fulfilled or a future obligation is being created by the act.

Where obligations are implicit rather than explicit there need be no direct return, nor need there be a favour in the recent past which is being returned. Moreover, third parties may be involved – the observed actors may be merely the agencies of repayment of favours between other actors. All of these considerations militate against Granovetter's use of frequency of contact as defining the strength of a tie. Rather, I would turn the argument on its head: the fact that employment aid is being given without any immediate expectation of return and without frequent contact is evidence of the strength of the tie, or of another set of ties lying behind the exchange, rather than of its weakness. I am thus arguing that transactions in the central economic area of employment information and aid provide us with a trace on the social networks that overlap and interact with the employment sphere.

There is, however, a rather simple explanation of the conflict between Granovetter's findings and the balance of contrary evidence presented here. In order to square the two sets of findings, we must start by asking what set of labour-market circumstances favour the use of weak ties in employment search and how these differ from those favouring the use of strong ties. Granovetter's research was conducted at a time and in an area where there was an acute labour shortage in the sector of employment he was examining. Under these circumstances, and in a sector where training is linked with formal credentials, weak ties are not surprising. However, in situations where skill is important but formal credentials are weak or in situations of recession, that is situations of labour surplus, strong ties are of importance. Granovetter fails to consider the special circumstances of the labour market he studied and it is this which explains the difference between his findings and those of many other studies. His thesis on the role of weak ties in employment search thus requires substantial qualification and modification.

The concept of 'proxy' is absent from Granovetter's analysis despite the presentation of material which indicates its relevance. Granovetter is not alone in his failure to theorize the influence of third parties in social exchange, for the work of Hill demonstrates the same tendency.[12]

In common with many exchange theorists, Hill's focus is on dyadic ties:

> The essence of [the preferential hiring] relationship, in the pure type, was the way it bound together people who interacted together on a personal, face to face basis. This was a dyadic tie which linked together pairs of individuals and not groups.
>
> (Hill 1976: 22)

Hill fails to discuss, as do many of the exchange theorists who focus on the dyad as the relevant unit of analysis, the manner in which the formation of and interactions between such dyads are themselves products of the surrounding network of relations.[13] Yet much of the evidence presented by Hill lends itself to this approach:

> Take the Big Boot gang – got all the cream on those ferry boats at 33 shed but you had to be a green scarf [Irish Catholic] to get in there. Any time Father X [the local priest] found someone in trouble – you know, the kiddies without clothes or the wife sick – he told the shipworker and the man got a couple of days with the gang.
>
> (Hill 1976: 19)

The problems inherent in conceptualizing social interaction as dyadic purely upon the basis that only two parties are immediately present or formally involved in any event or 'contract' are clear.

Social exchange, and we take the preferential hiring practices documented by Hill to be processes of such social exchange, takes place typically within a moral context which involves, and is seen by the actors to involve, other parties. Thus the involvement of the Catholic priest in the procurement of employment is no aberration. To conceptualize the resulting relationship between the hired man and the existing workers as dyadic is problematic, for it cannot accommodate the initial and continuing influence of the priest on the relationship. Ties are not only ties between individuals but also between groups where agencies outside of the dyad can influence the behaviour of either party or the content of the relationship. The focus on linked pairs is unduly restrictive – at the very least, Hill's earliest statement on the role of 'good families' as being central to the professional hiring system is not compatible with his later dyadic account of employment and kin relationships. The weaknesses of the dyadic account, although apparent in uses such as that of Hill, is particularly clear when migrant labour is studied – and it is to this aspect of the family and employment connection that I turn in Chapter 4.

Conclusion

Despite a growing, albeit fragmented, body of evidence on the role of kin and friendship links in the employment context, mainstream social-network analysis and mainstream industrial sociology have failed to develop a theoretical paradigm for the understanding of the family/friends–employment/work nexus. In the light of this evidence, I have looked at the rationale – for employers and employees – of using family and friends as a recruitment and job-search channel, and further evidence has been presented on the screening role that kin/friendship networks can provide for the employer.

The direct recruitment implications of the above theory and evidence are taken up later in Chapter 4. A major object of this chapter, however, has been to examine the implications of this evidence for mainstream social-network analysis and mainstream industrial sociology. The main methodological conclusion is the limited role of observed frequency of contact in identifying an occupational community outside work. First, most studies focus on contact between males and thereby miss out the network implications of female contact. Second, even within a dyadic perspective, a strong tie between a pair of individuals does not necessarily need to be accompanied by high frequency of contact – the strength of the tie is indicated by employment aid and information transfer, and this can happen through proxies.

I have thus taken issue with Granovetter's thesis that it is weak ties that are important in employment information transfer, and I argue that his data allows for my interpretation. I have also taken issue with Hill's conclusion, in the mould of the dominant paradigm, that an occupational community does not exist outside work.

Finally, I have argued that the dyadic perspective – present in most studies – is an inadequate theoretical base from which to establish community. My theorizing, my interpretation of existing evidence, and my presentation of my own primary material all point towards dyadic interaction being a product of the overall network structure, and I have pointed to the theoretical and empirical implications of this perspective. The next chapter of this book continues this line of investigation.

4
Migration, kinship, and recruitment policies

Introduction

In this chapter it is argued that the analysis of the previous chapters of the role of kin in gaining employment is considerably strengthened when the part played by social networks in accomplishing migration is considered. Once again the orthodoxy runs counter to my analysis. An integral part of the Parsonian thesis of the decline of the extended family appears to be the dispersal of family owing to the high degrees of geographic mobility induced and required by industrialization.

Even Litwak, whose position is concerned with the ability of the middle-class family to retain its structure and meaning over distance, appears to accept implicitly the necessity of the geographical dispersal of the component units of the family in complex, industrial societies (Litwak 1970). Within his work there is no evidence that components regroup and re-establish geographical proximity over time.

Adams, while accepting that kin networks are important for the immobile working class, has this to say of their counterparts in the mobile working class:

> We recall that Parsons's paper, which referred to the middle classes, asserted that chances of residential separation from kin are great, and intimated that residential separation really means isolation. This should be altered to read that the chances of middle class separation from kin are moderately great, but that this eventuality does not result in isolation from kin of orientation. On the other hand, working class migration and separation from kin, though less frequent, is apt to result in virtual isolation from all kin except parents where it does occur.
>
> (Adams 1971: 133)

From a position diametrically opposed to that above, this chapter argues that it is precisely for the mobile working class that regrouping and relocation of the kin network is the likeliest. The distinction should be made between middle-class career-related mobility and working-class job-related mobility. Career-connected dispersal contains within it no particular geographical familial constraints; as dispersal takes place on the basis of social advancement, the protective or insurance reasons for regrouping diminish in importance.

However, where family dispersal is concerned with the maintenance rather than advancement of position, as in the case of 'employment-push' migration, the migration is experienced as forced. Much working-class migration is of this forced character (see Petersen 1970; Taylor 1969; Schaffer 1970; Laurie 1975; Brody 1979). In such circumstances, regrouping of the family in a new location is likely to take place.

This is not to suggest that the complete family network of relations will be transferred to the new location but that some significant part of this network will gravitate there. This provides a further twist to the perspective provided by Litwak, and away from the Parsonian vision; for instead of individual component units being in contact with one another, more elaborate and complex structures appear to be interacting over distance. Indeed, this is precisely what we observe in chain migration.

Migrants who have been successful in obtaining employment transfer resources and information on employment opportunities back to their families in the area of origin (Richmond 1969). These 'spearhead' migrants are important in inducing further migration from the home area to that particular work location. Eventually, a clustering of family members in the new location occurs.

Chance is transformed into system by the character of the family information network. Systematic connections between regions are established precisely on this basis: information elicits migration, while migration generates remittances back to the area of origin (Ballard and Ballard 1977). Thus success is not best attained by severing kinship linkages but by consolidating them. The success of one family member creates a chain of opportunities for the kin network. Chain employment and chain migration, I will argue, are intimately connected.

Chain employment and chain migration: historical evidence

An important source of historical evidence on the links between family, employment, and migration is the classical study of Ireland by Arensberg and Kimball ([1940] 1968). In the context of a peasantry gaining its experience of the industrial world, they provide us with strong evidence of the ability of the family to regroup, on the basis of the 'capture' of sets of employment opportunities. They point out that migration of some members of the family does not necessarily weaken family ties:

> Nevertheless this necessary dispersal of the members of the family at its reorganisation does not necessarily destroy the family ties. The bonds of

affection and family obligation still hold. If they have migrated, the family members send back remittances and passage money for nephews and nieces and brothers and sisters left at home.

(Arensberg and Kimball 1968: 143)

They find considerable evidence of chain migration and provide some colourful illustrations of it:

There is a marked tendency for emigration from a local region to perpetuate itself, sons and daughters of each generation going out to join members of the last. . . . One district round Cross to the west of Carrigholt, a little settlement on the Loop head peninsula which juts out from Clare into the Atlantic at the Shannon's mouth, is said locally to be supported by sons in the Shanghai police force. The first to go became Chief of Police in the international settlement there and many places in the force have gone to the men of Cross.

(Arensberg and Kimball 1968: 143)

Clearly, family can turn chance into system. Arensberg and Kimball's account does raise the question of where precisely the resources necessary to the financing of migration are generated. As we shall see, this has a large influence on the nature of migration and on the social structures that result.

For instance, in certain cases of nineteenth-century English migration to America, Erikson finds that resources are transferred from the area of origin to the 'newly arrived' migrant (Erikson 1972). This reflects an interest by the kin network in the development of increased opportunity in the long term. Most of the migration in which this peculiar remittance pattern occurs is craft migration – it provides the migrant with the opportunity to set up a business or enter smallholding agriculture rather than to engage, of necessity, in wage employment.

However, the traditional Irish pattern of migration financing was based on remittances directed from America to Ireland, and afforded no such period of experimentation with new opportunity. Members of the family arrived in America one by one, with wage employment being taken up immediately – this was essential to meet the migration costs of the remaining members of the family.[1]

Irish migration was not financed solely by the sending back of the wages of the migrant individual or group, for another agency was involved. This agency was the American employer who hired Irish labour on a contract basis, meeting the cost of the passage and guaranteeing employment on arrival (Arensberg and Kimball 1968; Kennedy 1973).[2]

Irish labour already in the USA often made the arrangements for the employer, recruiting and vouchsafing labour from amongst their own kith and kin. But contract labour had little opportunity to arrive in cohesive family groups; pure labour migration preceded family migration.

One consequence of such a mode of entry is that the whole of the ethnic group is to be found within the same section of the labour market and that this mode of entry, with its consequent depression of wages, is not likely to find support amongst the indigenous labour force. Under pressure from organized labour the US government passed a law in 1885[3] placing a barrier to the direct contracting of labour by employers whilst simultaneously requiring that immigrants have a sponsor within the USA (Macdonald and Macdonald 1962). The consequence of this was to further strengthen the role of kin networks, with employers seeking to use these in their recruitment procedures.

The intersection of employer and employee interest, given the framework of the law, thus resulted in the strengthening of kin networks over distance rather than in their weakening. It was the interaction between employer and kin networks which permitted the development of chain migration in a context where the law was hostile to long-distance direct recruitment by employers. The Irish historical experience highlights the importance of the funding base of chain migration in determining the duration of a migration stream and for the occupational placement of migrants.

Other studies of migration to the USA also emphasize the role of kin in chain employment (Ianni and Ruess-Ianni 1972; Yans-McLaughlin 1971; Macdonald and Macdonald 1964). But a novel source of evidence on the links between chain employment and chain migration is Mormino (1982). Mormino informs us that the core of Tampa's Italian community originates from three villages in south-west Sicily and one village in Palermo.[4] Thus four specific Italian villages generated the late-nineteenth-century and early-twentieth-century Italian migration to Tampa. Information was being transmitted along a highly specific route. Mormino testifies that 'Sicilians came to Tampa, not as uprooted and alienated individuals, but in chains of related individuals or households. . . . The movement of friends and kin generated knowledge about local labour conditions' (Mormino 1982: 402).

A further useful source on the relationship between migration, kin, and employment in the USA is the work of Hareven (1975b). Her work on New England mill towns encompasses three distinct ethnic groups: the Irish, the Italians, and French Canadians.

> French Canadians were streaming to Manchester in response to systematic recruitment propaganda issued out of Manchester through their own ethnic organisations and through communications from relatives. Their kin met them on arrival, placed them in their first job and located them as temporary boarders until they found a corporation flat or rented an apartment in the growing French Canadian section of the city's west side.
>
> (Hareven 1975b: 374)

The involvement of these kinship networks in job placement was not confined to Manchester but was pervasive throughout the entire industrial region of New England, with considerable mobility occurring between the main mill towns:[5]

> Family has thus formed a network of employment opportunities as well as

temporary and permanent stations for migration. Migration did not destroy the family and kin group. It transposed a formerly localised family pattern over an entire industrial region in New England.

(Hareven 1975b: 374)

Clearly, Hareven's material demonstrates that the family is capable of retaining its position as an organizing principle in the workplace within industrial employment. It provides evidence that geographical separation does not of itself signal or necessitate the weakening of social ties. Kennedy, Mormino, and Hareven all provide evidence on the importance of strong ties in employers' recruitment strategies and do so within an American context. This represents a divergence from Granovetter's material which argues the importance of weak ties in occupational mobility. The historical evidence indicates the extent to which migration occurs along highly specific routes, a process in which kinship, in conjunction with a specific employer, plays an organizing role.

Comparable historical evidence also exists for the UK. Anderson recognizes the importance of kin aid in employment search during the nineteenth century in industrializing Lancashire. Thus he argues:

Recruitment to jobs in the factories or labouring gangs was similarly influenced by kinship considerations. 'Asking for' a job for kin was normal in the factory towns and the employers used the kinship system to recruit from the country.

(Anderson 1971b: 90)

Anderson goes on to explicitly link kinship, employment, and migration. Industrial employment not only provided a basis for meeting the obligations to kin, but also possessed potential for widening the definition of kinship. Where resources are constrained, the definition of kinship is likely to be narrow; by harnessing the recruitment process of a large employer, the social group can afford to expand its definitions of kinship beyond the boundaries that would pertain if income had to be derived, for instance, from smallholding agriculture or cottage industry. Employment aid is not only widening the definition of kin, but also intensifying it:

Many employers consciously set out to recruit whole families, or all the younger members of the families as they reached working age, or at least welcomed especially relatives of their employees. An employer of Parish assisted migrants noted that he could 'now, without any trouble, supply myself from Bledlow, by mentioning to my Bledlow hands that I am ready to take more.' . . . Even where employers did not follow a deliberate policy of recruiting family members, workers, particularly if they were reliable, could often obtain places for children and other kin in the firm on a preferential basis. . . . Numerous other cases appear of persons in all stations of life soliciting employers for jobs for friends and relatives. Indeed, at a time when the demand for jobs frequently exceeded the supply, so that employers could take the pick of the field, this seems to have been the usual way of getting a job, and one which will have obviously reinforced kinship bonds to some degree.

(Anderson 1971a: 118–19)

The interaction between kin interest and employer interest generates the twin institutions of chain employment and chain migration. Geographical distance does not appear to have weakened kin ties, for despite a period of separation, aid is still being supplied within the framework of kin. Once again the ties involved in labour recruitment are strong in character, the strength of the ties constituting part of the employer's recruitment strategy for ensuring the hiring of appropriate and controllable labour. This is the implication of Anderson's evidence on the continuous resort of employers to those sources of labour vouched for and accessed by their existing workforce.

Anderson explicitly recognizes that geographical mobility does not necessarily weaken existing social ties and takes issue with what he takes to be the orthodoxy; that is, that migration is necessarily disruptive of existing social ties:

One can justifiably deduce that even the migrants were able to build up an important kinship net in the towns. ... This might at first glance seem slightly surprising in view of the widely held view that migration is a key source of disruption of kinship bonds. This view is however an oversimplification even if only the rural situation is considered. If the urban context is also taken into account then the common belief is often even more erroneous. .. Migrants had reasons specific to themselves for wanting to build up and maintain kinship links, for migration in all societies presents specific problems which must be met if the migrant is to adapt to a new life in his new community. He needs information about prospects and conditions to help him decide whether or not and where to go. If he goes, he is faced immediately with the problem of finding somewhere to live, of finding a job, and of adapting himself in hundreds of other ways to the new community.

(Anderson 1971a: 153–4)

Historical evidence of employers' ability to harness labour en masse from far distant parts is not confined to Anderson alone. Anderson's evidence is for the Lancashire cotton industry; similar historical evidence is available for the Scottish cotton industry.[6] A particularly useful, though little-known source is the work of Handley (1943). Handley has gathered together a body of nineteenth-century materials which document employer recruitment strategies in respect of Irish labour in Scotland. He demonstrates how the harnessing of particular sources of distant labour through chain migration benefited Scottish employers. He offers an employer's first-hand account of the benefits accruing from recruiting through his existing Irish workforce.

These are threefold: the introduction of plentiful supplies of labour, the provision of residential aid to new workforce entrants by this labour, and the provision of training to new recruits on the basis of social-network membership. This practice of recruitment, as Hareven's evidence suggests, was of considerable significance to large employers. Hugh Cogan, a nineteenth-century employer with a workforce of 800 weavers, had this to say: 'In the cotton trade, especially in the weaving department, we could not have done without the Irish. . . . The Irish send over for relations, or acquaintances or townspeople, and take them in as lodgers, and train them to the weaving' (quoted by Handley 1943). Although Cogan does not explicitly mention the control properties of this relationship between social networks and employment chances other employers cited by Handley do.

Whereas within the new American labour history, there is widespread recognition and discussion of employers' role in shaping their workforces by the intentional harnessing and switching of different sources of labour, there has been little discussion of such practices within the UK labour process or labour history debates. Handley's work provides material for the UK which is directly comparable to that discussed in the American literature, a particular example of which is his evidence on the deliberate exclusion of local Scottish labour from the workplace by Scottish employers. This strategy of excluding local labour from employment was dependent upon the long-distance recruitment of Irish labour. These recruitment strategies engendered divisions and enhanced sectional conflicts within labour. Our object here has been to indicate the role of chain migration and chain employment in the constructing of such conflicts.

Both the US and the UK historical evidence demonstrates that the relationship between employment and migration is poorly explained by concentrating solely on the motivation and behaviour of the individual migrant. There is also a need to focus on the involvement of employers in inducing mass and chain migration.

Family, employment, and migration: contemporary evidence

Rural–urban migration in developing countries
One of the most consistent findings in the large literature on rural-to-urban migration in developing countries is the importance of presence of family and friends in the destination area as an explanatory variable for the rate of migration from a particular area of origin (Anand 1971; Banerjee and Kanbur 1981; Banerjee 1982; Barnum and Sabot 1977; Caldwell 1969; Collier and Green 1978; Rempel 1970). Collier and Green rely on Rempel's data from Kenya (Rempel 1970) to emphasize the role of social networks:

> Of Rempel's sample 65 per cent indicated that their family or friends were their primary source of information on urban centres. . . . This is powerful evidence for the importance of social networks as channels of information in Kenya. Not only was the social network the primary source of information for two-thirds of all migrants, but for about half of the migrants it appeared to be virtually their sole source. Social networks are also influential in the choice of destination. Twenty-four per cent of Rempel's sample gave presence of kin or

friends as their primary reason for the selection of their particular destination, and 61 per cent gave employment opportunities as their primary reason.
Further, of this latter group 64 per cent of those giving a secondary reason
suggested presence of kin or friends.

(Collier and Green 1978: 33)

Caldwell provides similar evidence for Ghana (Caldwell 1969). While
the role of employers in harnessing kin networks cannot be adequately
studied using the data collected by Rempel (1970) or Caldwell (1969), the
fact that of those giving employment opportunity as the major reason
for migrating two-thirds also mentioned kin and friends is suggestive,
as is the explicit reference to kin help in employment search (Banerjee
1981). Collier and Green go on to spell out the possible role of social
networks in migration:

Social networks can be influential in the choice of destination for two reasons.
The network provides reception facilities for the migrant and it provides
information. While not denying the importance of the reception function of
networks we regard the information function as significant. ... The
proportion of the educated relying primarily on kin or friends for information
is only 74 per cent of the proportion of the less educated. If the major
importance of social networks as an influence upon choice of destination was
due to reception facilities rather than information, we would expect no such
difference in the proportion of the educated and the less educated giving
presence of kin or friends as their primary reason for choice of destination.

(Collier and Green 1978: 33)

The role of kin in transmitting information is one reason why
employers use kin networks as a recruitment channel. Although there is
no direct evidence of this in Collier and Green's (1978) work, their
findings on information transfer are suggestive. Collier and Green
(1978) do not discuss the consequences of use of kin for information and
aid, in terms of the strength of ties. The historical evidence suggests a
strengthening of ties as a result of such a contact, even over large
distances. Banerjee's evidence on remittance suggests a similar pattern
(Banerjee 1981), although this matter needs to be investigated further
with more detailed data.

Ethnic labour forces
Employer involvement in contemporary migration has been documented for New Commonwealth immigration to Britain. Thus Peach
comments as follows on West Indian migration to Britain: 'Emigration
to the UK was not only officially encouraged but sponsored recruitment, for instance, by London Transport and long term loans were
available for some migrants' (Peach 1968: 20).

Whether they were recruited directly in the West Indies (as were many
workers for London Transport and nurses in Barbados) or whether they
moved through their own initiative, the bulk of West Indians were destined
to fill vacancies for which there was either insufficient white labour available

or which white workers were insufficiently willing to fill.

(Peach 1968: 94)

The role of kin and friends in providing trustworthy information in either of the above two cases is emphasized by Davison (1962) in a study of Jamaican migration:

> The migrants are eager to obtain reliable information about Britain. . . . They are not interested in warnings and exhortations which run counter to the evidence of letters and remittances from people they know personally, who are already established in Britain.

(Davidson, quoted in Collier and Green 1978: 32)

Further evidence on the role of kin in information transfer and on kin-connected entry is provided by Alavi on Pakistanis (Alavi 1963), Desai on Indians (Desai 1963), Palmer on Italians (Palmer 1977), Watson on Chinese (Watson 1977), and by a number of other studies. Cavendish produces evidence of kin-connected entry and direct-recruitment strategies in relation to the use of female Irish labour in the UK car components industry (Cavendish 1982). Her material also demonstrates the continued importance of the family in the workplace for other groups – the employer concerned recruits the bulk of its labour force through its existing employees, using a West Indian and an Asian employment network as well as the Irish one.

A major recent contribution to the study of kin-connected entry which focuses on the workplace is the study of Brooks and Singh (1979). They document ethnic control over employment vacancies in the West Midlands, with preferential hiring policies and patronage systems. Brooks and Singh believe they have discovered an exception to the rule, but the evidence presented so far suggests that the phenomenon they have identified is far more general.

A close investigation of the clustering of Asians in the foundry industry in the West Midlands revealed that employees were highly involved in the recruitment practices of the employer, representing not only a major channel of information but also a major agency of introduction, and they further provide us with evidence of sequential or chain entry of members of the same network.

Brooks and Singh highlight the role of spearhead migrants who become patrons in the recruitment process. However, throughout the paper, they handle the transaction between the patron and the recruit as if it were a discrete and specific exchange between two parties. While this may be important in the early stages of the process, sequential entry would tend to reduce rather than increase the importance of the patron. Certainly, his importance to the employer declines, and this is the effective basis of his power, since each new recruit is connected into the same kinship net and is thus a potential channel of information and recruitment for the same quality of labour, and on the same principle, as that supplied through the initial patron.

Similarly, increased kin presence in the workplace provides the individual kin member seeking entry with a greater number of alternative channels of access or routes. However, this issue received no explicit consideration by Brooks and Singh. Nor do they consider the possibility of multiple lines of introduction, where the greater the number of present employees who speak in favour of the same potential recruit, the greater is the likelihood of that individual being recruited to the workforce. Increased kin presence further restricts the power of the single patron by re-establishing customary obligations *vis-à-vis* each other.

Brooks and Singh's patrons also hold position by virtue of custom, so that using their data we cannot separate out specific exchanges around employment and customary status or standing in the ethnic group involved. However, the overall theoretical point should be clear. As chain migration continues, we have to abandon the notion of a dyadic tie between the patron and the new recruit (even if this were relevant initially), and move over to the concept of a process of generalized exchange.

Information and introduction services are not only exchanged in repayment for past favours between the two individuals directly involved but are afforded to proxies in repayment for such debts. While being a departure from the North American–British sociological tradition, this view is highly congruent with continental thinking, most particularly the work of Mauss and Lévi-Strauss. This theoretical argument is taken up again later in this chapter and my own empirical evidence from fieldwork on these processes is advanced in support of it.

Employer recruitment in Britain
The historical evidence indicates that the harnessing of chain migration processes by employers as a recruitment method is frequently preceded by recruitment drives outside of their local labour markets. There are a number of contemporary UK studies which identify employer use of this recruitment strategy in the present period. My argument is that such practices of direct recruitment are likely to accommodate the subsequent harnessing of social networks by employers with future labour requirements being met by processes of chain employment and chain migration.[7]

Not only does labour search for employment but employers also search for labour. Much of the literature assumes that employers merely advertise the existence of vacancies and that as a consequence of labour's search, labour is drawn to the workplace. Little consideration has been formally given within the literature to the conducting of recruiting drives by employers in advanced industrial societies into areas geographically removed from the plant or workplace. Where employers undertake such recruitment drives, typically they are concerned to recruit labour in bulk.

Bulk recruitment of labour provides the opportunity for group migration; that is to say, it enables the simultaneous migration of individuals who are connected to one another to the same destination. *It permits the transportation of sets of ties or networks over distance.* Furthermore, where employers undertake such recruitment drives, it is usually in order to establish the basis of more extensive recruitment through the chain migration mechanism already discussed. Neither direct recruitment nor the chain employment it calls forth has received the sustained attention of the literature.

Chapters 6 and 7 discuss the way in which adopting such recruitment practices permits employers to shape their workforces and to construct labour markets. For the present I will confine myself to establishing that such practices of direct recruitment, which are used in the UK still, bear a close resemblance to the practices I have detailed for the historical period. From my own evidence I will provide considerable detail as to how direct recruitment drives are conducted, having interviewed labour managers, government officials, and workers who have had experience of this form of recruitment. But now some secondary evidence will be considered.

First, I draw on evidence presented by Francis *et al.* in their study of the West Midlands car industry in the late 1970s and early 1980s (Francis *et al.* 1982). Unable to attract skilled labour locally at the existing wage levels, British Leyland at Longbridge were forced to search elsewhere for their supply of maintenance labour:

> For maintenance, management were obliged to use the external labour market due to continuing skill shortages within the Company because of the pay levels prevailing. Maintenance management toured the depressed areas of Merseyside, Scotland and the North East recruiting workers.
>
> (Francis *et al.* 1982: 17)

Francis *et al.* offer us no further detail on the social composition of these recruitment streams other than their area of origin. Here I am concerned to argue that this recruitment practice has the potential to accommodate kin-connected and friendship-connected migration. At a minimum, it indicates the extent to which working-class migration cannot be seen as the product of individual search.

An earlier and better-known study from which the existence of direct recruitment practices can be gleaned is the Affluent Worker study (Goldthorpe *et al.* 1968a, 1968b, 1969). Two of the employers, Vauxhall and Skefko, studied in the Affluent Worker project made use of such direct recruitment methods in their search for labour. Although the study team indicate these firms' involvement in this recruitment procedure, they make no attempt to assess the consequences of such practices for the composition of the workforce.[8] My own fieldwork discussed in Chapter 6 provides more detail on Vauxhall's use of this recruitment practice and considers the implications of such a recruitment method for some of the Affluent Worker arguments. Here it can be noted that although within the Affluent Worker study evidence exists on the use of direct recruitment methods, there is no attempt to investigate its possible chain-employment and chain-migration consequences. Within the data presented, however, there is considerable evidence of chain migration. These points are taken up in detail in Chapters 6 and 7.

Other evidence on direct recruitment, though over a shorter distance, but once again in the car industry, is that offered by Friedman (1977). Friedman makes the explicit connection between employers' attempts to change the character of the existing workforce and the use of this method, though once again he does not do so in any great detail:

> During 1971 and again in 1974/1975 both Chrysler and British Leyland (Coventry) laid off considerable numbers of car workers. In 1971 in particular, workers did not have to be laid off due to the technical unavailability of work. They were laid off as a disciplinary measure. . . . After layoffs at Ryton during 1971, when Chrysler began recruiting again, men were brought in from the dying hosiery industry around Hinckley, Leicestershire in spite of high unemployment in Coventry at the time. These workers had little tradition of militancy and were used to working very long hours.
>
> (Friedman 1971: 236–7)

Friedman provides us with no direct evidence on the involvement of kin in the contemporary workplace in his analysis, although his study also encompasses the historical role played by the family in the Leicester hosiery industry. Palmer has noted the dependence of the employer on the family as a recruitment and skilling agency in the US hosiery industry (Palmer 1954). Taking together Friedman's evidence on the nineteenth-century Leicester hosiery industry, Palmer's evidence on the twentieth-century US hosiery industry, and Manwaring's (1982), Jenkins *et al.*'s (1983) and Lee and Wrench's (1981) work on the importance of the family in employment search in the East and West Midlands, it is not unlikely that kin linkages were involved in this move from Hinckley to Coventry.

Further evidence on direct recruitment strategies within the car industry is, however, contained in the work of Beynon (1973). Friedman indicated that Chrysler had recruited outside the Coventry area in order to obtain supplies of green labour. Beynon finds evidence of Ford's attempt to adopt the same strategy in Halewood, Merseyside. In its attempt to produce a plant without militants the company recruited in the first instance a workforce on the basis of its inexperience of factory work. Sixty per cent of the workforce had no experience of factory work previously, and furthermore they were recruited from distant locations.

The car industry has not been alone in its use of direct recruitment; the Coal Board has also made extensive use of the practice. Kahn, studying job search in the context of redundancies in the car industry, found that special recruiting teams were sent to the British Motor Corporation in order to recruit labour for the coal industry (Kahn 1964). Kahn had indeed found evidence of kin connection within the workforce studied. Furthermore, she found evidence of the use of kin connection in the search for and obtaining of subsequent jobs.[9] Kahn does not provide evidence on the uptake of such direct recruitment schemes in any detail, and so we have no information on kin involvement in such schemes. Direct recruitment activities aimed at attracting the BMC workers was not, however, confined to the coal industry, for a recruiting van was stationed outside the works 'inviting men to join a concern of bus and lorry builders at some distance from Birmingham'.

Thus Kahn provides us with evidence on the recruiting employer's possession of an administrative base within companies shedding labour. Such companies, she tells us, were provided with offices inside the plant. Goodman and Samuel in the same period found similar practices, although they were studying recruitment into the car industry, not recruitment out of it (Goodman and Samuel 1966). They undertook an analysis of the first 3,000 hourly paid (manual) workers employed by a new factory in a development district. Their findings parallel those produced by other studies of the car industry cited in this chapter. First, the company undertook intensive recruiting drives in other development areas in order to obtain labour. Half of the labour imported in this manner was unemployed and thus eligible for state migratory assistance when moving to the plant. Second, recruits to the production line who had an immediately previous experience of factory production were in a minority – the labour was green. Third, in its new workforce, a quarter came from eight local firms.

Even when new workforces are formed this evidence suggests there are existing links holding between the membership, for the last employer may be a shared employer. Workers do not necessarily undertake occupational mobility as individuals; there may indeed be a group dynamic involved[10] – groups of workers may move together (in Ch. 8 I discuss in some depth precisely this situation). Direct recruitment may take place in situations of mass redundancy, greater numbers providing the searching employer with a highly cost-effective recruitment method. The sociological implications of this recruitment practice remain unexplored in the literature to date.

In case the car industry is thought to be unique in the British context, I also point to the work of Stacey *et al.* on migration in the context of the relocation of a plant, the first British re-study of a fieldwork site – Banbury:

> As the fieldwork continued we became increasingly aware of the complexity of the relationship between economic position and local social behaviour and realised that no simple and close association could be assumed between social and geographic mobility and particular sets of attitudes and behaviour.
> (Stacey *et al.* 1975: 27)

Banbury, like Luton (which I discuss in Ch. 6), enjoyed expanded-town status, providing overspill accommodation for London and Birmingham. Migration from Birmingham to Banbury was explained by the decision of a single employer, Bird's, to relocate the plant in the expanded town. It was, as Stacey points out, at the behest of a large organization that the individuals moved. Stacey herself makes no reference to kinship links holding within this workforce, although she notes that common place of origin provides the basis of friendship for this group.

However, Stacey's work is supplemented by that of Mann, who although in the main subscribing to the thesis that geographical mobility is necessarily disruptive of social ties, provides evidence of kin-connected migration within the Bird's workforce (Mann 1973).[11] Mann provides evidence not only upon the simultaneous migration of kin under the joint auspices of the employer and the local authority, which was responsible for the provision of housing, but also of subsequent chain migration by remaining family members to the new locale. His evidence on and his discussion of kin connection, in the spirit of the period, is confined to the footnotes.

Expanded-town status provided Bird's with access to new local authority housing for its workforce thus enabling the company to put together an employment/residence package. Bird's provided housing allowances which enabled their workers to enter the private housing market (Mann 1973; Stacey *et al.* 1975). Stacey, however, only mentions the involvement of the employer in workforce purchase in passing and provides no further detail on the topic. Her evidence is included here in order to highlight the extent to which employers are involved in the organization of working-class migration and to indicate the extent to which migration under such auspices can accommodate continuing ties.

Finally, I would like to consider the work of Taylor on migration from the Durham coalfields (Taylor 1969). He provides evidence of direct recruitment within the coal industry, that is for movement from one colliery to another in a different region. Taylor documents the operations of the Coal Board's inter-divisional transfer scheme. Recruiting officers were sent from areas hosting expanding pits to villages where pit closures had taken place, in order to recruit new supplies of labour. These schemes were widely advertised, making use of commercial broadcasting as well as mobile recruitment vans. Marsden, talking of the unemployed in the North East, says, 'The only transfer scheme they knew of was that run by the Coal Board, and was for skilled workers to go to Nottingham colliery jobs where working conditions were rumoured to be very unpleasant and unhealthy' (Marsden 1982: 62).

It was to these very same collieries that Taylor's migrants moved, with men from the same Durham pit applying in large numbers to work at the same colliery in Nottinghamshire, a situation of the last employer being a shared employer. However, the argument is strengthened further by recognizing that the Coal Board offered an employment/ residence package:

Most important are the many implications which stem from the provision of a house for every transferee. These houses form large estates which are usually situated alongside existing colliery settlements. These outlying estates are the real destinations of the Durham migrants and from Yorkshire to Somerset there is an impressive overall similarity.

(Taylor 1969: 104)

Within Taylor's account, then, migration is not serving to rupture ties with traditional social relations and forms of behaviour, for the simultaneous migration of linked individuals results in a reconstruction of old forms. His account presents a challenge to the mainstream literature, which assumed that working-class migration is necessarily an individualistic and isolating experience; yet, as we have seen, it is in step with the literature on chain migration which recognizes the importance of community in the migration process. Moreover, Taylor recognizes that the kin-based information mechanisms perform an important function in the transmission of employment information even when the employer himself is systematically providing information on the existence of vacancies. While 50 per cent based their choice solely on information provided by the Coal Board, 24 per cent based their choice on first-hand knowledge, while 26 per cent knew something about their destination from various second-hand sources. Furthermore:

Most of the first-hand information resulted from wartime service, extended work periods outside Durham and holidays with kin who had previously moved away from Durham: only occasionally was it the result of a specifically fact-finding trip. Second-hand information came mostly from friends and relatives who had this extra Durham experience.

(Taylor 1969: 127–8)

Thus Taylor is drawing attention to the importance of holidays as occasions for contact with geographically distant kin and the importance of such practices from the perspective of employment search and migration decision-making. Low frequency of contact does not necessarily mean the weakening of ties. However, Taylor does not develop his argument into an expressly network approach.

Social networks, employment, and migration: a theoretical formulation

It is the object of this section to draw together the various strands of analysis discussed so far into a theoretical formulation which considers explicitly the role of social networks in chain employment and chain migration, and the consequences of the employment relation for the link between migration and the strength of ties in social networks.

First of all I would like to consider the role of information transfer and social networks in transforming chance into system. In other words, I am interested in the mechanisms through which the migration of a single individual can be turned into a migration stream from the same area of origin, as in Arensberg and Kimball's account of the Shanghai police force (Arensberg and Kimball [1940] 1968). The role of employers in encouraging this process once the initial migration has taken place is highlighted.

Second, I would like to consider situations where employers systematically search for labour at a distance. As opposed to a spearhead being formed by an initial move from a worker, this is the situation where the spearhead itself is fashioned by employers.

Third, I will discuss the implications of the above processes for migration theory – in particular, I will argue that simple accounts of push and pull in migration theory have to be reformulated. Finally, I will consider the role of migration in further strengthening the ties that exist in a network – as opposed to the migration stream resulting from the strong ties that already exist in such networks.

Chance into system
Consider, then, a situation where for some reason an individual or a small group of individuals migrates in search of employment and secures this employment. It is this migration to which economists' theories of generalized search, incorporating general information about the area of destination and involving high risk in the absence of specific information, are most appropriate. However, once this migration has taken place, the character of the subsequent migration is essentially different with regard to information and, hence, the risk associated with it. Subsequent migration from within the same social network in the area of origin is likely to be directed towards this particular destination.[12]

At the very least members of the network in the area of destination provide more specific information than can be gleaned from general reports about the region. In effect, search can be conducted at a distance for those members of the network still in the area of origin. Thus specific information flows along particular channels – those in existence because of the network.[13] This information is more likely to be trusted by members of the network in the area of origin, again given the strength of ties implicit in a network – the degree of trust being one measure of this strength.

Moreover, when a new member of the network arrives in the area of destination, the existing members will provide aid while employment is being secured, if necessary. These processes depend on the density of the network as well as reachability in the network. The former measures the extent to which there are ties between all members of the network – it is the number of ties that actually exist relative to the number of ties that could potentially exist. The latter refers to the number of steps that need to be taken, on average, for one member of a network to be tied to (or to reach) any other member of that network. One would expect density and reachability to be greatest among kin, and one would therefore expect the role of kin networks to be particularly marked in migration over large distances. However, most empirical studies do not distinguish between family and friends – the two being lumped into a single category.

So far I have focused on the role of network members in transferring specific information along particular channels to other network members who will trust this information. This on its own can generate particularism in migration and turn chance into system. However, the particularism inherent in network information transfer is greatly strengthened by the fact that network members can help in securing employment at their own place of work for other network members.

Network members are at an advantage because they can be provided with information on vacancies in advance of general advertisement of these vacancies. Even in local labour markets, as we saw, this time advantage can be crucial. Over distance, its importance is further increased. Also, existing members of the workforce can provide detailed information about job specification and the nature of the interview, which can also help in securing employment. The implicit training, or tacit skills, to use Manwaring's terms (1982), which can be given to network members places them at an advantage over other candidates.

The above factors work to the advantage of network members securing employment in the same place even if employers themselves have no interest in tapping the network for labour. But the evidence suggests that employers do indeed use the networks of existing workers to recruit over distance. The use of networks provides a cost-effective method of generating an already screened labour force – already screened because of the expectation that the particular characteristics evident in the existing workforce will also be present in members of the network.

Employers are interested in a ready pool of labour that can be tapped at least cost. Hence the evidence that personnel departments – thought to be the epitome of modern, bureaucratic universalistic hiring procedures – actually make particularistic and ascriptive use of networks. Another important inducement to employers to use networks in hiring is that it provides an extra dimension of control over the workforce. The employment of the new recruit who is connected to an existing worker can be a reward to the latter for past loyalty, as in the case of Hill's dockers (Hill 1976), and is a control on the new recruit because of the ties that hold between him and the sponsoring worker, as in Lee and Wrench's 'lads of dads' (Lee and Wrench 1981).

There are, therefore, good reasons in theory as to why chance could indeed turn into system, both because of properties of networks and because of employers' use of them once the initial spearhead has been established. Notice that the processes identified here go beyond simply predicting residential proximity of network members in a new area – it predicts the presence of network members in the workplace. Also, all of the processes discussed are linked to the strength of ties in a network, not to their weakness, in contrast to Granovetter's position (Granovetter 1973, 1974). Moreover, the features of networks determining these processes are strongest in kin networks, as opposed to friendship networks. The above theorizing does suggest, however, that empirical work should indeed make this distinction – and this is done in my case study.

Systematic spearhead: direct recruitment
In my theoretical discussion so far, the role of employers has been limited to the use of networks into which existing members of the workforce are linked, thereby helping to turn chance into system. However, there is further evidence, both in my data and in the work of other authors, that employers deliberately set out to recruit labour over distance. Recruitment over distance can, for example, take place on the basis of skill complementariness between the regions from which the labour is derived and the character of the enterprise. Employers requiring special skills may have to locate in or recruit from regions in which those skills are present; in Chapters 6 and 7, for instance, I discuss the transfer of Scottish steel labour in bulk to Corby in Northamptonshire.

Apart from skill requirements in different contexts there is also evidence of the conscious recruitment by employers of labour over distance on the basis of its 'greenness' – labour unacquainted with the disutilities of industrial production, or possessing a docile industrial profile. Beynon's work on Ford's Merseyside plant revealed that in an attempt to produce a plant without militants the company recruited in the first instance a workforce on the basis of its inexperience of factory work (Beynon 1973). As one of Beynon's respondents said, 'they were a really green bunch of lads. Not a typical Merseyside labour force at all. Y'know, they weren't objecting or complaining' (Beynon 1973: 89).

Moreover, companies wishing to avoid high levels of labour turnover in 'dirty industry' may recruit migrants in order to enforce job stability. In such cases, local labour is perceived as possessing access through its local network to alternative sources of local employment whereas migrant labour is perceived as 'trapped'.

For these reasons employers may wish to recruit labour in bulk from distant regions, thereby systematically creating the spearhead of migration. But given the arguments in Chapter 1 on the role of social networks in local labour markets, sorties by employers into a particular market are likely to lead to recruitment of a labour force which is already connected. As we shall see in Chapter 6, the information and recruitment mechanisms used, in particular the involvement of the state employment agencies in the UK, will strengthen this tendency. Once the initial, already connected, labour force is transferred to the new region, the chain-employment and chain-migration processes discussed previously come into their own and will further strengthen the presence of network members in the workforce. A detailed empirical investigation of direct recruitment and its role in constructing a workforce – and the implications of such procedures for mainstream studies in industrial sociology such as the Affluent Worker study – are discussed in Chapter 6.

Implications for migration theory

Much of the focus in the mainstream study of labour migration is on responses to opportunity at the regional level; it is the general level of employment vacancies which is regarded as being important. My theoretical discussion, and empirical evidence, suggests that while the general employment conditions may determine the total number of migrants to be accommodated, they cannot of themselves determine the composition of that number – that is, the nature of the migration.[14] In order to understand the composition of in-migration, we have to identify and analyse the underlying mechanisms in greater detail.

Information on employment opportunity is not received simply on a broadcast model, nor is it gained as a consequence of highly individualized search behaviour. Rather, it is transferred through various systems of networks – both locally and, in particular, over distance. Moreover, networks are important not merely in information transfer but also in the securing of employment. Thus I argue that in contrast to the standard reliance on a competitive opportunity model, migration should be analysed in terms of a particular guidance model.

Moreover, along with Petersen,[15] I would view some types of migration activity as essentially conservative in character; while the initial migration may represent an attempt to break free from a structure (and it may not if direct recruitment is involved), the subsequent pattern of chain employment and chain migration leads to a preservation of social structure.

To develop these arguments further, consider the standard division between push factors and pull factors in the analysis of migration. The former are usually viewed as inducing migration of a conservative, security-maximizing nature, while the latter are viewed as inducing income-maximizing and risk-taking migration. For example, in Goldthorpe *et al.*'s work on the car industry (Goldthorpe *et al.*, 1968a, 1968b, 1969) and in Taylor's work on the coal industry (Taylor 1969), migration is categorized as being essentially of the pull variety where the individuals interviewed were not unemployed at the time of the migration. Such migration is then seen as maximizing behaviour on the part of the 'affluent workers'.

My argument is that even where the individual was not unemployed at the time of the migration, attention must be paid to the overall climate in the region of out-migration. In order to capture the migratory perspective of the individual, it is essential that we understand the migration in the context of anticipated unemployment.[16] Rumoured redundancy is an industrial fact, the role of social networks in transmitting this information being paramount. Workers frequently (though by no means always) anticipate changes in the circumstances of their present source of employment, registering changes in the level of orders, maintenance, and recruitment policies. In the USA there is evidence that unions train workers to read managerial strategies by such measures (see Bluestone and Harrison 1982). Where redundancies have occurred or are anticipated, even if the individual himself has not yet been made unemployed, the movement from such a context constitutes push migration.

In situations where the initial migration has a strong push dimension and direct recruitment is involved, further care is required in characterizing the quality of information possessed by the individual or group at the point of migration. In Chapter 6 this argument is developed more fully, demonstrating that the interaction of communal push factors, involvement of state employment agencies, and direct recruitment can result in migrants being channelled into far distant employment locations upon which they have no information other than that provided by the employer. Once this initial migration has taken place, then channels of information transfer and employment aid to subsequent migrants can be laid. The important theoretical point is that the information resources of migrants at different points in a migration chain are very different and require different types of analysis. Let us turn, therefore, to migrants in the middle of a migration chain – that is, where some part of the network has already migrated.

Even where a migrant both is employed and does not anticipate unemployment, so that one might appropriately characterize him as a pull migrant, I would argue that such migration may also be essentially conservative. Wrong notes the cohesive, as opposed to the individualizing and disruptive, influences of migration (Wrong 1965). The pull of social ties was such that '"the principal cause of emigration was prior emigration" and it was no longer relevant to "inquire concerning the individual motivations"' (Petersen, quoted in Wrong 1965: 89).

Wrong and other observers of international migration to the USA are overall more sensitive to the chain qualities of population movement, as are authors who have written on ethnic migration to the UK. Ethnicity renders these properties more immediately visible. But my argument is that such processes are also evidenced in internal indigenous migration. Networks are indeed maintained and reconstituted over distance. The social structure being entered by later migrants is different to the original structure of the new location and will bear some resemblance to that of the area being left, with some part of the social forms of the area of origin having been established in the new area. Early migrants experience different patterns of exposure to new social structures than do later migrants. The social and emotional costs of migration to later migrants are likely to be less, therefore, than those to early migrants. Early migrants must be viewed as the primary and major risk-takers, whereas later migrants may be viewed as being of more conservative character.

Any discussion of risk must be related to comprehensiveness/non-comprehensiveness of information, and investment at stake. Any individual migrating within a context well structured by family or friendship contact must be seen as taking less risk than any individual who migrates and sets up such contacts. Movement over physical space does not of itself constitute risk. Although historically this may have been true – and if one is considering nineteenth-century patterns of migration the chances of death on voyage have to be considered – the character of transport in the twentieth century makes this aspect of risk minimal. The second assumption frequently built into the risk–distance equation is the notion that information necessarily decays over distance; once again the nature of modern communications makes this less of a self-evident proposition.

The contagion model of information diffusion stresses the principle of physical adjacency in the process of information diffusion. I seek to modify this physical distance model by introducing the concept of social distance in the context of the transmission of employment and residential information. Whilst physical contact may be imperative in the transmission of disease, it is not imperative to the transmission of information. Both the migration literature and the labour-market literature have over-emphasized the importance of physical adjacency in the securing of opportunity. Information does not necessarily decay with physical distance.

Proximity may provide the optimum circumstances for the dissemination of information within a homogeneous group, but the proximity of weakly linked groups may provide no conditions for information spread whatsoever; information may be contained within each group. A strongly linked social group may be spread over more than one location, as a consequence of migration in the past, and the information circulation, and relevance, may be greater in volume between such groups than between those remaining in the old location. Proximity of itself does not provide an indicator as to the information transactions likely to occur. Any consideration of information spread must pay attention to the dimensions of both proximity and linkage.

I am concerned with two main types of information transactions, contacts between workforces and employers and contacts between workforces and their networks which take place locally and over distance. It is argued that the interaction between the two types of transaction diminishes the risk involved in migrational activity. Where migration is itself search activity, then almost definitionally a high degree of risk pertains; however, where search has been conducted before migration, through some other agency in a position to vouchsafe the existence of opportunity in the new location, migration can only be regarded as risk activity in a minimal sense.

Competitive opportunities necessarily involve migration then search, whereas particular guidance to employment opportunity involves search then migration. It is on this basis that I argue that the characterization of pull migration as risky and innovatory is too simplistic, at least after the point when the initial spearhead migration has taken place.

Finally, my theory has implications for the study of return migration. The standard characterization of return migration is in terms of failed search: an attempt is made to search for employment in a distant location, the attempt fails and return occurs. However, I would argue that there exists the possibility that return migration to the area of origin is occurring as a natural consequence of change in the structure of employment opportunities.

My case-study evidence, presented in Chapter 8, details the mechanisms underlying return migration from Corby to Scotland, but at the theoretical level it is clear that if the social network is present both in the area of origin and in the new area, a sudden decline in employment opportunities in the new area will lead naturally to a consideration of return to the network remaining in the area of origin. Furthermore, out-migration itself may generate the release of opportunities which occasion the return of previous migrants. However, even without loss of employment and consequent permanent return migration, the presence of the two parts of the kin network in the two areas can lead to a pattern of labour circulation, which I present evidence of in Chapter 8. Chapter 8 also considers the reasons why the return to the area of origin is more easily accomplished than forward migration elsewhere – in brief, it is the location of the individual's best employment contacts that determines the migrant's destination.

Chain migration, chain employment, and Corby: the role of kin in long-distance job search and procurement

Corby steel works has special characteristics which accommodate high rates of chain migration and chain employment; management's recruitment practices and the one-industry, one-employer nature of the town are two such features which receive more detailed attention in Chapters 6, 7, and 8. Although these features undoubtedly accentuate patterns of chain migration and chain employment, my major argument is that such social processes are not confined to one-industry sites alone but are more general in character.

The object of examining the processes of chain migration to Corby is, however, to address the more general issue of whether geographic mobility necessarily disrupts family ties. Sufficient evidence is available from the USA to question the old 'uprooting' orthodoxy of geographical mobility as a necessarily isolating and atomizing experience, but this evidence is largely provided for ethnic communities rather than for the mainstream population. The impression given by the literature as a whole is that ethnicity provides for stronger ties which combat the isolating dynamic of geographical dispersal.

Within this section I argue that kinship rather than ethnicity may be the more fundamental organizing principle of migration. In Chapter 7 I argue that a mainstream labour force may be converted into an ethnic labour force as a consequence of particular employer recruitment policies. Here I am seeking to establish that kinship as opposed to ethnicity is the prior factor in chain migration. Ethnicity merely renders the dynamic of chain migration and chain employment more visible. Recruitment to Corby steel works was disproportionately Scots (see Chapter 7); it is the Scots origin of labour which provides a trace on the extensiveness of chain migration and chain employment in this site.

Corby, I argue, represents the extreme end of a more general phenomenon, for similar processes exist elsewhere within UK industry and society. The difference in patterns of chain migration and chain employment to Corby and to Luton, for example, is a matter of degree not of kind – a position I shall argue for in the coming four chapters. In this section I will discuss the migration/employment/kinship nexus for three Scots/Corby kinship networks. After presenting the basic field-work evidence, I will analyse the structure of each of these nets, paying attention to both direct and indirect linkages. I will then consider, in greater detail, the precise nature of employment help given in these nets. Finally, I will discuss the paucity of friendship–employment–aid linkages in our evidence.

Buchanan, Buchan, and McConnell: three kinship–employment nets in Corby steel works
In Chapter 2 I defined employment net as a group of individuals linked by kinship or friendship and sharing place of employment. I now define a kinship–employment net as a group of individuals who share place of employment but are linked solely by kinship ties. These kinship relations may be either consanguine or affine – I refer to the former as a direct kin link and the latter as an indirect kin link. The Appendix to this volume describes in detail the collection of the primary material.

For each of the three networks – Buchanan, Buchan, and McConnell – I have identified all persons who are currently employed, or have ever been employed, in Corby steel works, the exact kinship relations holding within each net, their place of origin, their date of departure from Corby where relevant, the destination on departure, and the source of information and agency of introduction to Corby steel works.

Figures 4.1, 4.2, and 4.3 provide a visual appreciation of the size and complexity of these kin/migration, destination/workplace overlaps. Thus in Figure 4.1, the Buchanan net, the nine circles (1, 2, 3, 4, 5, 6, 10, 11, 13) represent nine kin-linked individuals who are currently present in the steel works. The six numbered triangles (7, 8, 9, 12, 14, 15) represent six individuals who used to work in the steel works – the nature and method of their departure is indicated below their name. Thus individual number 7 arrived from Peterhead in 1957, but emigrated to Canada in 1971, while individual number 14 came from

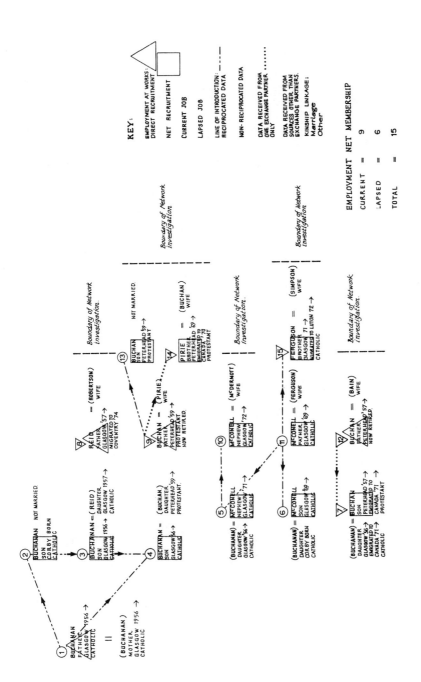

Figure 4.1 Buchanan: Corby-based employment net, March 1980

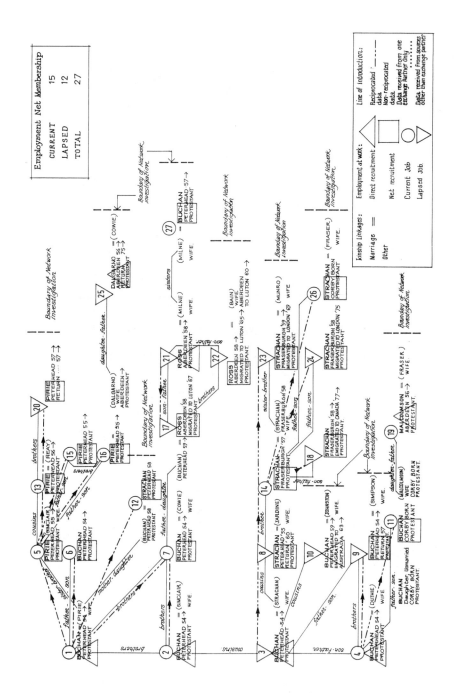

Figure 4.2 Buchan: Corby-based employment net, March 1980

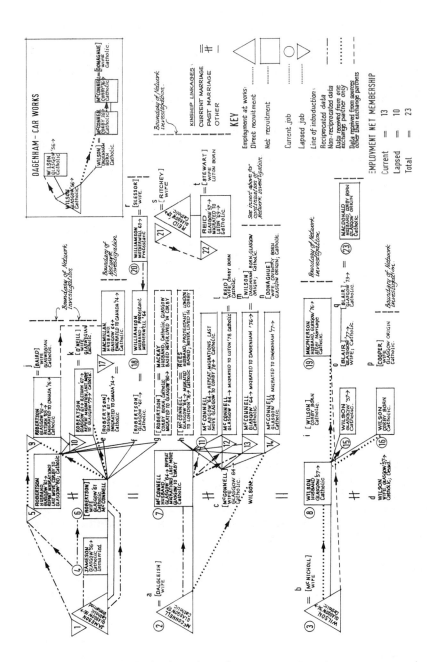

Figure 4.3 McConnell: Corby-based employment net, March 1980

Peterhead in 1969 but emigrated in 1970. The total number of direct and indirect kin-linked individuals in the Buchanan net is thus fifteen. Also indicated in Figure 4.1 is the line of introduction to Corby steel works – who helped whom in getting the job. This information will be particularly important when the nature of employment aid in our nets is considered in greater detail. However, I have also indicated in the figures whether the information on line of introduction was reciprocated data (i.e. confirmed by both parties) or not.

Figures 4.2 and 4.3 present analogous information for Buchan and McConnell – two nets which are larger than the Buchanan net displayed in Figure 4.1. The employment nets of these three kin networks in Corby, taking current employees at the steel works only and including both direct and indirect kin, are nine in number for Buchanan, fifteen for Buchan, and thirteen for McConnell. Given that the sample is primarily composed of Scots migrants, then these figures taken alone suggest that migration is other than an isolating and atomizing experience at least with regard to kin relations in the workplace. Furthermore, even taken at their barest these figures suggest that either processes of chain migration and chain employment are in play, or that marriage is taking place within the same occupational community, as all three employment nets are larger than is possible on the basis of recruitment from the nuclear family alone.

By including indirect kin, kin involvement in migration and job procurement is much extended as marriages within Corby increase the size of the total employment net, although the migration of the two kin lines are likely to have been independently organized. Indeed, this is the case for a number of the family groups contained within the networks studied. Here it is important to note that the one-employer character of Corby and its relative isolation from the surrounding hinterland, discussed in Chapter 7, most probably give rise to the high incidence of endogamous (to Corby) marriage found within our fieldwork. The prevalence of endogamous marriage will necessarily increase the size of the total employment net.

In some respects, then, Corby shares features with the fish-processing industry discussed in Chapter 2 in that isolation – social in the case of fish processing, physical in the case of Corby – is serving to produce and maintain occupational community through endogamous marriage within the industries.[17] Before moving on to measure the size of the employment net in terms of direct kin links alone, note that it is only by including both direct and indirect kin links that we gain an impression of the full mobilization capacity of kin in the workplace. Briefly, the basic argument is that employment aid is provided by both consanguines and affines; the literature in general has concentrated on the role of the former as an agency of introduction to the exclusion of the latter, thus greatly underestimating the degree of economic co-operation by kin in the modern industrial environment.

Tables 4.1a, b, 4.2a, b, and 4.3a, b extract from Figures 4.1, 4.2, and 4.3

information on kin links. The (a) tables refer only to individuals currently present in the workforce while the (b) tables conduct the analysis for both current and past individuals in the net. Thus Table 4.1a represents the kin links between current members of the Buchanan net (individual 1, 2, 3, 4, 5, 6, 10, 11, 13). The number of direct relationships (dk) possessed by each individual in the Buchanan net are as follows: individuals 1 (3 dk), 2 (3), 3 (3), 4 (3), 5 (3), 6 (3), 10 (3), 11 (3), 13 (0). Note that whilst no individual's personal network of direct kin relations is greater than three, the size of the aggregate structure is three times larger.

The number of direct kin relationships possessed by the current individuals in the Buchan net (Table 4.2a) tend on the whole to be somewhat greater than those occurring in the Buchanan net; they are individual 1 (7 dk), 2 (5), 4 (7), 5 (4), 6 (9), 7 (5), 11 (7), 12 (0), 13 (4), 14 (3), 15 (5), 16 (5), 19 (0), 26 (3), 27 (0). Note once again that whilst the maximum personal direct network is of nine connections, the size of the aggregate structure is substantially larger at fifteen.

Table 4.3a shows that the number of direct relations currently employed in the steel works possessed by each of the individuals in the McConnell net is somewhat smaller than that holding in the Buchan net. They are 2 (2 dk), 3 (3), 4 (1), 6 (2), 7 (3), 8 (3), 11 (2), 15 (3), 16 (3), 18 (1), 19 (0), 20 (1), 23 (0). The largest personal network in this employment net contains only three direct links, whilst the size of the aggregate structure is more than four times greater at thirteen.

Scott and his colleagues in their work on kin presence in the enterprise, a study which was also of the steel industry, provide two summary statistics on the matter (Scott *et al.* 1956). One statistic is for kin currently employed in the same workplace, the other is for all kin related to the current workforce,[18] both currently and previously employed, in the same place of work. Including such lapsed employment data increases the reading of the scale of kin presence in the workplace dramatically. Thus Scott found that on average steelworkers had 2.7 relatives currently working with them in the same plant, but if family members who had previously worked in the same plant were included then the average figure for relatives in the plant shoots up to 4.7 – almost double the current total.

These average figures are the sole statistics provided by Scott on kin presence in the workplace. There is, for example, no attempt to trace out or estimate the size of the aggregate structure which may result from the interlinkages given by marriage within this occupational community. Furthermore, these average figures exclude female relatives and male cousins employed in the workplace. I include both these categories as kin, as does Walker in his 1950s study of an American steel town.[19] Walker found seventy-two first cousins in a sample of sixty-one workers in the plant studied. Note that the exclusion of cousins from the category of kin is, given these rates of presence, problematic. Taking Scott's measure of kin presence in the workplace for the Buchanan net,

Table 4.1a *Kin linkages in the workplace: current only – Buchanan net*

	1	2	3	4	5	6	10	11	13	Total dk	ik	nk
1	0	dk	dk	dk	ik	ik	nk	nk	nk	3	2	3
2	dk	0	dk	dk	ik	ik	nk	nk	nk	3	2	3
3	dk	dk	0	dk	ik	ik	nk	nk	nk	3	2	3
4	dk	dk	dk	0	ik	ik	nk	nk	ik	3	3	2
5	ik	ik	ik	ik	0	ik/dk	dk	dk	nk	3	5	1
6	ik	ik	ik	ik	ik/dk	0	dk	dk	nk	3	5	1
10	nk	nk	nk	nk	dk	dk	0	dk	nk	3	–	5
11	nk	nk	nk	nk	dk	dk	dk	0	nk	3	–	5
13	nk	nk	nk	ik	nk	nk	nk	nk	0	–	1	7
										24	20	

Average no. of direct kin in workplace: 2·7

Average no. of indirect kin in workplace: 2·2

Average no. of all kin in workplace: 4·9

Key:
dk – direct kin connection
ik – indirect kin connection
nk – no kin connection

Table 4.1b Kin linkages in the workplace: current and lapsed – Buchanan net

	1	2	3	4	5	6	7	8	9	10	11	12	13	14	15	Total dk	ik	nk
1	0	dk	dk	dk	ik	ik	ik	nk	nk	nk	nk	nk	nk	nk	nk	3	3	8
2	dk	0	dk	dk	ik	ik	ik	nk	nk	nk	nk	nk	nk	nk	nk	3	3	8
3	dk	dk	0	dk	ik	ik	ik	ik	nk	nk	nk	nk	nk	nk	nk	3	4	7
4	dk	dk	dk	0	ik	ik	ik	ik	ik	nk	nk	nk	ik	nk	nk	3	6	5
5	ik	ik	ik	ik	0	ik/dk	ik	nk	nk	dk	dk	dk	dk	nk	nk	3	6	6
6	ik	ik	ik	ik	ik/dk	0	ik	nk	nk	dk	dk	dk	nk	nk	dk	4	6	5
7	ik	ik	ik	ik	ik	ik	0	nk	nk	nk	nk	dk	nk	nk	nk	1	6	7
8	nk	nk	nk	ik	nk	nk	nk	0	nk	nk	nk	nk	nk	nk	nk	–	2	12
9	nk	nk	nk	ik	nk	nk	0	nk	0	dk	nk	nk	dk	ik	nk	1	2	11
10	nk	nk	nk	dk	nk	dk	nk	0	dk	0	nk	nk	nk	nk	nk	3	1	10
11	nk	nk	nk	dk	nk	dk	nk	nk	dk	nk	0	nk	nk	nk	ik	3	1	10
12	nk	nk	nk	nk	nk	nk	dk	nk	nk	nk	nk	0	nk	dk	nk	1	–	13
13	nk	nk	ik	nk	nk	nk	nk	nk	nk	nk	nk	nk	0	dk	nk	1	1	11
14	nk	nk	nk	nk	nk	nk	nk	nk	nk	nk	nk	dk	dk	0	nk	2	1	12
15	nk	nk	nk	nk	nk	dk	nk	nk	ik	nk	nk	nk	nk	nk	0	1	1	12
																32	42	

Average no. of direct kin in workplace: 2·1

Average no. of indirect kin in workplace: 2·8

Average no. of all kin in workplace: 4·9

Key:
dk – direct kin connection
ik – indirect kin connection
nk – no kin connection

Table 4.2a *Kin linkages in the workplace: current only – Buchan net*

	1	2	4	5	6	7	11	12	13	14	15	16	19	26	27	Total dk	ik	nk
1	0	dk	ik	dk	dk	dk	dk	ik	nk	dk	dk	nk	nk	nk	nk	7	3	4
2	dk	0	dk	dk	dk	dk	dk	nk	nk	nk	nk	nk	nk	nk	nk	5	–	9
4	dk	dk	0	nk	dk	dk	dk	nk	nk	dk	ik	dk	nk	nk	nk	7	1	6
5	ik	nk	nk	0	dk	nk	nk	nk	dk	nk	dk	nk	nk	nk	nk	4	1	9
6	dk	dk	dk	dk	0	dk	dk	ik	dk	nk	dk	nk	nk	nk	nk	9	1	4
7	dk	dk	dk	nk	dk	0	dk	nk	nk	nk	nk	nk	nk	nk	nk	5	–	9
11	dk	dk	dk	nk	dk	dk	0	nk	nk	dk	nk	ik	dk	nk	nk	7	1	6
12	ik	nk	nk	nk	ik	nk	nk	0	nk	nk	ik	nk	nk	nk	nk	–	4	10
13	ik	nk	nk	dk	dk	nk	nk	nk	0	nk	dk	nk	nk	nk	nk	4	1	9
14	nk	nk	nk	dk	nk	nk	dk	nk	nk	0	nk	nk	dk	nk	nk	3	–	11
15	dk	nk	dk	dk	dk	nk	nk	ik	dk	nk	0	dk	nk	nk	nk	5	1	8
16	dk	nk	dk	dk	dk	nk	ik	nk	ik	dk	dk	0	nk	nk	nk	5	1	8
19	nk	nk	ik	nk	nk	nk	nk	nk	nk	nk	nk	nk	0	nk	nk	–	2	12
26	nk	nk	dk	nk	nk	nk	dk	nk	nk	dk	nk	nk	nk	0	nk	3	–	11
27	nk	nk	nk	nk	nk	nk	nk	nk	nk	nk	nk	nk	nk	nk	0	–	–	14
																64	16	

Average no. of direct kin in workplace: 4.3

Average no. of indirect kin in workplace: 1·1

Average no. of all kin in workplace: 5·3

Key:
dk – direct kin connection
ik – indirect kin connection
nk – no kin connection

Table 4.2b *Kin linkages in the workplace: current and lapsed – Buchan net*

	1	2	3	4	5	6	7	8	9	10	11	12	13	14	15	16	17	18	19	20	21	22	23	24	25	26	27	*Total* dk	ik	nk
1	0	dk	dk	dk	ik	dk	dk	dk	dk	dk	dk	dk	ik	nk	dk	dk	dk	nk	nk	ik	nk	nk	nk	nk	nk	nk	nk	10	4	12
2	dk	0	dk	dk	dk	dk	dk	dk	dk	dk	dk	dk	dk	nk	dk	nk	nk	nk	nk	nk	nk	nk	nk	nk	nk	nk	nk	8	–	18
3	dk	dk	0	dk	nk	dk	dk	ik	dk	dk	dk	nk	nk	ik	dk	nk	nk	nk	nk	nk	nk	nk	nk	nk	nk	ik	nk	8	5	13
4	dk	dk	dk	0	nk	dk	dk	dk	ik	dk	dk	dk	dk	dk	nk	dk	dk	dk	dk	dk	nk	nk	nk	nk	nk	ik	nk	13	1	12
5	ik	nk	nk	nk	0	dk	nk	dk	dk	0	nk	nk	nk	dk	nk	dk	dk	nk	nk	dk	dk	nk	nk	nk	nk	nk	nk	5	1	20
6	dk	dk	dk	dk	dk	0	dk	nk	dk	dk	dk	dk	ik	dk	dk	dk	dk	nk	dk	dk	nk	nk	nk	dk	nk	nk	nk	12	3	11
7	dk	dk	dk	dk	nk	dk	0	dk	nk	nk	0	dk	nk	nk	nk	dk	ik	nk	nk	nk	nk	nk	nk	nk	nk	nk	nk	8	1	17
8	dk	dk	dk	dk	nk	nk	dk	0	nk	dk	dk	dk	nk	nk	ik	nk	nk	nk	nk	nk	nk	nk	nk	nk	nk	nk	nk	7	1	18
9	nk	nk	ik	dk	nk	dk	nk	nk	0	dk	nk	dk	nk	dk	nk	dk	nk	dk	nk	nk	nk	nk	nk	dk	nk	dk	nk	13	–	13
10	dk	dk	dk	dk	dk	dk	dk	dk	dk	0	dk	nk	nk	nk	nk	nk	nk	nk	nk	nk	nk	nk	nk	nk	nk	nk	nk	8	–	18
11	dk	dk	dk	dk	dk	dk	dk	dk	dk	dk	0	dk	nk	nk	nk	dk	ik	nk	nk	nk	nk	nk	nk	nk	nk	nk	nk	13	1	12
12	ik	nk	nk	nk	nk	ik	nk	nk	ik	nk	nk	0	nk	nk	nk	ik	ik	nk	nk	nk	nk	nk	nk	nk	nk	nk	nk	–	4	22
13	ik	nk	nk	nk	nk	dk	nk	nk	nk	nk	nk	nk	0	nk	dk	dk	nk	nk	nk	dk	nk	nk	nk	nk	nk	dk	nk	5	1	20
14	nk	nk	ik	dk	nk	dk	nk	nk	nk	nk	ik	nk	nk	0	nk	nk	dk	nk	nk	nk	dk	nk	nk	nk	r	nk	nk	7	2	17
15	dk	nk	dk	nk	dk	dk	nk	nk	nk	ik	dk	nk	0	dk	0	dk	nk	nk	nk	nk	nk	dk	nk	nk	r	nk	nk	6	1	19
16	dk	nk	nk	dk	dk	dk	nk	nk	nk	nk	nk	nk	dk	nk	dk	0	nk	nk	nk	nk	nk	nk	nk	ik	r	nk	nk	6	2	18
17	nk	nk	nk	nk	nk	ik	ik	nk	nk	nk	nk	nk	nk	nk	dk	nk	0	nk	nk	nk	dk	dk	nk	nk	r	dk	3	2	21
18	nk	nk	nk	dk	nk	nk	nk	nk	nk	dk	dk	dk	nk	dk	dk	nk	nk	0	nk	nk	nk	dk	dk	nk	dk	ck	nk	8	1	17
19	nk	nk	nk	nk	nk	nk	nk	nk	nk	nk	ik	nk	nk	nk	nk	nk	nk	nk	0	nk	nk	nk	nk	nk	nk	r	nk	–	2	24
20	ik	nk	nk	dk	nk	nk	nk	nk	nk	nk	nk	dk	nk	dk	nk	dk	dk	nk	nk	0	nk	nk	nk	nk	nk	r	nk	5	1	20
21	nk	nk	nk	nk	nk	nk	nk	nk	nk	nk	nk	nk	nk	dk	nk	nk	nk	nk	nk	nk	0	dk	nk	nk	nk	r	ik	2	1	23
22	nk	nk	nk	nk	nk	nk	nk	nk	nk	nk	nk	nk	nk	nk	nk	dk	nk	nk	nk	nk	dk	0	nk	nk	nk	r	dk	3	–	23
23	nk	nk	nk	nk	nk	nk	nk	nk	nk	nk	nk	nk	nk	nk	nk	nk	ik	nk	nk	nk	nk	nk	0	dk	nk	ck	nk	3	1	22
24	nk	nk	ik	dk	nk	dk	nk	nk	dk	nk	nk	nk	nk	dk	nk	nk	nk	dk	nk	nk	nk	nk	dk	0	nk	ck	nk	8	1	17
25	nk	nk	nk	nk	nk	nk	nk	nk	nk	nk	nk	nk	nk	nk	nk	nk	ik	nk	nk	nk	nk	nk	nk	nk	0	nk	nk	–	1	25
26	nk	nk	ik	dk	nk	nk	nk	nk	dk	dk	dk	nk	nk	nk	dk	nk	nk	dk	dk	nk	dk	nk	dk	dk	nk	(	nk	8	1	17
27	nk	nk	nk	nk	nk	nk	nk	nk	nk	nk	nk	nk	ik	dk	nk	nk	nk	dk	nk	nk	nk	nk	nk	nk	nk	nk	0	2	1	23
																												171	43	

Average no. of direct kin in workplace: 6·2

Average no. of indirect kin in workplace: 1·4

Average no. of all kin in workplace: 7·8

Key:
dk – direct kin connection
ik – indirect kin connection
nk – no kin connection

Table 4.3a *Kin linkages in the workplace: current only – McConnell net*

	2	3	4	6	7	8	11	15	16	18	19	20	23	Total dk	ik	nk
2	0	nk	ik	dk	nk	dk	nk	nk	nk	nk	nk	nk	nk	2	1	9
3	nk	0	nk	nk	dk	nk	dk	dk	ik	nk	nk	nk	nk	3	1	8
4	ik	nk	0	dk	ik	nk	nk	nk	nk	nk	nk	nk	nk	1	2	9
6	dk	nk	dk	0	nk	ik	ik	nk	nk	nk	ik	nk	nk	2	3	7
7	nk	dk	ik	nk	0	dk	dk	nk	nk	nk	nk	nk	nk	3	1	8
8	dk	nk	nk	ik	dk	0	nk	nk	dk	nk	ik	nk	nk	3	2	7
11	nk	dk	nk	ik	dk	nk	0	ik	nk	nk	nk	nk	nk	2	2	8
15	nk	dk	nk	nk	nk	nk	ik	0	dk	dk	ik	nk	nk	3	2	7
16	nk	ik	nk	nk	nk	dk	nk	dk	0	nk	nk	dk	nk	3	1	8
18	nk	nk	nk	nk	nk	nk	nk	dk	nk	0	ik	nk	ik	1	2	9
19	nk	nk	nk	ik	nk	ik	nk	ik	nk	ik	0	nk	nk	–	4	8
20	nk	nk	nk	nk	nk	nk	nk	nk	dk	nk	nk	0	nk	1	–	11
23	nk	nk	nk	nk	nk	nk	nk	nk	nk	ik	nk	nk	0	–	1	11
														24	22	

Average no. of direct
kin in workplace: 1.8

Average no. of indirect
kin in workplace: 1.7

Average no. of all kin
in workplace: 3.5

Key:
dk – direct kin connection
ik – indirect kin connection
nk – no kin connection

Table 4.3b *Kin linkages in the workplace: current and lapsed – McConnell net*

	1	2	3	4	5	6	7	8	9	10	11	12	13	14	15	16	17	18	19	20	21	22	23	*Total* dk	ik	nk
1	0	nk	nk	dk	ik	dk	ik	nk	dk	nk	nk	nk	nk	nk	nk	nk	ik	ik	nk	nk	nk	nk	nk	4	4	14
2	nk	0	nk	nk	ik	dk	ik	dk	nk	dk	nk	nk	nk	nk	nk	nk	nk	nk	nk	nk	nk	nk	nk	5	1	16
3	nk	nk	0	nk	nk	nk	nk	nk	dk	dk	nk	nk	nk	nk	dk	nk	nk	nk	ik	nk	nk	nk	nk	3	1	18
4	dk	nk	nk	0	ik	dk	ik	dk	dk	dk	nk	nk	nk	nk	nk	nk	ik	nk	nk	nk	nk	nk	nk	4	4	14
5	ik	ik	nk	ik	0	dk	nk	dk	dk	dk	nk	nk	nk	nk	nk	ik	nk	nk	nk	nk	nk	nk	nk	3	4	15
6	dk	dk	nk	dk	dk	0	ik	dk	dk	dk	ik	ik	dk	dk	nk	nk	nk	nk	nk	nk	nk	nk	nk	6	7	9
7	ik	dk	nk	ik	nk	ik	0	nk	ik	dk	dk	dk	dk	nk	nk	nk	nk	nk	nk	nk	nk	nk	nk	6	4	12
8	nk	dk	nk	dk	dk	dk	nk	0	ik	ik	dk	dk	nk	nk	nk	nk	nk	nk	nk	nk	nk	nk	ik	3	5	14
9	dk	nk	dk	dk	dk	dk	ik	ik	0	nk	dk	dk	nk	nk	nk	nk	nk	nk	nk	nk	nk	nk	nk	5	3	14
10	nk	dk	dk	dk	dk	dk	dk	ik	nk	0	nk	nk	nk	nk	nk	nk	nk	nk	nk	nk	nk	nk	nk	5	3	14
11	nk	nk	nk	nk	nk	ik	dk	dk	dk	nk	0	dk	dk	nk	nk	nk	nk	nk	nk	nk	nk	nk	nk	5	2	15
12	nk	nk	nk	nk	nk	ik	dk	dk	dk	nk	dk	0	dk	nk	nk	nk	nk	nk	nk	nk	nk	nk	nk	5	4	13
13	nk	nk	nk	nk	nk	dk	dk	nk	nk	nk	dk	dk	0	nk	nk	nk	nk	nk	nk	nk	nk	nk	nk	5	2	15
14	nk	dk	nk	nk	nk	dk	nk	nk	nk	nk	dk	dk	dk	0	nk	nk	nk	nk	nk	nk	nk	nk	nk	5	2	15
15	nk	nk	dk	nk	nk	nk	nk	nk	nk	nk	nk	nk	nk	nk	0	nk	nk	ik	nk	nk	nk	ik	ik	3	2	17
16	nk	nk	nk	nk	ik	nk	nk	nk	nk	nk	nk	nk	nk	nk	dk	0	nk	nk	ik	nk	nk	nk	nk	3	1	18
17	ik	nk	nk	ik	nk	nk	nk	nk	nk	nk	nk	nk	nk	nk	nk	0	ik	nk	nk	nk	nk	nk	nk	–	7	15
18	ik	nk	nk	ik	nk	nk	nk	nk	nk	nk	nk	nk	nk	nk	nk	0	nk	dk	nk	nk	nk	nk	nk	1	7	14
19	nk	ik	nk	nk	nk	nk	nk	nk	nk	nk	nk	nk	nk	ik	nk	0	nk	nk	nk	nk	nk	nk	nk	–	4	18
20	nk	nk	nk	nk	nk	nk	nk	nk	nk	dk	nk	nk	0	nk	nk	nk	nk	nk	nk	nk	nk	nk	nk	1	–	21
21	nk	nk	nk	nk	nk	nk	nk	nk	nk	nk	nk	nk	nk	nk	nk	nk	nk	nk	nk	0	dk	nk	nk	1	1	20
22	nk	nk	nk	nk	nk	nk	nk	nk	nk	nk	nk	ik	nk	nk	nk	nk	nk	nk	nk	dk	0	nk	nk	1	1	20
23	nk	nk	nk	nk	nk	nk	nk	nk	nk	nk	nk	ik	nk	nk	nk	nk	nk	nk	nk	nk	nk	0	nk	–	1	21
																						74	70			

Average no. of direct kin in workplace: 3·2

Average no. of indirect kin in workplace: 3·0

Average no. of all kin in workplace: 6·3

Key:
dk – direct kin connection
ik – indirect kin connection
nk – no kin connection

one gets an average of 2.7 direct kin currently employed in the work-place (see Table 4.1a), a figure which is identical to Scott's own total figure of 2.7 if our supposition is correct; and an average of 2.2 indirect kin currently employed in the workplace, giving an overall average of 4.9 kin currently employed in the workplace. This figure is approximately double that obtained by Scott, but comparable to that of Walker, who found a figure of 4.3 relatives per worker–wife unit in an American steel town in the mid-twentieth century.

Moving to Scott's second measure, which includes both present and past employees who are relatives of the current workforce, one gets an average of 3.0 direct kin in the workplace, an average of 3.3 indirect kin in the workplace, and an overall average of 6.3 kin in the workplace (calculated from information given in Table 4.1b). Thus, whereas Scott's present and past employee average was almost twice that of his current-employment-only figure, in the Buchanan net the difference between the two figures is proportionately less – 4.8 and 6.3.[20] If, however, one looks at the size of the aggregate structure or employment net, including past employees who are kinsmen makes a considerable difference. Thus taking current employees alone gives a network of nine individuals or information and influence sources whereas including past employees gives a network of fifteen.

Applying Scott's measures to the Buchan net and examining current employment only, one gets an average of 4.3 for direct kin in the workplace, 1.1 for indirect kin, and an overall average of 5.3 for kin in the workplace (see Table 4.2a). Examining the data for both current and lapsed kin employment in this net, one gets somewhat higher figures, with an average of 6.9 direct kin, 1.7 indirect kin, and an overall average of 8.6 (calculated from Table 4.2b). This also represents a somewhat higher set of figures than those given by Scott. This is partly attributable to our inclusion of cousins as relatives; however, there are other factors in play. Although Scott explicitly discusses the role of kin in chain migration and chain employment to the steel industry, the only mention he makes of direct recruitment practices is for the early twentieth century (Scott *et al.* 1956: 44). In Scott's study, there is no evidence to suggest that the systematic establishment of spearheads for chain migration, found in Corby, had ever achieved the same dimensions.

It seems probable that direct recruitment provides the best explanation of the higher rates of kin presence in the workplace found in this section of my data as compared with those of Scott for the same industry. Furthermore, although historically the steel works studied by Scott had been the sole large employer in the area, this was no longer the case – whereas for Corby it remained the case even in the late 1970s. This would tend to push rates of kinship presence up. Note that these figures are also higher than those of Walker, who was studying a settled one-employer site.

The size of the aggregate structure for the Buchan family is fifteen if current employees only are counted but twenty-seven if both current and lapsed employment are taken into account. Note that Scott's measure can tell us nothing about interlinkages between the different sets of individual network data collected. The size of the employment net taken together with the average number and the total number of relations provides a better though not perfect indicator.

The McConnell net exhibits a somewhat smaller set of figures. The average figures for direct kin currently employed in the workplace was 1.8, for indirect kin 1.7, with an overall average of 3.5 kin currently employed in the workplace (see Table 4.3a). Using the Scott measure and anchoring on current employees, the average figures for current and lapsed kin employment taken together are almost double those of the current alone. They are 3.0 for direct kin, 3.0 for indirect kin, and 6.0 for all kin (calculated from Table 4.3b).

Averaging across current employment within these three nets, one gets a figure of 2.9 for direct kin, 1.7 for indirect kin and 4.6 for all kin. Note that the overall figure is almost identical to that of Walker, 4.6 as compared with 4.3. Averaging across past and present employees in the three nets, on Scott's method one gets an average figure of 4.6 for direct relations, 2.8 for indirect relations, and 7.1 for all relations. Scott's data is, as I have noted, not strictly comparable with my own; however, even if I make the data directly comparable by removing female relatives and cousin relationships, I still find a significantly stronger relationship between kin and the workplace – 3.2 as compared with 2.7, and 5.1 as compared with 4.7. Note that whereas Scott's sample was random, within certain departmental constraints, my sample was chosen on the basis of probable kin connection, using surname as an initial indicator. Scott and Walker's figures taken together suggest that the kin structures which I have identified are common within steel. Even if one considers direct kin in current employment only, my data suggests that the relationship between kin and the workplace in the steel industry, first identified by Scott *et al.* in the 1950s, persisted into the late 1970s even in a highly migratory context.

Earlier I quoted Wedderburn (1965) arguing that kinship ties are to be expected in any long-established plant or workplace; the thrust of this argument was that kin presence in the workplace was a feature of a settled community. My evidence on Corby suggests that such practices are by no means confined to the settled context and to the purely local environment, but rather the same dynamic may occur within a highly migratory context. Wedderburn views the relationship between kin presence and the workplace as principally a matter of time, of custom, and of tradition. My evidence suggests – whilst not wishing to diminish the importance of time in the generation of social ties, for example, with endogamous marriage – that bulk recruitment practices may accomplish the same demographic outcome as the passage of time in terms of producing high rates of kin presence in the workplace.

Networks and employment aid

My fieldwork thus establishes that kin is indeed present in the workplace – and this account fits with those furnished by a number of more general analyses of labour mobility to Corby (see Chapters 6 and 7). But how was this kin presence in the workplace established? I have discussed the role of kin in conveying information and the mechanisms involved in securing employment in earlier chapters. I now move to a detailed analysis of such employment aid for the three nets.

Figures 4.1, 4.2, and 4.3 indicate the line of introduction of each member of the workforce to his job. Figures 4.4, 4.5, and 4.6 convert this data into summaries of the exchange of favours within the nets. The literature assumes that kinship structures possess no sanctions in the economic/industrial sphere and thus, having no economic basis of control, have a generally weakened role in modern social life. The evidence in Figures 4.1, 4.2, and 4.3 and the additional material included in Figures 4.4, 4.5, and 4.6 directly challenge this perception (see pp. 90–2). Within the three nets, there were fifty-three instances of 'speaking for' a relative directly at the Corby works, that is fifty-three instances of social exchange between kin, or fifty-three events in which familial sanctions were explicit and in which familial social control adhered. Interestingly, all of these acts of introduction had a successful outcome; no 'patron' reported any lack of success in obtaining employment for any 'client' spoken for.

There are three reasons why such high rates of success should pertain in Corby. First, individuals may very well under-report their sponsoring failures. Second, during this period demand for labour in Corby was very high. Management had a stated preference for Scots labour (Thomas 1969: 858), and all the workers contained within our nets are of Scots background. Finally, and most interestingly, it may be the case that experience leads individuals only to sponsor clients who have a high chance of success, or alternatively leads individuals to time their interventions so as to maximize the chance of success. Thus our workers are sufficiently experienced to know whom to push and when to push them. Within the Sheldrake net, reported in Chapter 2, patrons waited for a recruitment drive and then pushed their candidate forward; the chances of an individual being hired outside these periods was known to be low. Similar processes appeared to be at work in Corby:

> I heard they'd started taking people on. I went over to personnel and said 'What about my son-in-law? His form's been with you for ages. And you're taking other people on in front of him. How's that?' So they looked for the form and they couldn't find it. Well it wasn't surprising really. I'd never filled one in. But he got up the front of the line and he got the job. It's the only way, you have to push if you want something, don't you.

> (Corby worker)

My argument here is that we should be careful not to over-read influence by simply looking at an individual patron's successful placement rates. Influence is not absolute; it is, in Wolf's terms, interstitial (Wolf 1966), depending upon an ability to correctly assess the match of the candidate to present labour-force requirements and upon the accurate timing of the intervention.[21] Interstitial influence cannot promise the delivery of a service on demand and precisely requires the scheduling of obligations. We take up this theme in more detail in Chapter 5.

An important property of the recruitment situation just described for the debate as to whether the family retains any social control over its members in the modern period is the extent to which harnessing new opportunities – jobs for the next generation, for instance – is predicated upon the employer's perception of the collective work behaviour of family members already in the workplace. It is not a matter purely of the individual reputation of the initial or current patron but of the group as a whole which sets the boundaries to the exercise of influence.

Let us now consider the matter of multiple lines of introduction to the workplace. There are two ways of approaching this issue. We can confine our attention to the situations in which more than one individual is known to have spoken for a new member of the workforce. Thus nine of our sixty-five workers (14 per cent) found employment as a consequence of verbal references given by at least two existing members of the workforce. Or we can follow the practices of British employers and combine verbal references with an analysis of the behaviour of all kin in the plant.[22] Many British employers have a standard question on their application forms: 'Do you have any relatives already working in this organization?' Some of the larger companies[23] keep computerized records of family connections within their workforces.

Let us return for the moment to Chapter 2 and to the Sheldrake net employment at Carreras Rothman, a large company with a bureaucratic personnel department which asks about kin connections in the workplace on its application forms. Thus, although Mary Murray (number 3 in Sheldrake net) and George White (number 13 in Sheldrake net) both made independent personal direct applications to the firm, at the point of their respective enquiries this firm contained five and seven members of their kin network. The expectation that both these workers would be satisfactory is related to the density of kin presence already contained within the factory. Thus, although Mary Murray and George White did not directly involve kin in their applications and did not therefore generate any new direct obligations, and although neither they nor the other members of their kin network viewed them as having received direct employment aid on this occasion, from our point of view they were recipients of indirect aid. Family reputation helped in the obtaining of these positions.

Within the Corby nets I have no examples of such direct applications at the gate, although it is known from other sources that this does indeed occur. Everybody within the nets attributed the gaining of their employment to the state employment exchange or, with one exception, to kin. It is tempting therefore to leave the story there, but multiple lines of introduction of influence must also be viewed as operative in Corby. That family reputation was important in the hiring decision was confirmed by an interview with the personnel officer and labour manager of the steel works. Family reputation not only provided the grounds for hiring a worker, it could also provide the reason for refusing a worker employment. Thus, whilst some individuals were concerned to demonstrate their kinship linkages as a way of facilitating entry to employment, others were concerned to conceal them as these sets of linkages represented a barrier to employment.

With each additional member of a family recruited to a particular workplace, an employer gains better quality information on the labour source, until the point of information redundancy is reached. As more members of a family enter the workplace, the importance of pivots diminishes in terms of both their screening and control functions.[24] Both functions become properties of the group as whole. Exchange is no longer dyadic but takes a generalized form. That this is the case can be seen from the practice of other kin members acting as patrons in situations where for one reason or another the natural patron is not able to perform this service. Here are two typical examples. First, there was a father who had acted as employment broker or patron for two sons and who was unable on account of illness to perform the same service for a third. The service was provided by the brother of the jobseeker. In a different instance of essentially the same situation, the introductory role was taken by the candidate's uncle, the brother of his father.

Three factors should be noted here. First, there is an etiquette to sponsorship; there is a notion of who should be approached first in the search for help. There are natural patrons – though this should not be confused with Brooks and Singh's notion of pivot, a concept which implies a monopolistic agency of introduction (Brooks and Singh 1979). Second, this concept of natural patron constitutes the social ground in which the practice of using proxies is founded. For in the two examples studied not only has a favour been performed with regard to the candidate but a favour has also been performed with regard to the natural patron. Third, although the natural patron is not physically able to perform the task of introduction in the two examples given, he is not entirely absent from the exchange either even from the employer's perspective, for his reputation remains part of the transaction despite physical non-presence. Hence, these situations are also to be categorized as involving multiple lines of introduction.

Having received employment aid not only generated an obligation to repay the aid donor if the relevant occasion arose, but also generated an obligation to provide aid to other kin members in the same way as it was provided to oneself. All our respondents regarded themselves as obliged to provide such services within the kin network. Group membership was the fundamental basis of exchange, not personal preferential pairings. Thus kin were viewed as having priority claims on aid as compared with friends. This is not to suggest that within the kin networks studied preferences for particular exchange partners were not being exercised – they were. Preferences could however be overridden by need. Thus three of our respondents housed kin of whom they were not fond, in situations of crisis. The direction of aid as dictated by preference and the direction of aid as dictated by need often vary. Thus, of the forty-nine workers interviewed, four had provided employment aid to kin members whose companionship they would not actively seek. These ties are deemed by the individuals interviewed as strong though the friendship content is small. Customary obligations generate strong ties.

Up to now I have concentrated only on employment aid given with respect to entry into the Corby steel works. But why was this aid given? Put differently, is it possible that such aid was given in repayment of past debt? And what obligations did this aid create for the future? Of course, the information given in Figures 4.1, 4.2, and 4.3 cannot shed light on employment aid prior to Corby or subsequent to Corby. However, one of the objectives of my interviews was precisely to reconstruct such a pattern of aid, if it existed. This pattern is presented in Figures 4.4, 4.5, and 4.6. Thus Figure 4.4 details employment aid within the Buchanan net. The columns represent aid donors while the rows represent aid givers. Hence at the intersection of row number 3 and column number 2 there is a 'C' – which indicates that 2 helped 3 into the Corby steel works. All the C's, therefore, represent the information already present in the main Buchanan diagram, Figure 4.1. However, Figure 4.4 also has P's, which represent aid given prior to Corby. Thus the P in row 5 and column 10 indicates that 10 helped 5 secure employment in a period earlier to arrival in Corby. Notice that in row 10 and column 5 there is a C. The P and C have been joined together to represent the payment of a past debt. The same is true of individuals 11 and 15 in the same Buchanan net: 15 helped 11 in the past, and 11 helped 15 secure employment in Corby.

In Chapter 3 I was critical of Granovetter's measure of the strength of a tie – namely, frequency of current contact – because it cannot take account of obligations incurred in the past. Nor, of course, can this approach shed light on obligations incurred for the future. Consider Figures 4.5 and 4.6, which represent patterns for the Buchan and McConnell nets respectively. Here again we see instances of obligations incurred and discharged. In particular, as 'S' indicates, employment aid is being given subsequent to employment in Corby. Thus in the McConnell net (Fig. 4.6) individual 17 helped individual 9 subsequent to Corby, that is in migrating out of Corby. However, individual 17 had himself been helped into the Corby works by 9. Clearly, therefore, a simple snapshot view of aid understates the role of past obligations leading to current help which in turn generates future obligations.

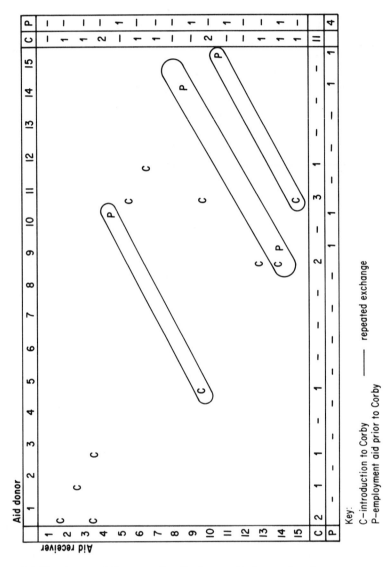

Figure 4.4 Employment favours: the Buchanan 'balance sheet'

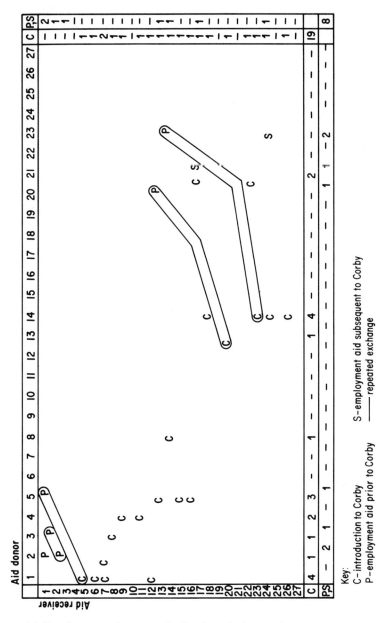

Figure 4.5 Employment favours: the Buchan 'balance sheet'

Key:
C – introduction to Corby
P – employment aid prior to Corby
S – employment aid subsequent to Corby
—— repeated exchange

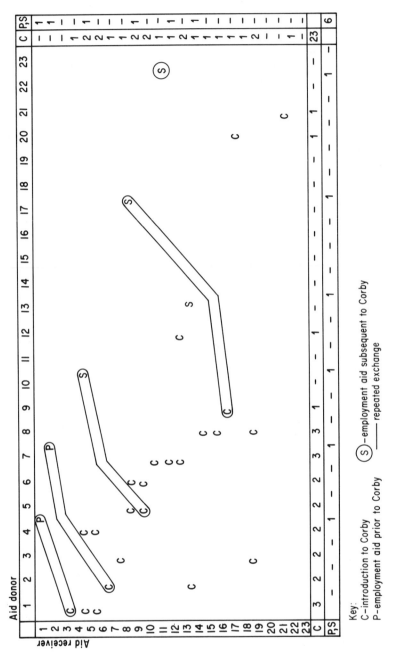

Figure 4.6 Employment favours: the McConnell 'balance sheet'

Friendship and kinship

Although my object in this section has been to highlight the kinship links in the Corby steel works, one striking feature of the employment aid investigation is that out of a total of sixty-five workers in the three nets, only one is known to have helped a friend find employment in Corby. This occurred in the McConnell net (see Figure 4.3), where number 9 (Robertson) helped number 17 (Macmillan) – and this relationship subsequently converted to kinship through the marriage of Macmillan to Robertson's sister (neither of these two workers were available for interview, both having emigrated to Canada; the information was provided by other members of the Robertson family).

As to why employment aid to friends is so rare in the Corby context, two lines of enquiry are of importance. First, how far is it the case that the absence of friendship-based employment assistance is a feature of our sample, and second, how much of the situation is explained by special features of Corby. While there are no cases of long-distance assistance to friends amongst the older workers interviewed, all of these workers have been helped by friends and given help to friends in employment search. This assistance occurred in every case outside of the Corby labour market. Of the younger workers interviewed, only those who had worked outside Corby had ever given or received employment help from friends. Once again this help had been within the context of a local labour market other than Corby. This should not be taken to mean that there are no friendship–workmate relationships in Corby – indeed, there are – but rather that they must be examined in terms of the special character of Corby, and it is to this we now turn.

Young Corby workers are unlikely to be required to give their friends help in the local employment context, as given the one-employer character of the town and the links holding between residence and employment (see Ch. 7), their friends are likely to have their own set of equally dense kin linkages to the works. Arrival in Corby indicates, in the main, an existing connection to the works.

Within the sample, then, removal to Corby appears to have tightened the link between kinship and employment rather than having weakened it. Some of this tightening of linkages can be attributed to the one-employer character of the town, combined with the recruitment practices which resulted in friends having parallel paths of access to employment. The other part of the explanation resides in the nature of migration itself. Providing employment aid to friends in the local labour market is less costly than providing aid in distant markets. Within the local labour market, native individuals have, as Marsden has most pertinently indicated, their own familial support structures (Marsden 1982).

Put differently, and using Davanzo and Morrison's terminology, individuals' resource networks can be viewed as location-specific capital (Davanzo and Morrison 1978). Thus, encouraging friends to migrate to a destination where they themselves have no relatives or alternative network contacts independent of the friend-informant, and where consequently no such familial safety nets are present, is likely to result in claims upon the sponsoring individual's resources which the limits of the relationship will not tolerate. The provision of aid to friends in the local labour market is thus fundamentally different to that provided over distance; limiting information provision effectively reduces the claims on aid.

In the local labour context, if the tip on a better job proves to be a bad one, little has been disrupted – residence remains the same, contact networks are unimpaired, knowledge of the local environment is still high. If, on the other hand, employment aid over long distance turns out to be bad advice, then the migrating individual is severed from the contact networks necessary to gaining another job and is highly dependent on his one information source, which has already proved unreliable.[25] Furthermore, the claims on aid that this individual is permitted to make of his information source are highly circumscribed – a prospect which is radically different from that facing kin.

There are high risks encountered, therefore, on both sides of the friendship exchange in assisting migration. As I have already remarked, within the employment nets kin were believed to have an entitlement to help, most particularly when accompanied by need. Furthermore, need was typically declared by a kin member other than the party requiring assistance. Thus assistance was offered rather than requested. Kinship accounts, so to speak, were subject to different balancing principles than friendship accounts. This point is reinforced in Chapter 8 in the context of residential aid in return migration. Migration upon a kinship basis may thus usefully be regarded as a survival strategy.

To summarize then, my argument is that the degree of aid required in long-distance migration and employment search is substantially greater than that involved in local search and that this requires only strong ties be used. Migration, rather than serving to disrupt kinship ties, may be viewed as intensifying them, for the aid required and supplied is likely to be greater than that needed in the local context. I suggest that had Granovetter applied his weak-tie analysis to labour mobility over distance, it would immediately have broken down. Migration as an atomized individual results in severance from those networks of contacts essential to job search and survival under adverse conditions, especially in the blue-collar sector. Chain migration protects against such severance, especially where it is accomplished upon a strong tie basis. Within the nets there is some evidence of chain migration taking place out of Corby in anticipation of imminent redundancy to Luton, Dagenham, and Coventry. Once again, it is upon a kinship basis, confirming the importance of strong ties in geographical mobility.

Conclusion

This chapter has argued that the major counter-example to Granovetter's conception of a weak tie (i.e. low frequency of contact), and its strong role in employment search, is the existence of chain migration, where information and aid are transferred from one agent to another without any necessary physical contact between them. Indeed, the essence of the information transfer in this context is geographical separation – one member of the network conducts search on behalf of another from whom he is geographically separated, transmits information (which is trusted), and perhaps even secures employment. I posed the question: why should this process ever take place if the tie between the two individuals is weak? Moreover, it was noted that employers recruit network members because the obligations between network members provide an extra dimension of control – control which rests on strong ties between members.

In contrast to the assumptions of the literature, I suggest that processes of chain migration are likely to strengthen social ties. The process of migration of C from the area of origin to a job in the area of destination secured for him by A is the consequence of obligations felt by A to C, either directly or even perhaps through a proxy. This act of assistance or exchange, apart from strengthening the relationship between A and C, further strengthens ties in the area of origin itself, since the new obligation from C to A creates new obligations between those strongly tied to A and those strongly tied to C in the area of origin. This dynamic aspect of the process of strength of ties leading to a service which in turn strengthens ties is largely uninvestigated in the literature.

In previous sections case-study evidence was presented which highlighted this process. In the next chapter I present a formal analysis in terms of measures of network density. The consequences for both mainstream industrial sociology and social-network analysis should, however, already be clear. First, occupational and geographical mobility in modern industrial societies need not destroy kin networks. Employment aid can be and is given in working-class families in such societies – this can only serve to strengthen the role of family. Second, since one dimension of a tie in this context is the employment aid given to kin members, the sphere of kinship and the sphere of employment necessarily interact and overlap – even in modern industrial societies, relationships, far from becoming single-stranded, remain multiplex.

The conclusion of this chapter is that the arguments and evidence in favour of an overlap between kinship and employment relations, strong as they are in the context of local labour markets, must be further strengthened when migration is introduced into the picture. The role of kin in assisting employment-related migration is well documented in the historical evidence, and is apparent from a number of different contemporary literatures as well. Evidence has been brought together as a backdrop to a theoretical analysis of the network basis of employment-related migration – the role of kin in turning a chance spearhead into a systematic migration stream, and the role of employers in encouraging this process and fashioning the initial spearhead by means of direct recruitment have been documented.

I have argued that direct recruitment and chain migration are a feature not merely of Third World societies and ethnic labour forces in industrial societies, but that they constitute an important feature of internal, indigenous migration as well. There is evidence of such employment-related migration in the UK in the contemporary period, for a number of industries and regions. My empirical focus, of course, is the migration stream from Scotland to the Corby steel works.

My case-study evidence shows the existence of kinship employment nets in this industry, and argues that migration mechanisms lie behind the presence of kin in the workplace. The direct recruitment strategies of the steel employers and the planning context of Corby's expansion, both of which contribute to strong kin presence in the Corby steel works, will be examined in Chapters 6 and 7. In this chapter, however, I have detailed how, for three particular kinship employment nets, lines of introduction of kin to employment are strong and multiplex, and I have drawn out the implications of this for both migration theory and network analysis.

In this chapter I have focused on employment aid given to each other by kin. However, in the next chapter the analysis will be extended by using my interviews to reveal the pattern of residential aid given during the course of migration and employment search, and by applying a vacancy-chain model to understand the role of such aid in explaining the chain-like pattern of migration.

5
Vacancy chains and family networks

Introduction

> Conflicts among individuals over opportunities are central to many theories
> in social science. Less often noted is the regenerative nature of such
> opportunity. When one man buys a new car another man can acquire the first
> man's trade in and, in turn, pass on his old car, and so on.
>
> (White 1970: 1)

> The chain of movements of men is a series of pulls of a man out of one job into
> a more attractive one. It is natural to call this pull chain a vacancy chain; the
> vacancy is moving from the job appearing earliest in the chain to the one
> appearing last, whereas the dual series of men change jobs in the direction
> opposite to the flow of cause and effect. The beginning event – creation of a
> vacancy – . . . causes the chain; it generates the opportunity to move seized by
> the new incumbent, whose departure in turn generates a new opportunity.
>
> (White 1970: 16)

White, in his classical work *Chains of Opportunity* (1970), focuses on the
dynamic set up by the movement of an individual or group of
individuals from one location to another. White's major focus is on
career opportunities, or employment 'vacancy chains'. He pays little
attention, however, to the sociological mechanisms underlying chains
of opportunity – employment related or otherwise. Although the chain
dynamic highlighted by White is of great importance, particularly in
understanding the process of chain employment, however, greater
insights into the underlying mechanisms are gained by analysing the
interactions between vacancy chains and social networks. The former
alerts us to the regenerative character of employment opportunity in
general; the latter emphasizes that this regeneration is particularistic in
nature. In the labour-market literature, this interaction of job-vacancy
chains and social networks has come to be called *grapevine recruitment*.

My purpose here is to provide a theoretical account of how this social process operates and to indicate its consequences for labour-market discrimination.

The nineteenth-century statistician, Ravenstein, posited a similar chain model in his explanation of labour migration. This Chapter expands upon Ravenstein's understanding of the chain characteristics of migration (Ravenstein 1885) and relates them to recent research on the involvement of social networks in this process.

The next section takes up Ravenstein's migration model in the light of social-network analysis. The third section turns to White's vacancy chain concept and its application, in conjunction with social-network theory, to kin-connected migration, while the fourth section considers the effects of chains on the network. The fifth section considers a particular consequence of the joint operation of vacancy chains and social networks – the capture of an entire sequence of opportunities by a kin network. My analysis suggests such occupational closure by the white working class may be as important in the disadvantaging of ethnic minorities as direct discrimination by the employer. The sixth section concludes the chapter.

Ravenstein's law of migration

Ravenstein's second law of migration may be summarized as saying: the mobility opportunity of one individual is occasioned by the movement of another. His contribution is to note that mobility involves two fundamental components: location and incumbent. If the number of locations is fixed or changes relatively slowly, then advancement of an individual creates a vacancy in his current location, which is filled by another, thereby creating another vacancy, and so on. This is an important contribution lost to the literature till its rediscovery by Harrison White.

But Ravenstein's model of migration is essentially a mechanical one. Termed the 'gravity theory of migration' (Lee 1966), it assumes that centres of opportunity exert a pull on individuals, with the pull of the centre on individuals in the adjacent space being greater than that on individuals in the next adjacent space to that, and so on – effectively, the Newtonian square law. The strongest pull works first, and then knock-on effects occur by another physical analogy: 'nature abhors a vacuum' and rushes to fill it.

Transfer of information on opportunities occurs automatically, and this is to be expected in a model which understands *physical adjacency* as the determinant of mobility. As to why individuals should fill adjacent gaps rather than move directly to new centres of opportunity, Ravenstein provides no explanation.

My own data on migration (Grieco 1981), along with that of many other writers, suggests that geographical mobility often involves leaps over great distances. However, by focusing on the concept of *social adjacency,* and by paying attention to the manner in which information on employment opportunity is relayed to socially adjacent locations, Ravenstein's insight on chains of opportunity can be rescued and made consistent with the observed facts of migration. Social adjacency is to be thought of in terms of a social network, and this can be radically different from geographical or physical adjacency. Consider the following hypothetical network.

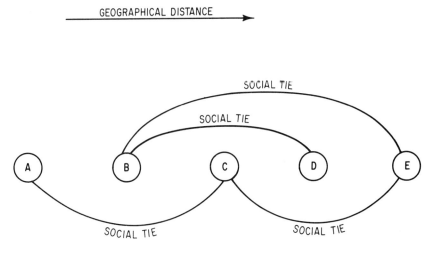

Figure 5.1

Points A through E are arranged such that A is one distance unit from B, B is one distance unit from C, and so on. The lines connecting the points *define* the network. In fact, this is the hypothetical network in Mitchell (1969: 16), but with the exception that the arcs are *not* directed – thus A can be reached from C and C can be reached from A.

We can write down the geographical distance matrix as follows:

	A	B	C	D	E
A	0	1	2	3	4
B	1	0	1	2	3
C	2	1	0	1	2
D	3	2	1	0	1
E	4	3	2	1	0

Figure 5.2

The social distance between any two points may be defined (Mitchell 1969) as the smallest number of steps needed for one individual to reach another through the network. The social distance matrix is, therefore:

	A	B	C	D	E
A	0	3	1	4	2
B	3	0	2	1	1
C	1	2	0	3	1
D	4	1	3	0	2
E	2	1	1	2	0

Figure 5.3

The disparity between social distance and geographical distance is depicted in Figure 5.4.

	A	B	C	D	E	Sum
A	0	-2	1	-1	2	0
B	-2	0	-1	1	2	0
C	1	-1	0	-2	1	-1
D	-1	1	-2	0	-1	-3
E	2	2	1	-1	0	4

Figure 5.4

D is closest to E geographically, yet, along with A, farthest from E *socially*. In particular, A is as close to E along the network as D, even though A is farthest from E geographically. Similarly, although the geographical distance from A to B is one, the social distance along the network is three. A new opportunity arises in the location in which E is situated. According to the Ravenstein model, D will move to the same location as E, C will move to D's location, and so on, till the situation looks like that shown in Figure 5.5.

Figure 5.5

If *two* opportunities arise in the location, Ravenstein's model predicts the situation shown in Figure 5.6.

Figure 5.6

Consider what the 'social distance' approach would predict in this case. E is closest along the network to B and C, and if two new opportunities arise in this location, these are the two who would be informed. Thus the new situation would be as shown in Figure 5.7.

Figure 5.7

This is clearly a different pattern of migration from that predicted by the Ravenstein model. Although D is closest to E geographically, he has not migrated because information has bypassed him on the network. Although the highlighting of the *sequential* character of migration is an important insight in the work of Ravenstein, an overly simple geographical model leads to predictions at variance with the facts. Migrants to Corby (Grieco 1985a) travelled great distances in their migration, despite the existence of towns of opportunity en route. On a measure of *social distance* Corby was closer to the centres of origin than the intervening towns. Note that this migration over social distance was indeed *chain-like* in nature.

Employment chains and chains of aid

The basis of Harrison White's emphasis on vacancy chains is that:

> Many jobs are social entities as stable and independent as men. This fact about social systems requires a new view of the nature of mobility. . . . Mobility among fixed jobs is highly constrained; movement must dovetail in order to maintain the fixed number of occupants. Mobility is enmeshed in a network of contingencies. When an incumbent leaves the job, one speaks of the creation of a vacancy and then the filling of the vacancy when a replacement enters the job.
>
> (White 1970: 1)

Although White applied his model to 'the movement of clergy among pastorates in national churches', the model is applicable to the housing market or other markets where discrete slots are filled with discrete incumbents. Let us go beyond the concept of chains and markets and consider a more abstract notion of a location, namely 'recipiency of aid' – and show how this type of vacancy chain connects with migration and employment chains.

White's analysis is restricted to the general properties of the vacancy chain, such as its average length. It is only in his penultimate chapter that White notes:

> Vacancy chain models are blind to particular ties among men. Moves between jobs for particular individuals are shaped by networks of acquaintances and sponsors which evolve over long periods in overlapping neighbourhoods. . . . What is missing is insight into 'in-breeding' in the system; that is, toward

certain arbitrary jobs marking the occupant for eventual success or failure, toward small sets of jobs capturing the whole careers of certain sets of men, and so on.

(White 1970: 298)

White did find some evidence suggestive of 'in-breeding', but as he admits, 'the book does not move far into the study of sociological network theory' (1970: xiii). However, it is this interaction between social networks and vacancy chains which is at the hub of the kin-connected and chain-like nature of employment and labour migration. Furthermore, it is precisely this interaction which serves to disadvantage out-groups in their search for employment. The macro implications of the micro social practice of favouring own-network members in the competition for resources are social segregation and indirect discrimination.

Job-vacancy chains
Consider the migration of an individual out of an area. This individual could be either a spearhead migrant – an initiator of the migration chain – or a later link in the migration chain. The point of interest is whether he leaves behind a job vacancy at origin. If he is unemployed, then clearly no job vacancy is left behind. If he was employed in the area of origin, then his migration creates a vacancy there. If the job slot does not close behind him, the regenerative character of migration through this channel is clear. The standard literature on migration focuses on the gain to an individual or family as the result of higher income or greater security attained in the new location. The vacancy-chain approach draws attention to the vacancies left behind – the opportunity set at origin has been expanded.

White's analysis is uninterested in the particularism of the chain, in who steps into this vacancy. Our analysis suggests that it will be a candidate socially connected to the departing individual. Networks play an important role in the filling of vacancies, both over distance and in the local labour market (Grieco 1982). Quite apart from the ability of the last incumbent to 'speak for' a particular person in his friendship/ kinship network, it is likely that the old incumbent is network-connected to other members in the workplace (Manwaring 1984). The existing workforce pass employment information on to other members of their network, and use influence to put network candidates at an advantage over other candidates for the vacancy. The implications of this analysis are clear: whatever the length of the chain, its *path* will be along channels given by the existing social network.

Apart from regenerating opportunity by the act of migrating, the migrant can regenerate opportunity further by seeking out and harnessing employment opportunities in the new area. This can happen in two ways. First, when the migrant moves on to a different (better) job and this creates a vacancy (the migrant becomes part of a vacancy chain in the area of destination), he can guide people into this vacancy by giving early information on the vacancy and perhaps using influence. The particularism of vacancy chains is perhaps most strongly indicated by their propensity to stretch over geographical distances. Second, and more importantly, when new jobs arise in the area of destination, information about these can be passed on through the social network to the area of origin.

However, aid is given not merely in terms of employment. Other forms of aid – such as residence – are important in migration and it is to these we now turn.

Aid vacancies
The focus of this book is on working-class migration, the role of networks in such migration, and the consequences for social segregation. One way of understanding the chain-like character of migration is through the employment connection – jobs are found in sequence and hence migration takes place in sequence. But there are other features of migration which reinforce this tendency, particularly in a working-class context. Resources for migration are limited and have to be generated period by period – the surplus left over to the migrant after meeting his expenses can be small in the initial stages. In a historical context the costs of migration were significant and the surplus generated in the area of destination would have to be used sequentially. Thus in a situation of restricted resources, recipiency of aid represents a *location*, the occupation of which by one incumbent prevents its usage by others. Over time, as the need for aid diminishes, the incumbent moves out of this vacancy and another incumbent moves in. Eligibility for recipient status is composed of a number of locations through which individuals move in accordance with the mobility of those in front of them. Aid is structured according to vacancy-chain principles.

An important factor in internal labour migration in the UK is accommodation during the initial period of job or residential search; this is a highly restricted resource. My evidence on migration from Scotland to Corby clearly demonstrates the operation of this type of aid chain. I would now like to turn, therefore, to the interaction between housing and employment within one particular migrant/kin network, the Robertson/McConnell net.

The Robertson/McConnell net: claims on residential aid
Elsewhere (Grieco 1985a) I have described the newly settled character of Corby New Town. In particular, attention was drawn to the manner in which labour for this English steel works was disproportionately recruited from Scotland. It was managerial policy to select in favour of Scottish labour throughout the post-war period. This recruitment pattern generated a distinct ethnic community in Corby which subsequently experienced *labour-market discrimination* in the surrounding area. This labour remained, on the whole, *socially unconnected* to the indigenous population and thus had limited access to local employment

opportunities. It had no access to the local grapevine and was directly discriminated against by local employers. It remained dependent on the large employer which had initiated the migration stream as the source of local employment. In this respect it shares in the experience of many long-distance ethnic labour streams.

The Robertson/McConnell network, or employment net, was recruited from Glasgow to Corby during this period. The net displays a pattern of labour oscillation or circulation which according to the orthodoxy is abnormal for modern industrial society – such patterns are normally identified with Third World or with historical material. This pattern of labour circulation is in part explained by the labour-market discrimination experienced by Scots Corby labour, in part by the seasonality of certain types of steel employment and in part by the information contacts between the two ends of the migration path described in the previous section. Changing jobs often meant changing area of residence (Grieco 1985a) and employment contacts were best in the area of origin (Grieco 1985b).

Through participant observation within this social network, we reconstructed the chain-like pattern of residential aid over a quarter of a century. In order to illustrate the relationship between labour circulation and residential vacancies, a diagrammatic representation of this information is presented in Figure 5.8.

Spearheading the arrival of the Robertson net in Corby were two unmarried uncles named Jameson. Initially, these two men had been in hostel accommodation, subsequently in lodgings, and had eventually been allocated a Corporation house. They advised their niece and her husband to come to Corby and helped to make the necessary employment arrangements for them. Both the husband and wife took up employment in the steel works immediately upon arrival in Corby. The uncles also made the initial accommodation arrangements, providing the married couple with a room in their own house.

Although the Robertsons initially left their children with relatives in Glasgow, having dependent children strengthened the couple's early claims on a Corporation house. Within six months the Robertsons had their own house and had moved out of the Jamesons'. Shortly after this the Jamesons and the Robertsons were both called upon to provide accommodation for the Robertsons' two married sons and their respective spouses. These two couples in turn were provided with Corporation accommodation of their own.

Subsequently, the Robertsons' marriage broke down and the husband moved in with his wife's uncle for the second time. The wife took a new partner, McConnell, and he and his adult son moved into the Robertson house, where the three lived together with Robertson's dependent children. Shortly after, McConnell's son successfully applied for a Corporation flat and moved out. Robertson lived with the uncles for one year before obtaining accommodation of his own. He subsequently left the property, returning to Glasgow, thereafter oscillating

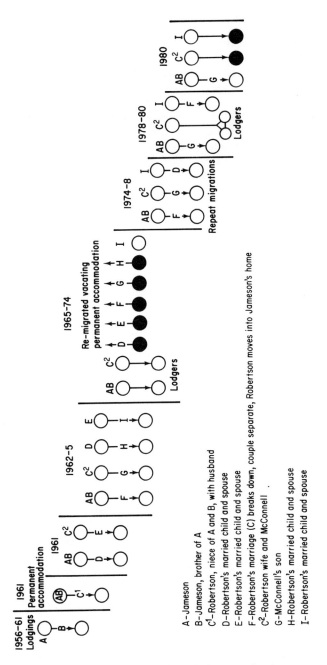

Figure 5.8 Robertson/McConnell: residential chain and sub-net, 1956–80

between Corby and Glasgow. Two of the Robertsons' daughters came of age, married, and moved into their siblings' homes with their respective partners, whilst waiting their turn for Corporation houses. Thus four of the Robertsons' children spent some part of their married life in either the uncle's, mother's, or siblings' homes. Of the four, only one retained permanent accommodation in Corby. Both the mother and the uncles have retained permanent accommodation in Corby. These three residential spaces or vacancies host the repeated migration of other members of this net from Glasgow to Corby. Eligibility for local authority housing is enhanced by the combination of residence and overcrowding, a combination of factors well used by this network in its strategy of accessing accommodation for its members.

Claims on the Robertson/McConnell domestic space also issue from the McConnell side of this alliance, where one son is involved in repeat migration between Corby and Glasgow. McConnell himself has also been involved in repeat moves between Corby and Glasgow. The latter are viewed as long working holidays and are typically occasioned by the need to attend to family matters in the home area.

The accommodation of repeated migration results in overcrowding. The official statistics suggest that the accommodation practices found in this network are fairly widespread. The census statistics for Corby show that over 11 per cent of households hold six or more members, 'the largest proportion in any new town and one resulting in the greatest occurrence of overcrowding in any new town outside Scotland' (Champion, Clegg, and Davis 1977: 155).

No doubt this exceptional proportion of large-sized households is in part attributable to the recruitment of Glasgow Catholic labour of child-bearing years. It is equally clear, however, that some part of this statistic is attributable to the pattern of labour circulation between Glasgow and Corby and its associated accommodation dynamic.

Accommodation in Corby, as with most New Towns, is limited to a few sources; as there is no private rental market of any significance, and as repeat migration generates a bad housing record, relatives and friends take on additional importance as major suppliers of accommodation. It is far more difficult to obtain public authority housing on a repeated cyclical basis, than it is to obtain lodgings with relatives and friends. Oscillatory migration may prove to be the best explanation of such ratios of overcrowding. These practices of overcrowding become in their turn a basis for further stigmatization of the new entrants to the locality. In this respect, Scots experience in Corby closely parallels that of ethnic entry to the inner city.

Family size does not disappear from the explanation altogether, however. For there is an important relationship between family size and network structure which bears consideration at this point. An increase in family size potentially permits an increase in the spread of opportunities captured; an increase in family size also increases the potential number of claims for aid on any one member. Thus, whilst large families reduce, in principle, the dependence of any one member on any particular other – a common feature of insurance practices – they also simultaneously expose individuals in particularly valued resource situations to a larger number of claims.

Let us relate this theoretical argument to the residential dynamic we have identified in Corby. Persistent overcrowding can be viewed as a measure of the number of individuals entitled to make claims on residential space and the paucity of individuals possessing it. Large families and labour circulation are interacting so as to generate recurrent overcrowding. Overcrowding, however, develops into a customary practice. In both the Robertson/McConnell home and the Jameson establishment, after the patterns of multiple-kin use had become common practice but in a period in which for various reasons there was no family need for accommodation, space was let to lodgers. The lodgers arrived by two main routes, the family or friends of friends, and through the housing officer at the works. The Robertson/McConnells helped their friends discharge their commitments when their friends were not able to directly undertake the provision of the service themselves.

What is clear from the Robertson/McConnell evidence on residential aid is the 'normality' for this group of close contact followed by geographical separation, which is followed once again by close contact, and so on. Their account of the pattern of ties, aid, and distance is strongly supported by the official statistics and sources, all of which note the strong and continuing connections between Clydeside and Corby.

The strength of ties is subject to periodic testing (the request for residential aid) and reinforcement (the provision of residential aid). Where the expected donor of aid experiences more demand for aid than she or he can *directly* supply in any one period, two strategies for coping are available: the use of proxies and the sequencing of aid. My fieldwork evidence shows that both strategies have been used in supporting chain migration into Corby. Proxies tend to be used most frequently in situations of crisis. The provision of aid is thus, not surprisingly, closely linked to the existence of strong ties.

Sharing residential space was both proof of a strong tie and generative of a strong tie; social proximity to kin was both a reason and a resource for migration. Circulatory movements maintained the active character of relationships but were also predicated in the ready reactivation of 'dormant' relationships. Using kin contacts as an accommodation resource must be viewed as both expressive and instrumental. Without these contacts there was no access to high-paying steel employment, but high-paying steel employment provided the resources to be with kin.

These residential practices served to strengthen the enclave properties of Corby New Town, which in turn served to produce sufficient bases of distinctiveness for labour-market discrimination to operate, which in its turn enhanced the monopsonistic character of the steel employer. Whereas for New Commonwealth entrants, colour often forms the basis of detectable difference, for Scots labour in North-amptonshire it was accent. The process of recruitment by a single employer to a distant location, accompanying chain migration, and subsequent labour-market discrimination by other employers in the new location have interacted to produce readily detectable difference which serves as a basis for further stigmatization. Scots labour became transformed into ethnic labour as a consequence of the interactions between the patronage dynamic within its own social networks, the recruitment policies of the employer, and the active discrimination of local employers against Corby Scots labour. In this respect it resembles the Irish experience in America and indeed the experience of many New Commonwealth communities in Britain.

Chains and networks

Chains of opportunity, contrary to the general thrust of Harrison White's work, are guided by network linkages. The giving of aid serves to strengthen ties in a network (Grieco 1982). Thus while the network influences the chain, the chain in turn has implications for the network. To see this, consider a highly stylized example with the network shown in Figure 5.9.

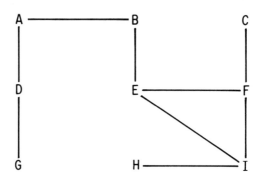

Figure 5.9

I do not want to inquire into how the links came to be. Suffice it to note that the links are *not* directed. Using the concept of network distance previously discussed, the distance between two individuals is measured by the smallest number of steps required to go from one to the other.

Let individual C have an aid vacancy in the network shown in Figure 5.9. What will be the chain of aid? Taking network distance to be the determinant of the sequencing of aid, aid will be given in the sequence shown in Figure 5.10.

Figure 5.10

Thus F is closest to C on the network and will be helped first. E and I come next and will be helped second – technically, there is equality between the two, and some other criterion will be used to distinguish which of E and I will be helped first. If, however, it is G that has the vacancy, the chain will be that shown in Figure 5.11.

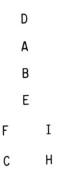

Figure 5.11

Hence the patterns of network linkages as well as the initial migration will determine the patterns of the chain. The latter, however, will in turn lead to a new pattern of linkages in the network.

The sociology of ties is such that the giving and receiving of aid serves to strengthen links between individuals. In the simple network here, let us represent this as the construction of a *direct* link where none existed before. Thus the chain which occurs if C has an aid vacancy leads to a new network where, along with the old ties, every individual is now directly tied to C. This is shown in Figure 5.12 with dotted lines representing the new ties.

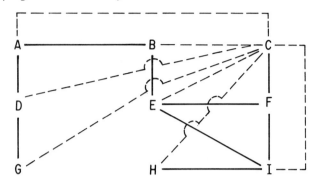

Figure 5.12

Following Mitchell (1969) and Barnes (1969), the density of a network is defined as the number of links that exist relative to the number of links that could exist. The density of the new network is clearly greater than the density of the old network. The Barnes measure of density is $\frac{200a}{n(n-1)}$ where a is the actual number of links and n is the total number of persons in the network. On this measure the density of the network in Figure 5.9 is $\frac{200 \times 9}{9 \times 8} = 25$ per cent, while the density of the new network in Figure 5.12 is $\frac{200 \times 16}{9 \times 8} = 44\,\frac{4}{9}$ per cent.

Above, it is assumed that there is a single vacancy, in the hands of C (or G), and the chain of aid through this one slot depends on the network connections of C. However, as individuals move through an aid vacancy they themselves become able to give aid. Indeed, I would argue, they are obliged to provide aid to other members of the network. Assuming that the new aid vacancy is allocated on the same principle, the pattern now is that shown in Figure 5.13.

Figure 5.13

Thus C helps F initially, and at the next stage both C and F have aid to give. Who will they help? F is directly linked to E and I. Assuming he helps one (let us say E), C helps the other. Now there are C, F, I, E with aid vacancies in the new location. E will help B, to whom he is most closely tied, I will help H, F will help A (given that B has already been aided by E), and C will help D – the closest person to C still in need of aid. In the next period, D will help G. The new network pattern resulting from this chain of aid is shown in Figure 5.14.

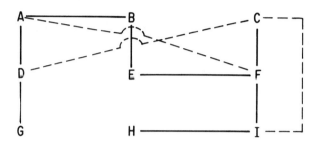

Figure 5.14

Comparing Figure 5.14 with Figure 5.9, it can be seen that the density of the network has increased. On the Barnes measure, the density of the network in Figure 5.14 is $\dfrac{200 \times 12}{9 \times 8} = 33\;\tfrac{1}{3}$ per cent. Thus, while networks give rise to particular chains of aid and opportunity, these chains in turn shape the pattern of the network.

The capture of opportunity by family

We move now from the regeneration of opportunity through a vacancy chain to the *capture* of opportunity through the annexing of an entire chain of employment.

Elsewhere (Grieco 1982; Grieco and Whipp 1986) I have presented evidence on the continuing importance of the family in the workplace and examined the role of this relationship in the organization of migration. Kin remains an important organizing principle in modern social existence. Assumptions about the erosion of the significance of kin in the organization of work are predicated on a misunderstanding of the needs, demands, and requirements of modern industry. Recent evidence from a number of quarters (Manwaring 1984) indicates that the importance of kin networks in determining employment location is greatest in the blue-collar sector. Within the context of industrial wage labour, blue-collar workers are better able to locate a range or set of opportunities which permit continued proximity and interaction for larger numbers of their members than are their white-collar counterparts. Why employers permit the possession of such occupational property has been explored at some length by a number of analysts (Rees 1966; Grieco 1982; Jenkins *et al.* 1983). A kin network may affect recruitment processes either as an agency of influence or as an agency of information or as both. Both these roles have parts to play in the capture of opportunities. Thus those analyses which focus only upon the transfer of material resources and fail to pay attention to influence and information as equally important resources, seriously underestimate the capacity of the working-class family to deliver aid and, consequently, to control behaviour.

To discuss the working-class family as the possessor of resources in the employment context is to diverge from the orthodoxy. Until recently it was assumed that unskilled manual work was a situation in which no control over recruitment numbers and types could be effected by present incumbents and therefore not a situation in which occupational closure would be expected to exist. Competition for such opportunities does exist, however, both within the socio-occupational range and within the locality, and it is precisely such competition which precipitates the need for closure on employment opportunities by kin networks. It is precisely by constructing imperfections in the information system of the labour market that the kin network best protects itself. The containment of employment information within the kin network is an important factor in the reduction of competition. By depriving potential competitors of information, kin can effectively protect their 'employment patch', especially where employers are using the kin-based recruitment strategies discussed previously.

Protected access to employment opportunities is a form of property; occupational property is, in fact, a concept long recognized by labour-market economists. Occupational property would appear to take two major forms. First, the control of information permits the capture of a set of opportunities. Second, the possession of particular and difficult skills is confined to the social group. The transference of skill takes place primarily on a family base, the transference of skill to non-family members being strongly resisted. An interesting instance of this is provided by Graves's account of pipeline construction workers in the USA (Graves 1958). His participant observation reveals the crucial role played by kinship in the recruitment and training of pipeline workers:

In-group workers (skilled pipeliners) are recruited for each new job by way of an informal grapevine which extends at least throughout the south west. Workers may be hired through phone calls or letters between themselves and friends or relatives at the job location. . . . Cliques of families and individuals travel together from job to job. In this way, the groups remain fairly cohesive in spite of the frequent moves which must be made.

(Graves 1958: 9–10)

Graves's account is a graphic statement of the capture of a set of employment opportunities by (largely) kin networks: 'First, and with few exceptions, the trainee must be a kinsman or a friend of some pipeliner who can either train him or to someone else who can have him trained' (Graves 1958: 10). Thus where kin networks have control over particular sets of vacancies, these vacancies may be deemed occupational property. Control of a vacancy is the ability of the worker or a worker's network to guarantee a friend or kinsman a job in the place of employment. The particular character of the intersection between employer and employee interest, here kin-defined, in many enterprises affords the family control over sets of vacancies. In such circumstances, the entire vacancy chain is contained within the network. Thus sets of employment locations become in effect 'family property'.

Graves's work shows us the extent of control over opportunities possessed by a ruling group or set of groups. It tells us about how such control is *maintained*. It does not, however, illuminate the manner in which such control is *acquired*. Here the work of Mormino is instructive (Mormino 1982). Discussing Italian migration to Tampa, Mormino throws light upon the way in which a kinship network trains its members *prior* to their entering the workplace. Initially, Italian labour was discriminated against by other labour in the cigar factories of Tampa. As a consequence, it accepted the rougher jobs in the workplace and expanded its 'capture' of jobs from this basis, little by little, until it had eroded the power of the existing workforce to enforce their discriminatory practices against it. Of particular importance is the mechanism by which this unskilled group taught itself cigar-rolling skills and thus 'robbed' the existing workforce of its advantages.

These Italians in low-skilled jobs 'cleverly smuggled scraps of tobacco from the factories to teach cigar-making to aspiring kin and paesani [countrymen] in the evening'. 'In spite of every opposition', a reporter observed, 'a few learned to make cigars and these in turn taught their friends and relatives' (Mormino 1982: 405).

We have here a classic description of the capture of a set of opportunities. First, the group enters the workplace, secures the information necessary to the acquisition of skill, trains itself and adjacent groups, finally occupying the workplace on the basis of skill advantage from an initial position of disadvantage. As Mormino reports, 'the practice was eventually institutionalised through the buckeye or "chinchal" system' (Mormino 1982: 405). Italians paid individual 'Spanish' workers (*chinchal* is the Spanish for bedbug; and it is presumably an indication of the low esteem in which these individuals were held by the Spanish community) to teach them and their offspring cigar-rolling skills. These *chinchales* ran apprenticeship schools *outside* of the workplace. Effectively, the Italians, by training themselves and by harnessing maverick Hispanics in their training arrangements, had broken the Hispanic monopoly on skill.

Mormino's evidence makes the point that positions conventionally regarded as unskilled and open do indeed have a skill base and as such are subject to social closure. His work evidences both the strength and the persistence of such monopolies and the mechanisms by which such arrangements can be disrupted.

The capture of employment opportunities is a threshold phenomenon. Once an enterprise holds so many members of a kin group, the probability of filling newly created vacancies with members of that group increases. Given the kin composition of the enterprise, information on vacancies is increasingly contained within the group. As the existence of the vacancy is not signalled to the outside world, it makes little sense to talk of general competition. Even if vacancies were advertised generally, the intersection of employer interest and kin influence would ensure that a vacancy chain took a particular route, whatever its average length.

The regeneration of employment opportunity, with the kin network plugging into the hitherto untapped employment vacancy chain, can thus become the capture of opportunity, with the entire vacancy chain being trapped inside the network, or at least a large part of it travelling within the network – an empty job merely calling for relocation by members of the network, with final entry by someone connected to the network. Consider two networks occupying nine locations (Fig. 5.15).

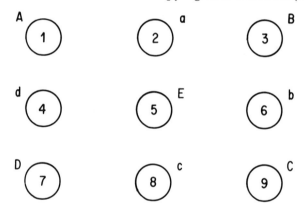

Figure 5.15

Numbers 1–9 give the locations, while A–E and a–d are the two networks. Suppose that the influence of a network on a vacancy in a location is determined by the number of network members *immediately adjacent* to the location in a horizontal or vertical direction – in case of a tie, the job goes to a member of the incumbent's network. Thus a vacancy in location 1 would be controlled by the network a–d, while a vacancy in location 2 would be controlled by the A–E network. Suppose that locations higher up the ladder are better, while locations at the same level are equally desirable. Suppose a vacancy arises in location 1. Since the lower-case network controls it, assume d moves into it (Fig. 5.16).

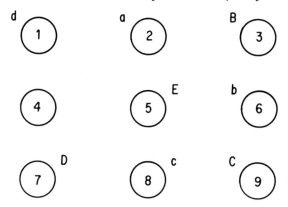

Figure 5.16

There is now a vacancy in location 4. The upper-case network controls 4 in Figure 5.16; assume D moves into it (Fig. 5.17).

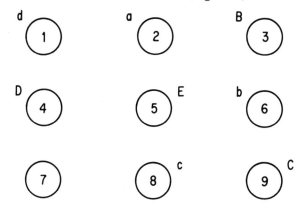

Figure 5.17

The vacancy is now in 7. D and E from the upper-case network both border it, whereas only c from the lower-case network is proximate. The upper-case network can thus make a stronger claim on the vacancy than the lower case; it is controlled by the upper-case network. F, a member of the upper-case network from outside the locations, is brought in to fill this. Thus control of the vacancy chain would alternate at different points in the chain. However, now consider the pattern of network and locations shown in Figure 5.18.

Now a vacancy arising in locations 1, 4, or 7 would always be filled by the upper-case network while a vacancy arising in 3, 6, or 9 would always be filled by the lower-case network. Locations 1, 4, and 7 are thus the occupational property of the upper-case network, while locations 3, 6, and 9 are the occupational property of the lower-case network – any vacancy chain originating in these locations will be

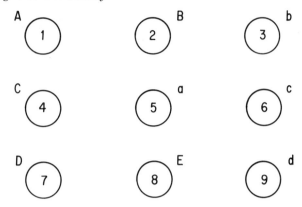

Figure 5.18

entirely controlled by the respective network. Vacancies occurring in 2, 5, and 8 in the next period are up for grabs, as there is an equality of claims for each of these slots. Subsequently, depending on who is successful, the other network's occupational property would once again be threatened.

The sociological significance of the capture of a set of opportunities by a network is that it highlights very clear situations where the opportunity of the individual is conditioned by the group to which he belongs. Brooks and Singh's work on Asian workers in the British foundry industry emphasizes this point (Brooks and Singh 1979). They identify a chain-migration and chain-employment dynamic similar to those sketched in this paper but regard it solely as a property of ethnic labour. My analysis and evidence suggest that these grapevine processes are as important in the employment search processes of indigenous groups as they are within the various ethnic communities. The rationale has been discussed elsewhere (Grieco 1982). Its consequence for the discussion of this chapter is that vacancies travel in chain fashion through kin networks.

This capture of employment opportunity perspective emphasizes the role of the working-class family in transmitting advantage to its members. The influence of such capture is not necessarily benign, however. As Lee and Wrench show, one reason why it is difficult for young blacks to get work is precisely because they are not tied in those social networks which mediate and control employment opportunity (Lee and Wrench 1982). Even without direct employer discrimination, therefore, the interaction of social networks with chains of opportunity can lead to discrimination of an indirect nature – that based on the capture of employment opportunity by a white family network.

Conclusion

The focus of attention in this chapter has been opportunity – in particular, employment opportunity. I have analysed the regenerative nature of opportunity by using White's concept of vacancy chains (White 1970), and brought out the regenerative nature of chain migration, as well as providing an explanation of it by extending White's concept to a more general notion of chains of aid. Effectively, I have modified Ravenstein's theory of step migration by directing attention towards social networks in the transmission of employment and residential information. Apart from considering the regeneration of opportunity – which is essentially a sequential, period-by-period, phenomenon – I have also drawn attention to the capture of an entire set of employment locations by a kin network.

It is often in an employer's interest to allow this to happen, and the information and influence mechanisms associated with employment facilitate its occurrence. When this happens, the vacancy chain is contained within the network, and the working-class family can indeed transmit advantage to its members, in terms of its occupational property. Where the existing composition of a workforce is drawn from a particular sector of the community, then subsequent recruitment will be from that same base. The process of chain employment or grapevine recruitment will serve to exclude those not socially connected to the existing employees from that source of employment. Indirect discrimination may be as powerful a constructor of disadvantage as direct discrimination.

6

Constructing a workforce: direct recruitment, labour migration, and the Affluent Worker study

Introduction

In previous chapters, attention was drawn, on the basis of historical and contemporary evidence, to employers' practice of direct recruitment of labour over distance. It was pointed out that the rationale for such practice goes beyond the simple notion of labour shortage in the local labour market. Employers search in distant locations which are likely to supply them with the labour characteristics they want.

In this chapter, this process, and its consequences, are considered in greater detail – using my fieldwork evidence from Peterhead in Scotland. My primary interest here is to describe the process of direct recruitment to the steel works in Corby. This description of direct recruitment represents the first stage in the analysis of the creation of a Scottish enclave in the heart of Northamptonshire.

The fieldwork also produced significant evidence of direct recruitment from the same area by Vauxhall to their car works in Luton – the very works which formed the basis of the famous Affluent Worker study.[1] Apart from presenting the evidence, my major object here is to discuss its implication, and the implication of direct recruitment in general, for the Affluent Worker study.

Direct recruitment in Peterhead

The material presented here is based on interviews with recruiting officers, employment-exchange officers, and individual workers being recruited. I concentrate on two main employers: Stewarts & Lloyds (who owned the steel works in Corby before nationalization) and Vauxhall (who owned the car works in Luton).

The Vauxhall and Stewarts & Lloyds recruitment drive occurred precisely during the period of a major depression in the north-east Scotland fishing industry. The companies brought recruiting agents into the area on an annual basis throughout the 1950s and early 1960s, and their recruitment drive took them all over the north-east of Scotland. The Vauxhall recruiting officers explicitly expressed a preference for north-east labour and, with the availability of this labour, ceased recruiting Glasgow labour through the employment-exchange network in this period.[2] Both the steel and car industries were recruiting 'green' labour.

Standing arrangements for the supply of labour held between these companies and the employment exchanges[3] of their preferred recruitment areas. The employment exchanges built up a list of individuals who possessed the skills and characteristics required by the employer and, when the collective lists warranted a visit, the employer's recruiting officers visited the area complete with medical officers to do health checks on the spot. Notification of vacancies was not through the local press but by circulation of information to the various employment exchanges involved in the scheme, for these companies made no use of advertising in this location.

Contact between the unemployed individual and the employer who was to take him out of the area could be made only through the employment exchange. The employer selected from the list the labour which he wished to interview, and unless an individual's name was picked he had no means of applying for the vacancy. In order for an individual's name to be picked, it had to appear on the list.

Where individuals were not connected to those being selected or had not themselves been selected for interview by Stewarts & Lloyds or Vauxhall, they would be unaware of the presence of these recruiters within the area. The recruiters themselves had no interest in signalling their presence in the area to any other than the already screened men. 'Jobs under the table' conveys very precisely the mechanics of recruitment as they were in play in Peterhead in the 1950s.

If, however, an individual was not himself selected but was connected to an individual who had been selected and was undergoing the interview process, then the recruiters would enjoy a visibility beyond that desired. Individuals could then make persistent and informed demands for election on to such lists. The evidence is that this did indeed occur, although even when workers had got on to the lists by virtue of their insistence, they often remained at a disadvantage *vis-à-vis* the exchange-picked candidates:

> Before we set off, they [the exchange] would have done a pre-sort of people that they thought were likely to be suitable. . . . We would go as a crew of three, the manager, who was the main interviewer, a clerk who would take the initial particulars and a doctor. . . . They [the exchange] would take the whole thing layer by layer, and they would take out the people who were not medically fit and those with enormous families who were likely to be

difficult. But if someone with an enormous family said they wanted to be put in [for the job] they would have to roll over and put them in. . . . They were really quite good about it. . . . [I]f somebody insisted on coming to see us whom they thought unsuitable, they would tell us. That wasn't true of everywhere, there were some of the exchanges in Ireland, for instance, that would put all the people who were likely to be extremely difficult on our list in the hope that we would pick them and take them off their hands. They [the Peterhead exchange] didn't behave like this at all, they were honest. And if it was a particularly good man, in their opinion, they would point him out to us.

(Corby labour manager)

My brother-in-law came home and said he'd been put on a list to be looked over by Corby steel works. They'd come up to Peterhead, with a doctor, and look people over for work in Corby. Houses were easy to get down there and the money was good. I'd heard that. There was no work at all in the north-east then. And I thought I'd give it a try. I thought it'd do no harm to put my name on the list. They weren't keen to take it, I mind. But they did and I got a job.

(Corby worker)

The effect of employers' preference for labour with certain standardized qualities is strengthened by the operations of the employment exchanges. Employment-exchange officers appreciate that employers prefer such standardized labour and shape their own recruitment behaviour to produce such a product. Individuals articulating their claim to consideration on the basis of kin linkage, kin reputation, and occupational similarity to those selected for interview could negotiate their entry on to the lists. Both the employment-exchange officer and interviewed migrant labour could well remember the occurrence of such a process:

We listed those we thought most suited, but if somebody was borderline, and we'd listed his father or his brother, nine times out of ten, we'd list him as well if he pushed it. More likely to stay if they went with somebody!

(Employment-exchange officer)

Well, my father and brother both had their names down. I don't know why I wasn't. Anyway that's the way I put it to them. If they're on the list I should be as well. Anyway, I got put on and passed the medical and got the job.

(Corby worker)

Knowledge of the process by the unlisted indicated a connection with the listed; it implied a homogeneity. The sense of homogeneity was compounded by the occupational similarity stressed by the soliciting individuals. Social network and occupational network often proved to be the same; shared information could be taken as an adequate indicator of shared skills and orientation, and frequently was. 'Speaking for' a member of family or for a friend in the context of job search is not confined to the conversation with employer or foreman alone, but may extend to the conversation with the middle man or recruiter. Moreover, labour not picked last time, or labour connected to that recruited last time, were alert to the sorties of employers into the area; they knew the structure of the recruitment drives and awaited their annual opportunity to migrate.[4]

It has become conventional in the literature to separate 'kin and friends' as an information channel from direct applications and from state employment agencies. However, the direct-applications category may in fact overlap with the kin-and-friends channel through the importance of internal notification procedures and word-of-mouth spread of information eliciting direct application. My evidence supports this argument, but also suggests that there is an overlap between the kin-and-friends category and the state-employment-agencies category.[5]

Despite the conventional perspective of the state employment exchange as an institution where all individuals have equality of access to employment information, this institution is substantially involved in screening labour in order to reduce the administrative complexities confronting the employer. It is not merely a matter of appropriate skills but also of 'suitability'. Furthermore, all vacancies are not publicly advertised. Individuals unaware of vacancies cannot take the first step towards presenting themselves for consideration. Thus the employment exchange itself may also be considered within the framework of the extended internal labour market, for individuals selected for consideration convey information on these low-profile recruitment drives to their kin and friends. Possession of the privileged information plus connection to those selected helps prospective candidates through the screening process. Thus even within the 'bureaucracy proper' kin and friends still play a role. However, it is a role likely to be under-represented in the official statistics.

Direct recruitment is a labour recruitment method which has received little attention in the standard literature. The prevailing model is one in which labour moves towards employers in its search for employment and not one in which the employer goes out and searches for labour with particular characteristics. The conventional understanding is that employers circulate information on particular vacancies within the local labour market through the vehicle of newspaper advertisements, notice boards both internal and outside the premises, the national press, and generally through employment exchanges.

The employers' assumed aim is to broadcast the message of existing vacancies to as great a number as possible, providing themselves with the widest field possible to choose from. On this view, information is generally available: the employer's intention is to reach the widest field possible possessing the requisite skill; his role is confined to feeding the information on vacancies into the broadcasting channels and to select labour from that which addresses itself to him in the location of the enterprise.

However, employers, even in advanced industrial societies, may play a far more active role in the recruitment of labour over distance.

Furthermore, the manner in which they proceed in this more active role may be very much removed from the conventional understanding. Instead of freely disseminating information as to the extent of their vacancies, they may attempt to minimize the amount of information available on the market generally. The screening process may be best served not by eliciting large numbers of applicants to be processed but by building in the prior screening of another agency into the selection process. The failure to advertise locally within the Peterhead area provides us with one example of such logic.

The direct recruitment strategy evidenced here bears a stronger resemblance to those recruitment strategies documented in the study of labour recruitment in Third World societies (Banerjee 1981) rather than any strategy documented for national labour in advanced industrial societies.[6] The employer has travelled a substantial distance to locate labour with characteristics of pliability. Can this journey be attributed solely to the desire to construct a workforce with the characteristics of non-unionization, pliability, and so on? Similarly, why does labour not merely bypass the employment exchange and apply directly to the employer in the location of the enterprise? Both questions owe part of their respective answers to the system of migratory aid in play during the period.

Employers, by recruiting labour from areas of high unemployment, could pass on some of the costs of their employees' relocation to the state. State aid, although in fact it was the right of the individual migrant, often appeared to the migrating workers as a benefit conferred upon them by the employer. The employer was perceived as meeting the cost of migration to the new workplace by the migrating worker even where the migrant had been in direct receipt of such benefit. Workers saw state migratory aid as tied to particular employers more than as tied to particular routes or paths of gaining such employment.

Although state migratory aid should be provided to any individual migrating from an assisted area to a job in another location, employment exchanges either fail or do not try to communicate to would-be migrants that such aid is available for individual migrations.[7] Marsden has documented the confusion that can exist around state migratory assistance and schemes (Marsden 1982). Similarly, Wedderburn provides evidence on the perceived 'secrecy' of such schemes; as one of her interviewees notes: 'I would get subsistence money from the government. I'm not supposed to know that, but I do. If I could get a job and subsistence money, I would go and the wife could stop here' (quoted in Wedderburn 1965: 141).

My own fieldwork evidence confirms this perception of secrecy and the general confusion to which it gives rise:

> I got an allowance while I lived here and the wife was in Glasgow . . . and some money to help with the move when we got the house. A sort of package deal really, I suppose. It was the works that arranged it all then, them and the

labour together. It's government now though isn't it. You can't keep up with all the changes nowadays, can you?

(Corby worker)

We got money for moving when we came here, not a lot but it helped a bit. It was all part of the deal. I came first and got an allowance for being away from home. From the works that was. I don't think we'll get that this time round, not with the redundancy money and all. I'll just have to keep my ear to the ground and see what's happening.

(Corby worker)

Thus even if the individual's preference is for individual search and migration, resource barriers may stand in his way merely because he does not have the necessary information on eligibility.[8] Clearly, from the point of view of the employment exchange it is more advantageous to 'export' groups of workers than individual workers (stragglers). It is administratively more convenient. Providing migration advice to the individual worker rather than as part of a scheme is seen as generating a greater probability of migration failures. The logic here is that migration failures render the system of aided migration less cost-efficient and also reflect badly on an exchange's record. It is in the interest of the employment exchange to ensure compatibility, security of employment, and so on, before making the administrative arrangements for migration aid.

By pulling the employer into the area, the exchange officials are able to ascertain the probability of stable employment, whereas if the search for an employer is left to the individual, then he may choose unwisely. He may choose a marginal enterprise with limited prospects of employment stability and thus increase the chance of return migration. Once it is recognized that for the employment-exchange officers the appropriate response to high unemployment in any particular area is migration, that is the 'exporting' of labour, then we should expect that the employment-exchange officials would provide information on that basis which generated the greatest migration and reduction of local unemployment.

It is in the interest therefore of exchange officials to convey the impression, or let the mistaken perception persist, that migration assistance does indeed take place at the discretion of the employers. Furthermore, it would appear that employers recruiting en masse actually administered the distribution of such assistance on the behalf of the exchange.[9]

Thus the employer was partly encouraged to the area because of the advantages accruing to the recruitment of labour from areas of high unemployment – that is, migratory assistance. But this is not the sole explanation for recruitment in this area. On the information provided by the employment-exchange officers, the docility of the local labour force was a major factor in one company's preference for locating in this area and for the deliberate bypassing of Glasgow, where the same scheme of migratory benefits applied. In order to qualify for migratory assistance, applicants had to be unemployed.

Mainstream industrial sociology of Britain stresses that the period of the 1950s to mid-1960s was a period of full employment. Full employment did characterize the national economy as a whole, but nevertheless there remained pockets and regions of high unemployment. For employers trying to reduce labour turnover and to construct workforces with more manipulable characteristics than those present in the regions of persistent full employment, such areas provided important recruitment locations.

Some indication of the extent of direct recruitment is given by the fact that from this one employment exchange area in Peterhead, during the five years from 1956 to 1960, 845 workers went to either Corby or Luton. This does not include recruitment drives by other employers or by the same employers in other areas of the north of Scotland. No record is kept of direct recruitment before 1956, and no record is kept of the separate numbers for Corby and for Luton. However, the interviewed official recalled the proportion as being half and half to either location. Thus over this period more than 400 workers were recruited directly to Corby and Luton respectively from one employment-exchange area in Scotland. Further evidence on the importance of this method of recruitment from north-east Scotland is given by Pocock (1960), and is discussed in Chapter 7 below.

Follow-up fieldwork in Corby – at the other end of the migration chain – revealed that in the 1970s the same approach was used to take labour out of Corby.[10] An exchange with high unemployment will actively attempt to attract bulk employers of labour to the area on recruiting drives.

The exchange is not concerned with the consequences of the 'exporting' of particular skill groups or categories for the remaining workforce, yet its consequence is clear: a diminished ability to attract permanent employers to establish workplaces within the area. The employment exchange's concern is to reduce the number of unemployed by placing them in existing vacancies. If there are no vacancies immediately available within the area, its remit is clear: labour must be exported. There is thus no strategy for holding on to precisely that quality of labour which might attract employers into the area.

Direct recruitment took place in Corby shortly after the intention of running down the works was finally and publicly declared. From the point of view of the recruiting employers, the strike in the steel industry which occurred shortly after the redundancy announcement was an unexpected bonus. Six recruitment drives by major employers took place in this period. Despite the open-display character of the new Job Centre, interviewing by the employer did not take place at the open counter, but rooms were set aside downstairs. Lists were used, and not all individuals wishing to be interviewed had their preferences met.

Before seeing the employer, applicants were interviewed by the employment exchange's officials to ascertain whether they met the employers' requirements. Employment-exchange officials were not just taking the names of individuals in order to allocate an interview space but were in fact part of the screening process. Thus, although in Corby, unlike Peterhead, employers did advertise in the windows of the Job Centre, it was strongly felt by many of the Corby respondents that this was still a case of 'jobs under the table'. The policy consequences of direct recruitment of labour into Corby, and the subsequent direct recruitment out of Corby, will be considered in detail in Chapter 7. But I would now like to turn to the analytical consequences of direct recruitment to Luton for the Affluent Worker study.

Direct recruitment, selective recruitment, and the Affluent Worker study

Focusing on direct recruitment highlights the processes whereby workers and jobs are brought together. This is a highly selective process which, in a given location, creates a workforce with special characteristics. The processes which led to the construction of the workforce have to be taken into account before we can interpret any data derived from the workforce as it stands currently.

I have already pointed to a number of studies which, because of a lack of appreciation of these processes, either misinterpret their data or are insensitive to the implications of the recruitment of labour over distance for the shaping of a workforce. A leading case of this is the Affluent Worker study, and here we consider the analytical consequences for the study of the existence of direct selective recruitment.

The Affluent Worker study by Goldthorpe *et al.* (1968a, 1968b, 1969) has held sway as one of the most important works in British sociology. Many analyses of industrial behaviour, political behaviour, family behaviour, and community behaviour take the findings of the Affluent Worker study as their starting point (Mann 1973; Giddens 1973; Pahl 1968). While the work has not been without its critics (Mackenzie 1974), the centrality of the affluent workers of Luton to British sociology cannot be doubted. The object of this section is to take issue with the claims of typicality and prototypicality made for the affluent workers of Luton by the study team.

The basic contention of the Affluent Worker study is that prior orientation conditions or mediates the experience of work, and that in the case of the affluent workers this orientation is instrumental in character. It is on the basis of this instrumental orientation that particular types of work come to be selected. The burden of the argument is that the affluent workers of Luton have traded job satisfaction for increased income (see Goldthorpe *et al.* 1968b: 33; 1969: 183).

However, a close examination of the recruitment and selection practices of Vauxhall, the employer of the Luton affluent workers, produces major problems for these arguments.

Recruitment from the periphery and the full-employment error

The peaceful industrial record of the Vauxhall workforce was taken as a starting point of analysis by the study team. Why was the workforce 'passive' in conditions of claimed work deprivation? The Luton workforce was a collection of individuals instrumentally inclined, and had arrived in Luton to further this instrumentality (Goldthorpe *et al.* 1968b: 18–20, 27; 1969: 42). The question as to how the workforce had been shaped by recruitment practices was never posed. If it was not so shaped, at the very least the manner in which a population homogeneous in its value orientations arrived in Luton requires a minimal sketching of mechanisms – a problem highlighted by the fact that the study team in fact found high rates of sibling presence[11] in the new location (Goldthorpe *et al.* 1969: 38).

The affluent workers of Luton are characterized as being in situations of choice with regard to the type of employment obtained (Goldthorpe *et al.* 1968b: 3). Moreover, employment chance is assumed to be equivalent for all migrants independent of regional derivation (Goldthorpe *et al.* 1969: 27). Full employment plays a very large part in the argument. As the national situation is one of full employment, it is assumed that all actors have a choice to make between low paying but satisfying employment and high paying but intrinsically unsatisfying employment. This, taken with the sample group's lack of direct experience of unemployment and with the sample group's experience of more satisfying employment in the past, leads the authors to the conclusion that those workers choosing to take up unpleasant employment are necessarily doing so on an instrumental base (Goldthorpe *et al.* 1969: 55–6). Furthermore, the longer the distance migrated, the more instrumental the sample are presumed to be.

Migration itself is taken as evidence of instrumentality; it is seen purely within the framework of free choice, with economic coercion playing no part (Goldthorpe *et al.* 1969: 78). A migrant man is a maximizing man; he moves in the attempt to maximize income and, moreover, in the attempt to maximize the value freedom to do so (Goldthorpe *et al.* 1968a: 154–5). The basic argument is that individuals have escaped from their moral community of origin in order to more fully pursue self-interest; it is preference not push which, according to this study, explains migration to Luton.

The major flaw in this argument, however, is that the structure of employment opportunity exhibits regional variations even in situations of full employment. Thus even when full employment may be taken as an adequate characterization of the national economy as a whole, this cannot be taken to mean that there are no pockets of unemployment (see, for example, the regional variations in unemployment shown in the *Ministry of Labour Gazette*, 1950–68). Most importantly, labour derived from such locations, even where there is no direct experience of unemployment on the part of the individual migrant, has been exposed to an atmosphere of employment insecurity: 'I've never been unemployed. I've always got out in time, sometimes just in the nick of time. I've been lucky really until now. It's better getting out of a place before you have to, it really gets to you otherwise' (Corby worker).

Perceptions of the structure of opportunity will vary, I wish to argue, between localities in which full employment is the norm and localities in which unemployment is present to some recognizable degree. Movement to a location of full employment, that is to an area of greater employment chance, on the part of the individual can in such a context be deemed a conservative and not an innovatory move (Mann 1973), even where the migrant himself has not experienced unemployment. As my evidence shows, migration can take place in anticipation of unemployment. It is the subjective assessment of the probability of unemployment which is of consequence (Martin and Fryer 1973).

What is the import of this line of thought for the Affluent Worker study? It was precisely in such pockets of unemployment that Vauxhall focused much of their recruitment activities.[12] Furthermore, the concentration of recruitment activities in such locations was not accidental but the consequence of a policy decision:

> They came back to us every year for more workers, they liked the north-east workers. No unions and eager for work, that is what they liked best.
> (Peterhead employment-exchange officer)

> No, no, the labour was sensible about it. I mean Vauxhall were recruiting and we knew because the labour told us and they must have told Vauxhall about us. But we were the two who were consistently taking advantage of the transfer workers scheme. Which was worth quite a lot of money remember.[13]
> (Corby labour manager)

Employment chances are not nationally but regionally conditioned; it is the impact of regional employment circumstances on the orientation to work which is of sociological significance in any thorough-going understanding of the behaviour of those affluent workers of Luton recruited from areas of high unemployment.

My evidence shows that when recruiting in areas of high unemployment, such as Peterhead, a preference was exercised on the part of the firm for non-unionized labour. A preference for non-unionized labour led the firm to recruit in areas of low union activity and membership, and this preference was so strong that areas of high unemployment which possessed a history of union activity – such as Glasgow – were deliberately bypassed in the recruitment campaigns: 'They preferred the north east; they bypassed Glasgow altogether in the peak years. No unions here you see and unemployment was high, we had as many men available as they could take' (Peterhead employment-exchange officer).

The significance of such direct recruitment is that non-union membership prior to arrival at Vauxhall becomes a regional characteristic and not merely a characteristic of the individual worker. Mackenzie recognizes the general significance of this point (Mackenzie 1974), but in the specific case being considered the preference for non-unionized labour led Vauxhall away from traditional working-class areas as potential recruiting grounds towards more peripheral locations.

We have seen how the collapse of the east-coast fishing industry in the mid to late 1950s induced an intensive recruitment campaign by Vauxhall to the affected area. In fact, 19 per cent of the Affluent Worker sample was recruited from the Celtic periphery (Goldthorpe *et al.* 1968b: 150), including Ireland. Moreover, not only were declining areas or regions an important source of labour, declining sectors and sectors of low union activity also provided a substantial source of labour – 40 per cent of the machinists and assemblers were derived from small-scale industry, agriculture, distributive, and other trades (Goldthorpe *et al.* 1968b: 33). As one of the employees who previously worked in the hat trade was recorded as saying, his reason for coming to Vauxhall's was that the hat trade 'hadn't picked up since the war'.

The above account, at least for labour recruited from declining areas and regions with a history of low union activity, would seem to be consistent with evidence presented on low union-membership charac-teristics of the sample prior to arrival in Luton (Goldthorpe *et al.* 1968a: 96). But the shaping of the workforce in this manner should give us cause for concern about to what extent the Luton workforce was indeed representative of the solidary working class. Given the recruitment strategy of Vauxhall, their workforce cannot be understood as being typical of the working class. Far from being the vanguard of the working class, a significant section of the workforce has to be understood as labour peripherally recruited and therefore untypical. Prototypicality, given this frame, would be an even more unsubstanti-able claim (Goldthorpe *et al.* 1968b: 9).

When we further investigate the information mechanisms and local pressures in the decision to migrate, the simple link between migration and instrumentalism advanced by the study (Goldthorpe *et al.* 1969, Ch. 4) can also be questioned. We have already argued in this chapter, and in Chapter 4, that labour migration from areas of high unemployment – whether or not the individual migrant has experienced unemployment – can be interpreted as a conservative rather than an innovatory move. However, when we consider long-distance migration, to work of which there is no previous experience, the quality of information is likely to be poor (Wedderburn 1965: 12), particularly where migration takes place outside the auspices of kinship and friendship networks.

Without full information on the nature of the work task, the requirements of instrumentalism cannot strictly be met, for it has to be a conscious trade-off between a more satisfying work situation and higher levels of income. Even critics of the Affluent Worker study, such as Mackenzie (1974) and Beynon and Blackburn (1972) accept this conscious trade-off.

However, the greater the distance migrated – in the absence of an operating social network in the areas of destination – the less the information and the more difficult it is to characterize migration as instrumentalism with the full theoretical strength given to the concept in the Affluent Worker study. Thus long-distance migrants are precisely the group whose behaviour is least adequately accounted for by prior instrumental orientation, even if the area of origin is one without high unemployment.

As distinct from poor information, the problem of misinformation must also be considered. How did Vauxhall locate their reserves of labour? Labour exchanges provided Vauxhall with the necessary information on areas of unemployment and performed initial screening operations for the company. The interviewing and selecting of would-be employees took place in the area of origin, and this would seem to be a factor of some significance when considering the quality of information possessed by potential migrants on the nature of the work situation and task before arrival. The major informant, indeed perhaps the only informant for the initial migrants, on the nature of work tasks and the disutilities of the assembly line under such circumstances, would be the employer.

A clear account of such misinformation is provided by Beynon on Ford's 'green' labour strategy during the same period (Beynon 1973). Labour was recruited to Merseyside from distant locations on the basis of inexperience of factory work:[14] 'They weren't used to factories, let alone the Ford assembly line' (Beynon 1973: 89). Beynon's account suggests that the initial choice by the migrants was conditioned by a lack of information, not instrumentalism. Given that employers put considerable effort into recruiting labour from an area, as in the case of Ford's or Vauxhall or Stewarts & Lloyds, the object is to persuade labour to migrate and not to dissuade labour with information on disutilities. It is unlikely in such a context that labour would be presented with a true picture of the disutilities of assembly-line employment. The link between instrumentality and migration should be treated with caution in such a context of misinformation.

Another problem with the characterization of migration as being on the basis of free choice concerns the role of the state employment agencies in migration. The policy debates of this period took their lead from Beveridge (1944) in stressing the need for the organized mobility of labour, that is migration.[15] In the field, my interviews revealed a similar view being taken by the employment-agency officers – migration being viewed as a necessary part of a process of adjustment to the relocation of employment opportunities: 'They had to go. There were no jobs here and no prospect of any. There was nothing else that could be done. And people were lining up to go. Good paying jobs against unemployment. There wasn't any choice' (employment-exchange officer).

It is common practice for firms wishing to recruit labour to be given facilities on the premises of a firm wishing to shed labour. Information on the coming of redundancies is, for example, passed on to local employment exchanges, who have been warned about redundancies in advance of their occurrence.[16]

Thus migration was the expected response to unemployment at the national level (see NEDC 1963), but at the local level the close co-operation of would-be employers and state employment agencies with such perceptions produced a situation in which it was difficult for migrants to resist the *pressure* to migrate:

> It was either go south or sit around twiddling my thumbs. There was no chance of a job. Not that anybody tried to do anything about bringing jobs in. So we had to move, there was no option. Now we'll have to move again, no doubt. Hasn't anybody thought of bringing jobs to people yet?
>
> (Corby worker)

The active direction of labour out of an area on the part of the state employment agencies constitutes a pressure on the locally unemployed, who are bound to make use of its services to migrate. In fact, during this period the same agency was responsible for administering unemployment benefit and for industrial placement. The locally unemployed would be effectively trapped, for not to migrate where the offer of employment in a different location has been concretely and visibly made was to be taken as non-serious in the search for employment.

In this context, migration has to be analysed with care. Achievement orientations cannot be assumed: migration does not of itself constitute evidence of a free-choice preference for migration.[17] Indeed, from this description of the context from which at least some of the affluent workers were recruited, it should be apparent that under such circumstances it is the refusal to migrate which constitutes strong preference.

Thus for at least one part of the Vauxhall workforce, a detailed investigation of the mechanisms whereby they arrived in Luton indicates a different interpretation of the data from that provided by the study team. This part of the workforce cannot be taken to be the vanguard of the new working class, furthering their prior instrumentality in Luton. On the contrary, they were recruited by Vauxhall from peripheral regions with high rates of unemployment and marginal sectors of the economy and migration for them took place under pressure and in conditions of less than perfect information – hardly a strong basis for claiming migration as evidence of instrumentality. Vauxhall's own account of why it recruited in areas of high unemployment and continues to do so is that it finds it difficult to attract workers:[18]

> We just couldn't get enough workers. We even went to Ireland. We met our recruitment targets all right but they just didn't stay on. There's always been a turnover problem. When we find a good supply in terms of numbers, then they're never suited to the work. They just move on, most times they even go

back where they came from. So all you can do is run a permanent recruitment drive, just to keep your numbers up. It's the nature of the work really, it's not pleasant by any stretch of the imagination. It wouldn't suit most people.

(Vauxhall manager)

It would seem, therefore, that finding workers who wish to be affluent at the cost of being on the assembly line is difficult. Whether Vauxhall recruited from the ranks of the unemployed as a consequence of labour scarcity or whether it recruited from within this category in order to obtain a pliable workforce, the consequence for the typicality and prototypicality of the instrumentalism argument is the same. So far as this part of the sample is concerned, the Affluent Worker findings have no necessary implications for the solidary working class. However, this is just one part of the workforce. What of members of the workforce recruited from the London area? Surely the study team's account of atomized entry to Luton by instrumentally oriented individuals is appropriate for them? It is to these questions that I now turn.

Selection of London labour: the role of housing
A substantial section of the Vauxhall labour force was recruited from London (Goldthorpe *et al.* 1968b: 150). Even for this labour, recruited from a region of low unemployment, screening procedures were applied which led to the workforce having special characteristics. Luton as an 'expanding town' provided local employers with special mechanisms for the screening of labour. Londoners wishing to move to a new or expanded town could do so under the auspices of the Industrial Selection Scheme. A basic attribute of this scheme was that registrants' housing needs and work experience were kept on record by both housing authorities and employment exchanges. Gee provides an account of how this process worked:

> This selection process begins when an employer in a new or expanding town has a vacancy which cannot be filled by a local person and notifies it to an employment exchange in the town. The employment exchange sends details of this vacancy to the London and South Eastern regional offices of the Department of Employment, who in turn notify the GLC and all the London employment exchanges. For each vacancy notified the GLC selects up to 20 names from the register, taking into account each registrant's housing need as well as his qualifications for the job. Selected names are sent to the registrant's local employment exchange, which writes to the registrant asking him whether he wants to apply for the job.

(Gee 1972: 3)

Thus London labour arriving in Luton through the Industrial Selection Scheme was screened on two counts (housing and employment history) and by four agencies (the GLC, the employment exchange of the registrant, the employment exchange of the company, and the company itself). It is clear that while housing need was an important screen, whether or not the labour met the 'employer's requirements' was also important: 'But before sending a man's name to an employer, both the London exchange and the new or expanding town exchange screen applicants to check that they meet employer's requirements' (Gee 1972: 29). Vauxhall, as an expanding-town employer, had available to it lists of would-be employees in housing need. In order to secure a local authority home in Luton, a would-be migrant had first to secure a job. A major advantage to Vauxhall of recruiting through this system was that each worker so recruited was provided with state-financed housing, a factor of major importance in the tight Luton housing market. But it is likely, given the screening mechanisms, that the employment histories of individual workers were used as well.

The implications for the Affluent Worker study are clear. While Vauxhall were recruiting labour from a region of full employment, the mechanism of recruitment was such as to allow them to construct a workforce of a particular type by selection – once again, the extent to which the Affluent Worker sample is representative of the solidary working class may be questioned.

The analysis of London labour and housing also has implications for the study team's interpretation of home ownership statistics. The percentage of home owners within the manual-worker category in Luton is taken as evidence of changing attitudes. As only London labour was eligible for local authority housing, labour derived from the periphery – the areas of high unemployment – even where it had a preference for public-sector accommodation, had no choice but to buy. Thus, unless it is shown that London labour possessing access to both private and public markets chose the former, these home ownership statistics have to be interpreted with care.[19]

Direct recruitment and selective recruitment have considerable implications, therefore, for the Affluent Worker team's interpretations of their data. Part of their sample was from peripheral areas and sectors, moving to Vauxhall under pressure of unemployment rather than to maximize income. Part of their sample, while being from a central area, moved to Vauxhall under housing pressure and was in any case provided with poor work information (Gee 1972: 25) and was highly selected by the employer on the basis of work history. The sample cannot therefore be taken to provide conclusive evidence of instrumentalism amongst British workers at large. However, a neglect of recruitment mechanisms also led the team to a misinterpretation of data on relationships in the workplace, and it is to this we now turn.

Direct recruitment and informal information networks: the importance for work-group relationships
The characterization of occupational entry to Vauxhall given in the Affluent Worker study is that of atomized entry. Atomized entry is congruent with instrumentalism and privatization as a theoretical set of relationships (Goldthorpe *et al.* 1969: 121). Where entry was atomized and took place on the basis of instrumentalism, the insignificance of

work relationships claimed in the study is comprehensible (Goldthorpe *et al.* 1968b: 48).

But assumed in this set of relationships is the proposition that on entering employment in Vauxhall no prior relationship existed between any section of the labour force. If workers in Vauxhall had either previously shared the same employer or been involved in the recruitment of one another to the labour force, then the absence of significant work relationships requires to be explained. The compartmentalization of life projected in the Affluent Worker study not only concludes that workmates do not on balance become friends but also assumes that friends and kin do not become workmates.[20]

That relationships in the work setting could become less instrumental through such a mechanism is clearly a possibility, since for compartmentalization to persist not only must work not enter social life but social life must not enter work.

Vauxhall offered bounties to its workforce in order to induce them to introduce friends and kin to employment in the firm:

> We pay a bounty to any worker introducing a successful candidate to the company. It helps in selecting; the chances are if they are being introduced by another employee then they know all the pros and cons before they start and are more likely to settle in quickly.
>
> (Vauxhall manager)

Thereby, it formally involved its workforce in its recruitment procedures. Given the existence of the bounty system, intuitively we would expect kin- and friendship-connected entry to the firm. That is to say, work relations and social relations are unlikely to remain compartmentalized. Furthermore, where an individual has been involved in recruiting another, the exercise of recruitment itself must be taken as indicative of some prior relationship. Infrequent contact outside of the workplace may be perfectly compatible with a strong relationship, for the workplace itself may provide the very forum for daily contact.

The Affluent Worker study assumes that families have no ability or desire to regroup in a new location. It is a static analysis based on a snapshot taken at one point in time. Jackson warns us against such an approach, for geographical dispersal may be a characteristic of a particular stage of communal migration (Jackson 1969). If the snapshot of chain migration is taken too early, the later features of network reconstitution cannot be captured. Where employers use employee networks to recruit, kin presence in the workplace is to be expected and should be explored. In the Affluent Worker sample (Goldthorpe *et al.* 1969: 38) 36 per cent of couples had a majority of close kin living in the town in what was predominantly a migrant context.

If kin-connected entry did not take place in Luton, when the employers were favourably disposed towards hiring labour introduced by members of their present workforce, this requires investigation. If kin-connected recruitment did take place, then the characterization of relationships holding between workers offered in the Affluent Worker study (Goldthorpe *et al.* 1969: 164–5) is inadequate.

The case-study literature surveyed previously demonstrates not only the way in which the industrial enterprise and the family can co-exist but the manner in which the workplace can contribute towards consolidating the family. It is my contention that the uncritical acceptance of the doctrine of the nuclear family and its relation to mobility resulted in the relevant questions not being posed by the study team (Goldthorpe *et al.* 1969: 33). We do not know from the Luton study whether the sibling presence in the sample was a consequence of independent arrival or whether siblings were involved in guiding the entry of one another into the area.[21]

Furthermore, we know nothing about kin presence in the workplace, for kin-connected entry to both geographical and occupational location has been neglected as an area of inquiry in both the interview schedules and the interpretation of the findings of the study. Questions were asked on the geographical location of kin, but where kin was present in Luton, no further questions were asked on how this came to be.

Conclusion

This chapter presented evidence of direct recruitment by Vauxhall car works at Luton – the very works that were sampled in the famous Affluent Worker series of studies. Material gathered from a number of sources shows this to be a persistent and continuous practice on the part of Vauxhall from the mid-1950s up to the date of the study. The particularism inherent in direct recruitment mechanisms has signifi-cant implications for these studies – the most important being that the Luton sample cannot necessarily be taken to be representative of the solidary working class. Particularism and selectivity were also shown to hold in the recruitment of London labour. On this count also, the claim of general validity for the Affluent Worker findings needs to be treated with caution.

Direct recruitment is thus shown to have significant implications for a major study in British sociology. I now examine the experience of the workers recruited from the same area and at the same time to the Corby steel works. What sort of labour market awaited them there? The next chapter takes up the construction not only of a workforce but of an entire labour market in a Scottish enclave in the heart of the Northamptonshire countryside.

7
Corby: migration, networks, and enclave development

Introduction

Jobless steelworkers cluster conspicuously in Corby's modern shopping piazza, the skyline dominated . . . by the now almost idle steelworks. . . . The 3,000 already laid off since early April were given £1,000 on account to tide them over. Most of it went on settling household and other debts incurred during the strike. Word has it, that three workers – Scots, like much of Corby's immigrant population – blew it by backing Scotland to beat Ireland in the soccer international. . . . Meanwhile, Corby, amid its green country-side, is a town full of hope and despair, enterprise and resignation, undoubted bitterness, but with a will to survive. It would be better and more healthy if it were not a one-industry town.

(*Daily Telegraph*, 10 July 1980)

The round of rationalizations in the British steel industry which took place at the beginning of the 1980s spelt mass redundancy for Corby.[1] In late spring/early summer of 1980, 6,000 redundancies occurred, pushing the local unemployment rate up to 24 per cent – more than twice the national average at that time.[2] The impact of the closure of major sections of the steel works was immediate and critical, for Corby was, to all intents and purposes, a one-industry town. For the redundant workers of Corby, there is little hope of ever gaining comparable employment within the town or surrounding area again.

Corby's situation has a special dimension because it is essentially a Scottish enclave in the heart of England. In previous sections I have discussed the direct recruitment of labour by steel employers from Scotland to Corby, and the subsequent kin-connected chain migration to Corby in the wake of this direct recruitment. Here we look at the Corby end of the migration stream, highlighting the extent to which the Scottish migrants to the Corby steel works were isolated from the surrounding area.

This occurred both because of the network properties of the pattern of migration that took place, and because of deliberate decisions by employers and planners to keep Corby a one-industry town. The analysis of the role of the state planning authorities in the encouragement of the enclave development desired by the employers is a major object of this chapter.

The logic of the intersection between employer and employee interests results in processes of chain employment. There is, furthermore, a tendency for some kin groups to put all their employment eggs in the one basket: that of the best employer. In the case of Corby, the situation is compounded by the distinctiveness of the community produced by long-distance migration from Scotland and by the 'seals' around the town which have developed as a consequence of social and economic planning designed to ensure the one-employer status of the town.

Under normal conditions, long-distance migrants are disadvantaged by their lack of the necessary local contacts to sample the local employment market. Frequently, their sole local employment contact is the employer who recruited them in the home area himself or members of that same workforce. However, a contact in the workplace is of great importance in getting hired. Our Corby migrants did not possess the contacts necessary to probe the local employment market as a consequence of the very planning which ensured steel access to the necessary supplies of labour.

It is in this sense that we are discussing the relationship between social networks and enclave developments. Bad planning prevented the emergence of those bridging networks which could have opened up the workplaces of the local hinterland for Corby labour. Under normal circumstances, and over time, long-distance migrants become locals and acquire the access to places of employment other than that which initially recruited them. Fifty years after the establishment of Corby, such contacts have not developed. This chapter investigates how and why this situation emerged.

Migration from Scotland to Corby

It is somewhat ironic that Corby is itself the product of previous rationalization in the British steel industry, which caused a small Northamptonshire village to grow into a major steel town. The initial expansion of Corby took place during the last great depression. The ironstone deposits of northern Northamptonshire attracted Stewarts & Lloyds to the area, and in the two years between 1933/4 and 1935/6, more than 3,000 employees had been recruited to the steel works in a village with an original population of 1,500 (see Thomas 1969; Scopes 1968).

By the time Corby had been designated a New Town, in April 1950, its population had increased to more than 15,000, and in the 1971 census its population was recorded at 48,000. Between 1951 and 1961, employment in the steel works increased from 7,100 to 12,164 and stabilized thereafter around the 12,000 mark (figures taken from the Corby Development Corporation's employment census).

With the rapid expansion of the steel works came the rapid in-migration of workers. In the initial stages labour from contracting or closing steel works was located en masse in Corby (Pocock 1959). As the company history of that time notes:

> In the depression of the 1930s the fortunes of Clydeside – and most of the Scottish works, for that matter – had been at a low ebb. A good deal of labour had gone south to Corby and there had been rumours that Stewarts and Lloyds might be pulling out of Scotland altogether.
>
> (Stewarts & Lloyds *c.* 1953: 88)

A contemporary observer provides us with more detail on the migration:

> Corby recorded no less than 2,875 'foreign' books, an absorption rate of 49.2 per cent, comprising nearly a quarter of the immigrants to the eastern area. Two-thirds of the newcomers to this mushroom township came from Scotland – a result of the planned migration which accompanied the location by Stewarts and Lloyds of their new iron and steel plant. Only a few years ago the Office of the Ministry of Labour at Corby had a very rustic appearance, and the officials had never seen a steel erector. Today the number insured at that Exchange is over 6,000 persons, the majority of whom gain their livelihood in the local steel works. Numerous families, complete with shop-keepers and even hairdressers, moved en masse from the Motherwell district, and recreated in this corner of Northamptonshire a vigorous and thrifty Scottish community.
>
> (Thomas 1938: 421)

There was little room for choice on the workers' part in respect of their move. They had the option of either migrating to the North-amptonshire village or being made redundant in both a local and a national situation of high unemployment. Whatever may have been their perceptions of improved wages in Corby, they were forced to move by redundancy, and once they got there their wage expectations were not realized:

> Workers transferred from other works of the company (mainly from Scotland) had the fixed idea that their wage rates and earnings should be higher than in their former employment, disregarding entirely the modernity of the Corby plant, its capacity, equipment and output.
>
> (reported in Scopes 1968: 237)

In the post-war period recruitment from Scotland continued, but the focus of attention was diverted somewhat from Motherwell and Glasgow to north-east Scotland and to the west-coast fishing ports, in the wake of the collapse of the fishing industry in these regions. Information on the practice of direct recruitment of this labour, and the role of state employment agencies in assisting direct recruitment, is provided by Thomas:

> Men without work in these areas were offered a job and were provided with a rail ticket and a subsistence allowance by the Department of Employment, while Stewarts and Lloyds gave them temporary accommodation in hostels near Corby. Those with families put their name on the Development Corporation's house waiting list and were able to obtain a house, usually within a fairly short period.
>
> (Thomas 1969: 857–8)

How significant was direct recruitment from north-east Scotland in Stewarts & Lloyds' overall recruitment? Neither the census nor the Corby Development Corporation's reports provide us with a detailed breakdown of area of origin within Scotland. However, from my fieldwork I identified a flow of just over 400 directly recruited workers from Peterhead in north-east Scotland to the steel works in Corby between 1956 and 1960.[3]

Over this same period, Corby Development Corporation's employment census tells us that employment in the steel works increased by just over 2,000. In other words, it is possible that around 20 per cent of the increase in the Stewarts & Lloyds workforce is accounted for by one area in north-east Scotland. My interview evidence indicates that intensive recruiting drives were taking place elsewhere in the region in addition to Peterhead.

To summarize, therefore, Corby's development displays striking characteristics. A phenomenally rapid expansion led to a trebling of population in the first fifteen years followed by further trebling in the next fifteen. This rapid expansion was almost entirely associated with the expansion of one industry – steel. Corby was a one-industry town. Finally, the in-migrants to Corby were not recruited from its surrounding East Midlands region but from farther afield. In particular, pools of Scottish labour have been tapped right from the start;[4] in the first phase of expansion it was north Lanarkshire and in the second phase – to which my fieldwork evidence speaks – it was from Clydeside and the north east of Scotland. What was the role of the state authorities in this striking pattern of expansion? The next section turns to this question.

New Town planning and imbalanced development

In the previous chapter, I detailed the role of state employment agencies in the direct recruitment drives conducted by Stewarts & Lloyds in Scotland. At the other end of the migration stream, in Corby, the state was also involved. The imbalanced development of Corby, with reliance being placed on one industry for jobs and on one area as a source of labour for these jobs, is all the more remarkable because during the second phase of its expansion, from 1950 onwards, Corby was a New Town. It would appear that the principle of balance, which was at the heart of the New Town ideology, found no place in the development of Corby New Town. In fact, I will argue that the New Town status was used in further accentuating the economic and social imbalance represented in Corby.

The structural imbalance of Corby, in its reliance on steel, is immediately apparent from an examination of the statistics. In 1971 half of the total jobs and two-thirds of male jobs were in the steel works. In 1961, at the height of New Town planning, more than two-thirds of all jobs were in the steel works, and of the increase in total employment of around 7,000 between 1951 and 1961, 5,000 jobs were at the steel works (these figures are taken from Corby Development Corporation employment census, cited in Coopers and Lybrand 1979). Although Corby was designated a New Town three decades ago, and the issue of over-dependence on one industry and, worse still, one employer was raised on a number of occasions,[5] it was decided that Corby's 'imbalanced' course of development should be permitted to continue. As the *Corby New Town Extension: Master Plan Report* noted: 'There is a fundamental identity between Corby and the steel works, the growth of one would not be possible without the development of the other, the existence of one is dependent on the existence of the other' (Corby Development Corporation 1965: 3).

This imbalanced development was defended not only on the grounds of the national interest but also on the grounds that Corby's centrality to British Steel production was its own guarantee of the continued prosperity of the town. (See Corby Development Corporation's Annual Report of 31 March 1966, p. 105, for an example of such a tone.) Further expansion of steel was consistently advocated as the best defence against the prospect of future mass unemployment, as early planning documents show:

> Moreover, economic vulnerability – the most powerful pre-war argument against a one-industry town – does not now seem to us to be a danger. Steel is likely to be needed in large quantities for as long as it is profitable to look ahead and if competition develops for a limited market, Corby is well placed to hold its own.
>
> (Holford and Myles Wright 1952: 38)

Even more detached observers, registering disturbance at the degree of imbalance present in Corby's employment and industrial structure, declared themselves comforted by Corby's centrality to the British steel industry:

> The conclusion to be drawn is that the deliberate creation and continued expansion of a large steel works in a centre formerly lacking any industry has produced a town of highly specialized character with an extremely ill-balanced industrial structure. . . . It is therefore fortunate that the industry is one of national importance.
>
> (Pocock 1959: 47–8)

Almost up until the point of closure itself, Corby was being reassured by way of commissioned reports and documents that the imbalanced employment structure of the town was neither pathological nor problematic:

> At present the New Town has an employment structure dominated by the British Steel Corporation and with a very small proportion of jobs in the service industries. The first type of imbalance is one that may not necessarily be cause for alarm.
>
> (Buchanan & Partners 1975: 88)

This was an astonishing conclusion to reach, given the existence of the 1973 White Paper on the proposed rationalization of the steel industry. It did little to advance the cause of developing policies of replacement employment. Indeed, this report argued against granting Corby Intermediate or Development Area status: 'We believe that this approach should be reserved for those areas whose very economic existence is threatened' (Buchanan & Partners 1975: 98). My fieldwork evidence further shows that in the last stages of the development of the Corby steel works, but before the destiny of the works had been made public knowledge, labour was still being attracted to Corby – this time from closing Welsh steel works: 'There's some Welsh boys just transferred here last year. Set up their homes, the lot, and now look where they are, redundant again, and what will they do this time? Go back to Wales!' (Corby worker).[6]

The above evidence on 'expansion to the point of closure' has serious implications for migration theory, in particular for the concept of efficient migration. Whilst from the point of view of the employer the transfer of labour from a situation of redundancy into a situation of imminent redundancy may be efficient, enabling or contributing towards the maintenance of a full workforce until the point of planned production stoppage (see Martin and Fryer 1973; Wedderburn 1965; Slowe 1978)[7] and minimizing the need for the recruitment of new labour and resultant contracting of new responsibilities, from the perspective of the migrant the move cannot be deemed efficient.

For both production and political reasons the steel employers concealed the imminence of redundancy from the workforce until the very final stages of production. That information, which would have alerted individuals to the very short-term character of employment to be had in Corby and caused individuals to consider the wisdom of investing in such a migratory move, was deliberately contained within the upper reaches of the steel decision-making hierarchy.[8]

The information which would have permitted steel workers to make efficient migration decisions, or at least more efficient migration decisions, was withheld. The cost of such concealment in terms of individual migration failure was high for workers migrating into Corby in the final stages of steel production there. Migration is a costly activity, as is job search; to migrate on the basis of certain employment, then to be rendered unemployed almost immediately, and thrown back into the pit of job search, with significantly reduced resources, must shake the understanding that encouragement of migration is the rational social response to unemployment: 'It's bad for us, we'll have to move again. There's no choice really. But what's the point? You move to find steady work and it only disappears again. Something's wrong somewhere. Don't you think?' (Corby worker). Much of the contemporary discussion of the appropriate response to unemployment assumes that the problems are caused by the resistance of labour to undertake geographical mobility. Such resistance is viewed as a traditional or customary response, ill-adapted to the requirements of a modern and rapidly changing industrial structure. The extent to which the experience of migration may itself produce such a resistance is rarely considered.

Where individuals have migrated in pursuit of stable employment, and such employment reveals itself almost immediately to be unstable, before even the cost of migration has been recovered and despite the assurances of the recruiting agency at the point of recruitment, then the whole business of locating accurate employment information is revealed as problematic and so consequently is the rationality of migration.

In a period of wide-scale redundancies and, therefore, employment uncertainty and systematic misinformation about such uncertainty in the particular enterprise by the individual employer, migration in search of stable employment opportunity may result in the diminution of resources without any consequent gains in employment security. The cost of migration may not be recoverable. This was the experience of the Welsh labour entering Corby in the mid and late 1970s. Similarly, the concealment of information as to when precisely redundancy will occur, or indeed that it will occur at all, results in a workforce being poorly prepared for the prospect of migration. Whilst migrational efficiency would be increased by a longer warning period, production would be more disrupted, and it is a concern with the latter rather than a concern with the former which dominates the British industrial scene.

In migration theory, 'poor' migration decisions are typically characterized as the outcome of poor search or wrong choice (Davanzo and Morrison 1978); the structural factors generating the experience rarely receive attention. Little work has been done on false employment signals operating in the market and the consequences of such signals for migration decisions.

It is of course one thing to neglect non-steel employment because of a misperceived faith in steel. It is quite another to deliberately exclude other employers from the town. There were, in fact, a number of critical points at which a change in the direction of Corby's development could have been effected. Corby's development as an enclave is not merely the outcome of one initial and crucial decision, but it is rather a consequence of recurrent decisions to steer the same direction.[9]

Steel was to be protected at all costs. Whereas in other New Towns a number and variety of employers were induced to enter, in Corby other employers were actively held out of the town. This was true before nationalization, when Stewarts & Lloyds owned the Corby steel works, as well as after nationalization. In 1952 Holford and Myles Wright, in their report to accompany the Corby Development Corporation Master Plan, stated:

> It is the main aim of the Corporation to provide for 10,000 workers in Messrs Stewarts & Lloyds. To expand services will help to obtain and especially retain the added numbers. Encouragement of alternative manufacturing industries on any large scale would have the opposite effect.
>
> (Holford and Myles Wright 1952: 38)

More directly, Coopers and Lybrand characterize the situation as follows:

> while Stewarts and Lloyds had several hundred job vacancies in the steel works, it was difficult and at times impossible for the Development Corporation to persuade either the Company or the Board of Trade to allow any major competitor for male employees to enter the town.
>
> (Coopers and Lybrand 1979: 4)

Not until the 1970s, twenty years after the establishment of Corby as a New Town, was the Development Corporation permitted to commence upon the diversification of the town's economy with respect to the employment of male labour. The Corporation was permitted to encourage some diversification of the Corby economy before this date, but diversification of significant magnitude was confined to the sectors of economic activity which utilized female labour (see Coopers and Lybrand 1979: 5). Needless to say, this diversification was limited and its occurrence coincided with steel's reduced demand for labour, and there continued to be examples of employers excluded on the grounds that their entry would be detrimental to the interests of steel. Thus Barber notes: 'One major manufacturing company was refused an Industrial Development Certificate in Corby within the past two years. The company was a German concern, who gave undertakings to employ 400 males in a car accessory plant' (Barber 1974: 12).

Even when the phasing out of steel was well under way, all attempts to obtain the necessary planning equipment to phase new employment into the town met with failure. Steel, it appears, was to remain the major employer in Corby right up to the point of planned production stoppage. The Corby Development Corporation's Annual Report for 1976 is revealing:

> In view of the unemployment in the town, the Corby District Council addressed a report to the Secretary of State for Industry asking for a meeting with the object of having Corby designated an Assisted Area. The Corporation while applauding the Council's zeal advised them that they considered this premature.
>
> (Corby Development Corporation 1976: 119)

It appears paradoxical that Corby's status as a New Town should have gone hand in hand with the pattern of imbalanced development described. The principle of balance attending most British New Town development – indeed the principle which was at the very heart of New Town ideology – found no place in the development of Corby New Town.[10] The national interest appears to have dictated that in the case of Corby this principle should be discarded. Moreover, my argument is that the endowment of New Town status on Corby was a device for accentuating the imbalanced company character of the town rather than an instrument for redressing the balance.

The inauguration of Corby as a New Town removed from the existing local authorities the ability to control the town's size and development – an objective they had pursued with some vigour, placing the power to determine the yea or nay of Corby's expansion very firmly within the province of the central state agencies, in the form of the Development Corporation. It is of crucial importance in understanding Corby's development to recognize that Development Corporations are appointed boards responsible directly to the government. Making Corby a New Town in fact enabled the bypassing of local opposition to the expansion of the town, an expansion directly related to the increase in the actual and planned labour demand of the steel works.

Local opposition to the development of Corby was advanced on more than one count, but it is clear that a significant factor in fostering such opposition was the cost Corby's expansion represented to the local authority. By rendering Corby a New Town, this particular basis of resistance was effectively removed, for the cost of Corby's development was directly transferred to central government. (One argument that has been put is that since the development of steel was in the national interest, it was only proper that the state and not the employer pick up the bill for the provision of housing via the New Town scheme.)

The consequence of this accountancy device, however, was to remove all serious opposition to imbalanced development. Local financial politics no longer had a role, so that although opposition remained throughout the local hinterland to the expansion of Corby, with the establishment of the New Town Development Corporation the vehicles for translating this opposition into effective resistance lost their place.[11] By establishing Corby as a New Town, moreover, the employers and the state had removed at a stroke the obstructions that the local authorities could have put in the way of expansion through the normal use of the old planning procedures, as indeed it seems they were prepared to do:

> At the time, the Urban District Council opposed the designation of Corby as a New Town. . . . Underlying these objections were reservations by the local elected members to the imposition of an independent Development Corporation with wide powers and governed by appointed board members reporting directly to central government.
>
> (Coopers and Lybrand 1979: 3)

Thus New Town status removed the barriers to the town's expansion, but it also permitted the articulation of the steel interest as part of the development policy of the town. The Development Plan, for example, was one of the instruments used to exclude all competitors for steel labour from the town. The planned character of Corby appears to be a crucial part of the rationale for holding other employers out. To permit the entry of employers other than steel would cause the town to grow beyond its planned size. Yet when steel demanded an increase in planned size, expansion appeared infinitely possible. Thus the Development Plan, normally an instrument for ensuring balance, was used to accentuate the imbalanced development of Corby. However, it can be argued that had Corby not obtained New Town status, the steel employers would have found it more difficult to maintain their employment monopoly.

That the Development Corporation operated unerringly in favour of the steel interest was as good as guaranteed by the composition of the Development Corporation. The employers of Corby, that is the steel employers alone, had direct representation on the Development Corporation Board. This was the case both during the period of steel under private ownership and during the period of steel as a nationalized industry. It would seem that this is the only case of a single employer being so represented on the board of a British New Town Development Corporation, and the steel interest was thus in a position to ensure that there would be no planning changes that could adversely affect steel.

Throughout the history of the town's development, local criticism has been two pronged: over-expansion on the one hand, and over-dependence on steel on the other. Had the local authority been in control of Corby's development, it would have been in its interest, as the ultimate inheritor of problems surrounding any closure of the steel works, to ensure that other employers *did* enter Corby and thereby reduce the town's over-dependence on steel. Ironically, the winding up of the Corby New Town Development Corporation and the closing of the steel works occurred almost simultaneously. The winding up of a New Town Development Corporation is customarily given as the sign that a town has accomplished a healthy maturity; it is the democratic time, as custom has it, for the 'planning guardians' to withdraw. In the case of Corby, the planned withdrawal of the Development Corporation coincided with the complete collapse of the local economic structure. The collapse happened suddenly and without adequate prior information, leaving a population and a planning system ill-prepared for coping with the immediate and subsequent impact of mass redundancy. The social imbalance of Corby further served to accentuate the problem, and we will consider this in the next section.

Manorial labour markets, networks, and ethnicity

A manorial labour market

In order to understand the present situation of Corby, attention must be paid to the role played by steel producers in determining both the industrial structure and social composition of Corby. The development of Corby is best understood as the development of a manorial labour market;[12] that is to say, employment and residence are tightly linked to one another, with employment determining right to residence. Furthermore, by manorial labour market I mean to indicate that there is only one major employer in the market. One agency controls both access to accommodation and access to employment. Corby, I argue, represents a deliberately constructed manorial labour market.

Although at different points in time different agencies have been responsible for funding the provision of steelworkers' housing – commencing with the direct provision of worker accommodation by the steel producers themselves, followed by a situation in which local authority provision augmented that of the steel producers and culminating in New Town Development Corporation provision of housing (Pocock 1967) – the principal qualification for housing remained, until fairly recently, that of possessing a job in the steel works. The hiring practices of one employer determined the social composition of a whole town; this is not the only case to be found of such a practice, but it is the only New Town case.

My account is comparable to that of Mullen on the relationship between employment and residence in Stevenage (Mullen 1980). Stevenage, however, is a situation where more than one major employer is present.[13] The steel employers of Corby not only shaped a labour force, they shaped a labour market, but even more significantly, they also shaped a planned town.

In the initial phase of its expansion, Corby was visibly a company town, with the steel producers, who at that time were a private company, occupying the joint role of employer and landlord.[14] Accommodation was tied to employment: loss of job resulted in loss of accommodation. With the advent of state provision of steelworkers' housing, a situation which occurred even though steel itself was in private hands, the relationship between job and accommodation was weakened but it did not disappear. Accommodation remained subsequent to employment; holding a job in the steel works was essential to the obtaining of state-provided housing, although leaving the employ of the steel works no longer necessitated the forfeiture of accommodation. Obtaining accommodation was tied to a particular employment base; remaining in the accommodation so provided was not.

This, however, represents a situation of apparent, rather than real, freedom to obtain employment elsewhere, for as we have already remarked, in the case of Corby, a policy decision was taken to hold other sources of substantial employment out of the town. Most particularly, the steel employers were concerned to reduce the effective competition for male labour. Thus, although formally Corby labour was free to leave the employ of the steel producers, in practice, decisions were taken to deliberately limit this freedom. Moreover, the planning history of Corby contains numerous explicit statements as to the desirability of separating Corby from its hinterland. Thus the 1952 New Town report argued that 'the journey to work in neighbouring towns, though arduous for the people concerned,[15] is in the best interests of Corby' (Corby Development Corporation 1965).

Corby's role was to house the steel works' labour; the planners' role was to ensure that labour, once recruited, was not 'poached'. There was always present the recognition that steel-works employment represents 'dirty work' and 'dirty industry'. The prevailing understanding was that labour presented with the option of employment in the cleaner sections of industry would desert the employ of the steel works.

Corby was constructed in such a way that this course of action was not open to its residents. The minimum space possible for the leakage of Corby labour into the local economy was provided. Coopers and Lybrand provide a detailed account of the poor road and rail communications between Corby and its surrounding region (Coopers and Lybrand 1979). The steel works were serviced by a branch line of the railway network and had little cause to argue for better road services. Corby's passenger rail service was closed in the 1960s even though the main line passes through Corby and despite the fact that the town represents a major population base. Added to this is the fact that 54 per cent of Corby households (in 1971) did not own a car, whereas the average for all New Towns is 45 per cent.

The 1971 census provides further evidence on the isolation of Corby (Champion, Clegg, and Davies 1977). The ratio of those living and working within the town to the sum of inward and outward commuters, an index of commuting independence, is 2.32 for Corby as compared to a New Town average of 1.20. On this index Corby is the third most isolated of the twenty-eight New Towns in Britain.

Further evidence on Corby's comparative isolation from its neighbouring region is provided by an examination of the extent to which in-migration to Corby from outside its region is large relative to in-migration for other New Towns from their region. Comparing Corby and Northampton New Town, both in the East Midlands region, the (five-year) migration tables of the 1971 census tell us that while of all in-migrants to Corby only 12 per cent were from the East Midlands region, of all in-migrants to Northampton more than 20 per cent were from the East Midlands. The situation is even more marked for out-migration.

Manorial labour markets potentially provide employers with extra degrees of control over their workforce. For the same reason that an employer would wish to create monopsony by keeping other employers out of a local labour market, he would wish to restrict the contact of his workforce with the surrounding region in order to diminish the chance of labour leaving.

Recruiting labour from a distance is of course another manifestation of this rationale – the 'leakage' of labour to the surrounding economy is minimized. Returning to the arguments of Chapter 1, securing a job is dependent on a contact in the workforce – often migrants' sole employment contact is the initial recruiting employer himself. One problem with the account provided above immediately leaps to mind: Corby's steel works had a problem of high labour turnover.[16]

There are two ways in which this apparently contradictory fact can be squared with the preceding account. First, and for reasons that will be stressed again presently, Corby labour remained highly connected to its area of origin and circulated between those locations and Corby:

> A lot of our family are still there in Glasgow. And here there's only the one job really. If you get fed up with it, and you're bound to aren't you, then there's nothing else. You can't get a job in Kettering for love or money, if you're from Corby. I know, I've tried. So I go back up to Glasgow now and again. Somebody always knows of something going. And they always had you back here. That'll change now. They were always glad of you back before.
>
> (Corby worker)

Part of high turnover is to be accounted for in the departure and return of the same individuals to the steel works' labour force, such individuals finding the distance between Corby and, most frequently, Scotland easier to negotiate than entrance into the local labour market.[17] My respondents had no contacts in the immediate surrounding hinterland who could help them find employment. Second, labour departing the steel works also departed from Corby: 'When they got dissatisfied with us they would go down to Luton for the week-end and pick up a job down there and not come back. Just write to us and say "Sorry chum, tarra, and send us my cards"' (Corby manager); 'Initial turnover is understandably high [in Corby works]. Many migrants more swiftly move on to better paid jobs with the motor industry in Coventry or Luton' (Thomas 1969: 858). High turnover does not of itself indicate that the labour market is other than manorial; for although turnover may be taken as an indication that labour is not completely trapped, it must leave the region in order to obtain alternative employment. High rates of out-migration necessarily accompany high rates of turnover in manorial labour markets.

Networks and ethnicity

Added to the manorial aspects of the labour market in Corby is the fact that the labour was recruited from a distinctive area – Scotland. Of course, other regions such as Merseyside and the north east of England were also visited, but the historical pattern and my own fieldwork evidence testify to the importance of the Scottish connection. The 1971 census shows one-third of Corby's population (not workforce) as born in Scotland. This does not include children born in Corby to Scottish parents, and the census cannot reveal this figure. Champion, Clegg, and Davies (1977) estimate the latter to form one-third of the population. Other estimates (e.g. Corby Development Corporation 1977) also put the figure for Scottish or Scottish parents (Scottish origin) at around 60 per cent. An interesting piece of evidence is provided by the 1981 census tables on usual residence. Of all the people enumerated as visiting Corby on the night of the census, over 60 per cent gave Scotland as their usual area of residence.

Thus Corby is not only a heavy-industry enclave, it is primarily a Scottish enclave.[18] The aggregative figures cannot give the same feel of Scottishness as anthropological observation. Corby represents a speech community which is distinct from that of the surrounding area. The Scottish accent persists in Corby even though the town is located in the heart of England. The impressionistic journalism quoted at the beginning of this chapter does indeed reflect the truth. Children born in Corby speak with Scottish accents.

The labour-market consequences of a distinctive Scottish community isolated from its surrounding region are of considerable interest.[19] I have already documented the kin-connected entry to Corby – whether it was because kin were recruited directly in the area of origin or because of chain migration following on from the initial recruitment. The Corby population is thus composed of numerous strong networks which are moreover bounded *vis-à-vis* the surrounding hinterland. As we discussed in Chapter 5, residents of Corby are more strongly tied to kin and friends in Glasgow and Peterhead than they are to individuals in the East Midlands region. A distinctive community, strongly connected within itself but poorly connected to adjacent communities, has significant labour-market consequences.

Employers encountering a Scottish accent within the Corby sub-region identify that labour as Corby labour and attribute to it the characteristics associated with heavy industry. In the case of Corby labour, accent acts as a signal, a signal which of itself is sufficient to preclude any deeper investigation of skill or competence. As the labour manager of the Corby steel works commented:

> Because they spoke with beautiful Jimmy accents they were immediately marked. . . . They were considered to be strange. They spoke with this marked accent and the accent is really a beautiful accent but you have to be very used to it to understand a word that people are saying.

Scottishness, and the Scottish accent, was used as a proxy for heavy-industry characteristics:

> There was that. Immediately there was the whole ambiance that they were tough people. They were difficult people and they themselves were very cliquish. They went around together. They didn't go and mix up with the Northamptonshire people who they probably found had very funny natures.
> (Corby manager)

The above evidence is backed up by interviews of employers in the region surrounding Corby. The details of the interviews are given in the Appendix to this volume. Sixteen employers were chosen in the sub-region and were asked about their hiring practices. The survey supported the labour manager's arguments quoted above: accent was identified as a primary signal. I have argued that the poor quality of contact between Corby and its hinterland was likely to result in indirect discrimination; Corby workers were not on the relevant grapevine for local jobs, but there was also direct discrimination against Corby labour – discrimination which owed much to the development of Corby as an enclave:

> I can always tell if they're from Corby – by the accent, broad, broad Scotch. I don't employ Corby workers, they're bad time keepers and a bad influence. You only have to go through Corby and see the vandalism to know what I mean. Whole streets of new houses completely wrecked. No, I don't want that here. No, thank you. No discipline that's the trouble.
>
> (Kettering manager)

The above fieldwork survey of employers was further confirmed by our interviews of workers in Corby. Workers were aware that Corby had a bad name, that steel had a bad name, that Glasgow had a bad name, and that the Scots had a bad name. Often measures were taken by labour to conceal its Corby address when applying for a job:

> There was a few of us trying for local jobs, like. We did the rounds in the one car. We'd had it up to the ears with the works – there was a gaffer who was pushing us around too much and we wanted out, so off we went to Kettering and Wellingborough, even pretended we didn't come from Corby. But no luck.[20]
>
> (Corby worker)

The analysis of responses from the Corby sample with regard to labour-market discrimination opens up the question of ethnicity in Britain. Typically, the analysis of ethnicity has been restricted to New Commonwealth minorities. But Wallman, in her introduction to a volume devoted to immigrant minorities, defines ethnicity as follows:

> Ethnicity refers generally to the perception of group difference and so to social boundaries between sections of a population. In this sense ethnic difference is the recognition of a contrast between 'us' and 'them'. . . . Ethnicity is not, therefore, the same as culture or race. It is not simply difference: it is the sense of difference which can occur where members of a particular cultural or racial group interact with non-members.
>
> (Wallman 1979: ix)

On this definition, the Corby Scots represent an ethnic minority in the heart of England. As we have seen, accent provides the basis for identification, and is perceived to do so by both parties – the Scottish community in Corby and the English community in the region. Wallman further identifies the relationship between ethnicity and work: 'In the sphere of work it is also possible to identify circumstances in which ethnicity is used as a resource managed for specific occupational goals' (Wallman 1979: xi). Brooks and Singh, in the same volume, provide a discussion of the above. As I discussed in Chapter 4, they have spotted a pattern of entry, among Asian foundry workers, largely similar to the pattern I have evidenced for the Corby Scots. Brooks and Singh assume that they have found an exception, and argue that such a pattern is confined to ethnic minorities alone. My argument is not simply that connected entry can take place on the basis of networks, but that employers' recruitment policies – and the chain migration that follows in its wake – are capable of rendering sections of the indigenous labour force ethnic. The manner in which such a labour force faces discrimination in the local labour market has received no attention to date either in the planning or in the sociological literature. The planners of Corby accentuated this process by failing to build the necessary bridges into the local labour market to combat this discrimination.

Thus direct recruitment, network-based entry, and planning procedures all combined to give Corby a highly imbalanced economic and social composition. The consequences of such a structure, for a town faced with mass redundancies, are severe. The concluding section of this chapter will consider some of the policy lessons of Corby's plight.

Conclusions and policy lessons

A variety of strategies for alleviating the misfortunes of Corby have been suggested by a variety of agencies, but all recognize that the respective strategies advocated would be insufficient for the accomplishment of a major recovery in the town's employment profile.

An attempt has been made to establish co-operatives involving British Steel and Job Ownership, but it is sufficient to indicate here that British Steel did not attempt to endow co-operatives but sponsored an initiative designed to encourage individual workers to invest their individual redundancy payments in small co-operative ventures. Although the co-operative form has on occasion provided something of a solution in redundancy situations, a handful of small co-operatives would not even have made a dent in the unemployment figures – although the sponsorship of the co-operative initiative certainly made a splash in the national press.

The individual redundancy payments made to Corby workers could never of themselves have provided the employment potential necessary to the soaking up of the steel labour force. And British Steel did not attempt to endow any enterprises, large or small. Furthermore, the departure of British Steel represented the departure of the major ratepayer in Corby – in 1973 the steel works directly accounted for 34 per cent of the rateable value. The drastic reduction in the level of financial income available to Corby had very real consequences for the town's ability to correct the high unemployment levels left by the withdrawal of steel. We have already discussed the extent to which Corby was over-dependent on the steel works for employment, but the local authority in Corby was also financially over-dependent on steel. Had there been other employers of substance in the town, the withdrawal of steel would not have had the same drastic effect on the rates as a source of income. Precisely at the point at which Corby most needs revenue in order to be able to attract new employers, it has been deprived of the necessary income base. It is an aspect of the development of a one-industry, one-company town which has received little comment.

The recruitment practice of Corby, and the social planning which accompanied it, resulted in the acceptance of dirty industry as the only possible future employment prospect for the town. Dirty industry, the experts agreed, was the cause of Corby's present problems, but, they argued, in a manner which sounds paradoxical, only dirty industry would be attracted to Corby, possessing as it does the characteristics and profile of a dirty-industry town. The pressure is on Corby to continue down the same problem-laden road, resulting in the ultimate expansion and not contraction of the dirty-industry problem. Involvement in dirty industry pushes individuals and groups, and in the case of Corby, even whole towns, on to a course of subsequent involvement in dirty industry, with the consequence of an increasingly weakening ability to resist such definitions and developments. Steel towns which have experienced mass redundancies and exhibited high levels of unemployment have been in a weak position to resist the entry of anti-social petro-chemical developments, developments refused and resisted by areas with lower levels of unemployment. Thus Shotton accepted a development refused by Darlington. So far no employer of this type has approached Corby with regard to location there, but were any employer to do so, no matter how undesirable the character of the development, the outcome of such an approach is certain: permission would be given. As Coopers and Lybrand note:

> At a time of high unemployment it is neither feasible nor desirable to exercise a high degree of selectivity in attracting new firms. The present policy of accepting any enterprise with reasonable employment prospects is therefore sensible. . . . [The strategy should be] to attract, with central government assistance, larger industries requiring unskilled or semi-skilled labour, possibly even dirty industry, and locate them, in co-operation with B.S.C, outside the designated area.
>
> (Coopers and Lybrand 1979: 29)

To date there has been little chance of local industry entering the vacuum created by British Steel, and the planners' reliance on the hope of a new dirty industry to sop up the high levels of unemployment can be seen as a consequence of the failure to attempt any integration of Corby into the surrounding economy.

The state likewise has dragged its heels with regard to resolving the problems experienced by Corby. The subject has not even merited an inquiry. The government's sole contribution has been to declare Corby an Enterprise Zone,[21] but without a significant improvement in Corby's communication network it is difficult to see how this can translate into any long-term concrete improvement in the situation. A minimum requirement, I had suggested (Grieco 1985a), would be the re-opening of the rail station; as this most certainly lay within the immediate power of government. This has now occurred (April 1987). It is essential if state investment in Corby New Town is not merely to be written off. It does not seem probable that the market of itself will bring about the recovery of Corby. There is a need for stronger intervention than merely labelling Corby an Enterprise Zone.

Within the politics of the sub-region, Corby is poorly placed to effect its interest in attracting employers over that of the local market towns competing for the same employers. The development of the problem was national in character, emanating from the expansion of steel in the national interest; the solution of the problem can only originate from as mighty a source.

> Since the root cause of its problems lies in its historical development and present position as a town dominated by a steel works serving the national economy, responsibility for providing this assistance should be shared between central government and the steel industry itself.
>
> (Coopers and Lybrand 1979: 2)

Six to seven years after its radical experience of mass redundancy and employment loss, Corby is now poised for major new improvements to its communications network financed by the EEC. Despite many calls upon national government and the steel industry to compensate for the disruption of Corby, at the end of the day it is an external agency which is about to provide the infrastructure for development.

The more general conclusion from our analysis is to caution against imbalance in terms of one major employer in a region. Given the recruitment, search, and information mechanisms I have highlighted and analysed in this book, it is likely – as in the case of Corby – that entire networks of kin and friends, or at least a substantial part of the network, will locate with the one employer. It is in the employer's and the employees' interest to do so, at least in the short term, and they have the mechanisms whereby this can be achieved. Industrial imbalance, acting through these mechanisms, leads to social imbalance. The consequence is that a sudden change of fortune leaves the entire network disadvantaged and isolated from the surrounding area. Return migration is one alternative, and I shall discuss this in the next chapter, but it is costly. Far better to ensure that the imbalance does not accumulate to an unmanageable level. Even where industrial imbalance cannot be countered because of the technological necessity, the planning authorities can still act to ensure social balance by (a) encouraging recruitment from a wide variety of locations and (b) purposively building bridges into the surrounding community so that the boundary of the network expands beyond the place of work. A communications network is clearly an important start in building a community network.

The suddenness of closure is also an important factor in determining the opportunities of redundant workers and their families. We have produced evidence of concealment of such information. This is clearly a device for securing high productivity in the run-up to closure, but its consequences for the ability of workers to find opportunities after redundancy are severe. Finally, the making of such information public earlier would encourage the employment exchanges to bring jobs to a location rather than export the unemployed workers quickly after redundancy is announced – by inviting direct recruitment from employers or otherwise.

8
Return migration from Corby: the role of information networks

Introduction

In the previous chapter, I analysed the genesis of the problems in Corby at closure; most particularly, attention was drawn to the poor quality of contacts with the hinterland and the consequences for job search. It has a workforce strongly linked to its area of origin but weakly connected to Corby's sub-region. The former is the result of recruitment practices, the latter the result of deliberate monopsonistic practices – in both, state employment and planning agencies have played their part (advertently or inadvertently). The consequence is that with closure the unemployment rate in Corby rose to 24 per cent – it is unlikely that attempts to attract new industry will produce a basic improvement in the situation for some time to come. One possible solution for Corby labour is return migration. In fact, my fieldwork in Peterhead, conducted in 1978, had located workers who had returned from Corby *in anticipation of redundancy*. On what basis did this return migration take place, and what were the information mechanisms related to it? The object of this chapter is to present an analysis of the role of information networks in return migration. Apart from shedding light on some questions in the migration literature, my theoretical analysis and empirical evidence should also give some indication of the possible responses of the Corby unemployed in the years following closure.

Return migration from Corby to Peterhead: information networks and anticipated redundancy

In 1967 Stewarts & Lloyds shelved their ambitious expansion plans and settled on the prospects of a more or less constant workforce size. However, employment at the steel works started declining in the 1970s, primarily through natural wastage. In the three years prior to 1978, employment fell by 1,000. Furthermore, although no actual redundancies were declared till right at the end of this period, discussions of the problems of steel were fairly frequent in the press after the 1973 White Paper on the future of the industry.

The twenty Peterhead respondents – the Reid net – interviewed in March 1978, had returned to Peterhead from Corby during the past fifteen months in anticipation of redundancy. Docherty reports that by the end of 1978 'rumours had been rife that steel making at Corby was threatened. . . . These rumours were confirmed in a B.S.C. statement on 8th Feb. 1979' (Docherty 1983: 136). None of the returnees had in fact been made redundant, nor were they connected to individuals who had been made redundant. Rather they had spotted a policy of natural wastage. Departing labour was not being replaced and this was taken to be 'the writing on the wall'·

> You can tell. Mainly you can. Things are allowed to run down, the machinery doesn't get the same attention. Jobs begin to go. Fewer people taken on. Nobody says anything official mind. It's just a hunch. You can't quite put your finger on it. But you know just the same.
>
> (former Corby worker)

The UK situation is somewhat different either from that in Germany, where the 1976 Co-determination Act requires West German businesses to give one year's advance warning of intended plant closures, or from that in the USA, where there is no such legislation but unions are developing methods to interpret signals of redundancy:

> Workers in the parts department of a plant know when replacement orders are being cut. Machine repair people are the first to become aware when management is cutting back on their programmed maintenance, because it is their ingenuity that is called upon to keep the old equipment functioning. Key personnel in a firm's real estate department can tell when the company has stopped searching for local space for expansion or is actually beginning to sell some of its property. Some unions and citizen labour coalitions are beginning to write 'early warning system' manuals for one another's use.
>
> (Bluestone and Harrison 1982: 243)

In the absence of legal requirements or formalized methods of interpreting signals, local information networks are crucial in carrying information on anticipated redundancy. One consequence of this is that, depending on the nature of the networks, information and anticipation may differ even within the same workforce.

Thus Wedderburn, investigating white-collar redundancies in Luton and Stevenage in the aerospace industry in the 1960s, found that 58 per cent said they did not anticipate redundancy while 40 per cent said they did (Wedderburn 1964). Wedderburn's interviews were conducted *after* redundancy had taken place, and she remarks that of those claiming to have anticipated redundancy, 'some . . . no doubt [were] wise after the event'. Here my own study is of particular importance, for the returnee respondents had indeed anticipated redundancies and as a consequence migrated *before* the event.

In the case of Corby, at least as experienced by our returnees, there was no one specific rumour of redundancy. Rather there was a developing impression of rundown in which information on the non-placement of departing labour played a critical role. Furthermore, discussions between departing labour and those remaining in the short term at least served to confirm suspicions – for the possession of information on the 'real state of affairs' was often attributed to departing individuals.

It was assumed that departure was informed by more concrete knowledge than seems indeed to be the case. My own sample was not privy either as a group or as individuals to such special information *but they assumed that others were*. The notion that there was 'something at the back of his going, something that concerns us all' was a common one:

> A couple of blokes left, all of a sudden like. People who had their heads screwed on, not 'wasters'. Left for no good reason. Well it started me thinking. And it wasn't long before I got to thinking about leaving as well. There'd been talk of redundancy on and off for years. But suddenly all the old hands seemed to be going. And I thought there must be something at the back of it all. So I started to look around as well.
>
> (former Corby worker)

Why was this anticipation of redundancy not more widespread? Asked about the extent to which the 'signs' of trouble had been a topic of group discussion, our respondents replied that it had indeed been a subject of great debate:

> Everybody had been talking about redundancy for years but nobody really believes it will happen. I think it's got to myself. Things are changing in steel and Corby's old now. God knows what they'll do when it happens. There's only steel at Corby. I wasn't taking any chances. I'm too old for that. This job doesn't pay so well but it's safe at least for the rest of my working life – what with the oil. Yes people talk about it all, but they don't face the facts. I don't give Corby much longer at all.
>
> (former Corby worker)

But not all workers read the signs in the same way; for example, younger workers tended to be more optimistic and to see the reductions in manpower as trimming rather than rundown activity. Although my evidence is second-hand, in the sense that it is my sample which is providing information on the perceptions of different groups prior to the announcement of redundancy, it does seem that these perceptions differed greatly within the workforce.

> Some people think Corby won't suffer with the changes in steel, and some think it will, but even most of those think it won't be for a while yet. You can't blame people for not moving till they have to, especially the young ones with

families. It must be easier to think everything will work out all right. I don't think it will – but there you are.

(former Corby worker)

At the theoretical level the above responses raise the question of why it is that some sections of the workforce receive the signals on the probability of redundancy, while to others it comes as a major shock. Here the theorizing of the anthropologist F.G. Bailey may provide us with some direction. In his well-known work *Gifts and Poison: The Politics of Reputation* (1971), Bailey argues that politics is pervasive throughout society and at every level of the social structure. He theorizes as to the generality of social closure and the role played by information management – the politics of reputation – in achieving such social closure.

Individuals transmitting information have to take care of their reputations. The transmission of unreliable information carries penalties, especially where it is acted upon with adverse effects. The individual has to make a decision about the responsibility which he is willing to take in being seen to be the originator of the message, that is in 'signing' it.

Bailey, from anthropological field study, though not in an industrial context, charts for us a number of strategies open to an individual wishing to transmit information to which varying degrees of certainty attach. He draws our attention to the use of 'in confidence' as a device for restricting the transmission of information, and the use of rumour as a device for restricting or evading responsibility for the transmission of information.

In earlier chapters it was suggested that information on opportunities is deliberately sealed into particular groups. Here, a slightly different dynamic is being considered, that is, how the information on disappearing opportunity is sealed into groups. Here the situation is slightly more complex for rumours are general, yet not acted upon. The literature on information diffusion clearly signals that in order for information to be acted upon it must be believed. The receipt of information is not sufficient in itself.

'Rumours' represent the circulation of that category of information on which no person is prepared to stand author, or, in Bailey's terms, sign. To transfer speculative information (and reading the writing on the wall is necessarily such) which retrospectively proves to be wrong, endangers reputation and perhaps even sets of relationships. These conditions, where an individual wishes to share the information which he is party to but where its reliability is uncertain, will precisely generate a rumour. To quote Bailey, 'In . . . conditions of uncertainty, we would expect to find devices by which S [sender of the message], so to speak, hedges his bets. The label of "rumour" frees him from responsibility' (Bailey 1971: 289). The sender behaves as a mere instrument, a channel of information and no moral responsibility attaches for its authorship.

Bailey attributes the rapid spread of rumours to this special feature: 'It is probably this quality of being without cost which enables rumours to be spread quickly and early' (Bailey 1971: 288). Thus where individuals are ready to provide their workmates with a hint as to redundancy, but are not prepared to make the issue a matter of their judgement with its attendant risks, we may expect rumours. In this way self-interest and altruism are both served as values. Rumours are then the general diffusion of information with low specificity and as such are unlikely to be acted upon.

A second way in which rumours may be generated is through the 'in confidence' device. The individual or sender has received information from an authoritative source but to reveal the source would result in punitive action being taken against the source. The message must be passed on without the 'signature', for it cannot be generally disclosed with the signature without risk to the author. Those individuals closely tied to the initial recipient of the message are likely to act upon it, but the more weakly tied to the recipient is an individual or group, the less likely the individual or group is to act upon it.

Effectively, as it passes down the information chain the message is weakening, and redundancy situations are likely to host such weakening messages. Indeed, the notion that such messages had been circulating lay behind my respondents' belief that although their own departure was not based upon any such specific message, the behaviour of others was:

> I'd heard that someone had seen some plans for closing Corby. It was just a rumour but it gave me a scare, I can tell you. No smoke without fire I thought and I asked my brother if he could do anything for me if the worst came to the worst. He found me this job. I didn't hang around. I gave my notice in a week after and came on up. The wife followed a couple of months after. I don't know if I've done right. I think so.
>
> (former Corby worker)

The in-confidence strategy may indeed seal a message within a group – and Bailey assumes that this will be the case. Placing an in-confidence restriction on the transmission of information, even where individuals do feel morally compelled to give the hint to others to whom they are linked, will, however, at the very least reduce the specific message to rumour.

Here further insights of Bailey's are of relevance to our discussion and return us once more to the debate on the importance of weak and strong ties in information diffusion. Bailey argues that where individuals are weakly tied, information is forced to be more explicit than where individuals are strongly tied and share codes. Yet explicitness where uncertainty is present carries risks. This is of importance in understanding why such divergent perceptions of the probability of redundancy exist within one workforce. Where individuals are strongly tied, there is less need for explicitness in the transmission of information and less need for the individual to expose himself in sending information. Thus Bailey argues:

> Those communities in which relations are relatively highly personalised, in which people treat one another 'in the round', in which relationships are multiplex and roles are particularistic should also be the communities in which the signalling system is most efficient – that is to say, in which the signals can be most laconic.
>
> (Bailey 1971: 12)

It is precisely such a structure which is most congruent with the relay of information which depends for its authority on the 'writing on the wall'. Strong ties lift the burden off the individual by requiring less explicitness.

The theoretical analysis above suggests that within the same workforce there are likely to be different perceptions of the probability of redundancy. My empirical investigations confirm this. All of the Peterhead respondents had anticipated redundancy and acted upon it, but they also gave information on differing perceptions among their workmates in Corby.

However, for the Glasgow–Corby Buchanan net, constructed from interviews in Corby, redundancy came as a complete shock; while for another net, Peterhead–Corby Buchan, beliefs were mixed.[1]

> It came as a shock, there's no doubt about that. Closing a whole town down. Whoever thought they could do that. What we'll do next I don't know. It's a good job my son got out of the steel or we'd all have been in the same boat just now. I can't believe it even yet.
>
> (former Corby steelworker)

> We knew it was coming. We just didn't know when. And there's no way of guessing. Whatever you do it can turn out wrong. But in a New Town, what a disgrace! What a shambles!
>
> (Corby steelworker)

Not only did perceptions as to the likelihood of redundancy differ, so did reactions and behaviour even within the same information net. Ten members of the Reid net remained in Corby up to the point of redundancy. What explains this difference in behaviour? Those returning to Peterhead were significantly older than those remaining in Corby – of our return migrants all but two were in their mid to late fifties, whereas the remainees were all within the 20 to 40 age category.[2]

This younger labour undoubtedly shared an understanding of the imminence of redundancy with its older counterparts but viewed itself as having different prospects in terms of its ability to secure new jobs with relative ease. It is this difference in circumstances which explains the difference in behaviour within the net, and not a difference in belief.

Age is a major explanation of migration in anticipation of redundancy. For this mid to late fifties section of the Corby labour force, delaying the search for replacement long-term employment until redundancy was actually announced could have jeopardized the prospect of success altogether, especially in a period of a high national rate of unemployment.

In fact, it would have involved a delay of two to three years as matters turned out. Clearly, for this group of workers to migrate before redundancy actually occurred meant forgoing sizeable redundancy payments; to remain would have most probably meant enforced early retirement or unemployment, for each additional year added to a man's age at this point in his working life would militate against his re-employability given current perceptions.[3]

The younger members of the networks saw their interest as being best served by remaining in Corby until the point of redundancy so as to collect their redundancy payments and indeed to continue in high-earning employment for as long as was possible. Thereafter they intended either to follow their fathers and older kin back north or to move elsewhere.

Of the ten direct links to our twenty returnees, only three were contemplating a return to the north whereas seven were contemplating migration elsewhere. Three were searching for work in the south of England and the Midlands, four were intending to migrate overseas, of whom two were following up on previous migrations by parts of their network and two were hoping to be sponsored by the Steel Company of Canada.[4] The latter was actively recruiting in Corby.

Direct recruitment and chain migration were once again the mechanisms by which out-migration was being accomplished. The three contemplating return to the north were hoping to find work through their local contacts or networks in Peterhead and Aberdeen, this group of individuals being linked into both of these centres of employment. The three seeking work in the Midlands and the south were hoping to get jobs in the car industry, having contacts in three sites, Coventry,[5] Luton, and Dagenham.[6] The actual outcomes of these decision-making processes are not known for at this point my fieldwork stopped.

Return migration from Corby to Peterhead: local networks and networks over distance

The period of rundown or impending rundown in Corby during the mid-1970s coincided exactly with a radical shift in economic opportunities in the area of origin of one group of migrants to the steel works. As documented in Chapter 6, throughout the 1950s and the 1960s the decline of the fishing industry in the north east of Scotland provided a ready pool of labour to employers in England, in particular the steel works at Corby. However, in the 1970s the North Sea oil boom increased employment opportunities throughout this area. Aberdeen became the oil capital of the North Sea, and all through the north east oil-related industry moved in. The censuses of 1961, 1971, and 1981 confirm for us the major decline in population of this region in the decade of the 1960s, followed by an even more spectacular increase in the decade of the 1970s.[7]

The census data cannot tell us to what extent the large increase in migration was return migration. However, the local employment-exchange officer in Peterhead, interviewed in 1978, calculated that 100 working-age males had returned from Corby within the previous year. The regional report for 1981 indicates that the population of the civil parish of Peterhead was 17,317 in 1971 as compared with 19,445 in 1981. How much of this increase was generated by in-migration and how much by natural growth is not known. If one assumes the increase was generated purely by migration, Corby is contributing 5 per cent to the increase – even if only male labour is considered. If an adjustment is made for spouses, then Corby's contribution would be closer to 10 per cent.

Apart from the aggregative census figures, anthropological fieldwork also established the prevalence of return migration. Local newspapers contained stories on return migrants, and local employers were rehiring return migrants. My network-based research focused on twenty of these return migrants and their respective contacts, which I have collectively termed the Reid net. The details on data collection are provided in the Appendix. All of these respondents were employed in five small oil-related engineering enterprises.[8] The network basis of return migration became abundantly clear during these interviews, and it is to these I now turn.

Employment and wage laws
The oil boom in Scotland and in Peterhead led to a massive increase in employment opportunities, an extremely tight accommodation situation, and moreover happened in a period of statutory wage restraint. Each of these factors worked towards encouraging network-based migration. The sudden increase in labour requirements by incoming firms was to a large extent met by large migrations from other areas – many firms brought their workforces with them. But local established firms, whether in engineering or in services, seem to have relied on the networks of their existing workforces. The rationale for this has already been discussed at length. The surest way of meeting the labour shortage was to tap the networks, which – because of the patterns of earlier migrations – stretched to Corby. Quite apart from the speed of information transfer along network routes, the network properties of sponsorship and control would also advantage network members.

It may be argued that an alternative to using networks would have been to offer higher wages and advertise as widely as possible. Even if this was a more efficient method of information transfer than the network, and we have argued that this is not necessarily so, we have to take into account the fact that for some part of this period statutory pay restraint was in force. This disadvantaged existing local companies severely in their attempts to attract or hold labour, for the new and incoming firms were able to 'redefine' jobs and thereby sidestep the codes. A number of local companies went to the extent of disbanding themselves and re-opening as new enterprises in order to subvert the codes and remain competitive in the local labour market (see Hunt 1975).

Even when pay restraint was removed, local companies still faced the problem of having to pay sufficiently high wages to hold labour in competition with the larger firms. One way in which this was achieved was at the expense of the taxman. Thus wages were made up of a number of components, not all of which passed through the books. Five of my respondents worked for engineering firms on a casual, black-economy basis which did not pass through the books:

> When they're very busy at . . . I go along after finishing my proper job and help out. It's all cash in hand, no deductions. My brother works there and he phones a message through when I'm needed. Their order book depends on a quick turn round – machine repairs for oil – so the boss is prepared to pay well for it. I can't complain – it's hard work but it's worth it. You have to be a bit careful about what you say. It's an extra wage really.
>
> (Peterhead returnee)

The employer thus obtained the flexibility necessary to meeting a highly fluctuating, but immediate, demand for his engineering services (a high volume of immediate repair work) without improving the formal wage necessary to the holding of labour.

It is in the context of strong competition in the labour market, therefore, that we can understand the network basis of return migration in this case. It is clear why small local employers should seek to recruit return migrants network-connected to the existing labour force. Given the formal illegality of wages offered and wages declared for tax purposes, new recruits have to be strongly tied to the existing workforce to ensure trust.[9] Severe financial penalties would be incurred if these practices were discovered,[10] and severe labour shortage would occur if they were not carried out; the solution was the hiring of return migrants connected to the existing workforce.

Residential aid: implications for network theory
The other major factor behind the network basis of return migration is residence. All of the return migrants in the study received residential aid from kin. Fifteen stayed initially with kin on their return and five found their accommodation through kin aid. This was a factor of some considerable importance in enabling the return, for all varieties of accommodation were in scarce supply at the time of return – even hotel places. Residential aid was given despite poor resources of kin in Peterhead.

There were some reports of 'tiffs' or 'rows', particularly when one couple were sharing with another, but these were considered 'natural, given the circumstances', and were not viewed as fundamental precisely because kin were involved:

> They stayed with us in Corby way back. We got on well but there was the occasional upset – but everybody has those don't they? It's only natural to let off steam, isn't it? Everybody has their own ways. We spent three months with them when we came back from Corby. We had a lot of laughs and one almighty row. But it blew over, a misunderstanding really. Between our husbands, it was. We can laugh about it now. It wasn't funny at the time though.
>
> (Peterhead returnee, of her sister and brother-in-law)

It is also interesting to note that help was given with equal frequency by both wife's and husband's family. Indeed, there was need to pay attention to protocol in taking assistance. Receiving too much aid from one side caused problems with the other, although individuals who had been directly helped by the returning couple had first claim on providing aid:

> When they came to Corby, we put them up. Them and the kids. So when we came back we stayed with them till we got on our feet. We've always got on together. Holidays together and that sort of thing. My brother got . . . his job down at the harbour there. They've been very good to us. Mind you, we've done the same for them.
>
> (Peterhead returnee, of her brother and husband)

The above account of return migration thus throws light not only on the role of strong network ties in securing and maintaining employment, but also their role in providing the important complementary input of residential aid. It shows that even within networks, the giving and receiving of aid is highly structured – considerations of balance and sequence predominate. The material also shows directly the greater importance of kin. Whilst the return migrants in the study felt that they could call upon the majority of their kin for aid immediately upon their return to Peterhead, they had reservations about making a similar call upon past friends:[11]

> You can't just walk back in on friends after fifteen years and say well what about a job then can you. You lose touch with friends after a few years; it's different with family what with weddings and holidays and people visiting you, you're always in touch one way or another. If you needed help you'll always get it and if it's needed I'd always give it. That's the way it is with us.
>
> (Peterhead returnee)

A further consideration appeared to be that kinship gave detailed knowledge of living habits. Holidays, spent together in the past, provided the necessary assurance as to compatibility:[12]

> We often stayed with them when we came back up for a holiday or a wedding or something like that. They came to us quite a few times too. Two weeks at most, but we know one another's ways. We've not had any problems, really, we've stayed together so often we all know when to shut up and get out of the

way. We never interfere in one another's business. That's the golden rule.
(Peterhead returnee of his brother and his wife)

The anthropologist Wolf notes that kinship has special properties: kinship relations 'are a product of social synchronicisation achieved in the course of socialisation. The private relation of trust may thus be translated into co-operation in the public realm' (Wolf 1966: 9).

It is this social synchronicization which is of consequence in the provision of domestic space for incoming kin. For the respondents, friendships were indeed being restored, and past friendship formed a basis for present friendship, but the lapse of the tie during the period of the returnee's absence inhibited immediate requests for aid. Thus friendship ties were viewed as having lapsed in a way that kinship ties had not.

Implications for migration theory

In a standard reference on migration, Lee theorizes what Ravenstein (1885) referred to as 'counterstream', as follows:

> A counterstream is established for several reasons. One is that the positive factors at [destination] may disappear, or be muted, as during the depression, or there may be a re-evaluation of the balance of positive and negative factors at origin and destination. The very existence of a migration stream creates contacts between origin and destination, and the acquisition of new attributes at destination, be they skills or wealth, often makes it possible to return to the origin on advantageous terms. Migrants become aware of opportunities at origin which were not previously exploited, or they may use their contacts in the new area to set up business in the old. Accompanying the return migrants will be their children born at destination, and along with them will be people indigenous to the area of destination who have become aware of the opportunities or amenities at the place of origin through stream migrants. Furthermore, not all persons who migrate intend to remain indefinitely at the place of destination.
>
> (Lee 1966: 55)

Thus Lee offers us six different explanations of return migrations:

1. An *objective* change in the opportunity structure of the two regions sets the current of migration in the opposite direction.
2. A *perceptual* change takes place in the assessment of the opportunity structures of the two regions, setting the current of migration in the opposite direction.
3. A change takes place in the *characteristics* of the migrants (the acquisition of skill and capital) such that the opportunity structure of the area of origin is transformed for them.
4. *Dynasty* return which involves the return of migrants' offspring born elsewhere.
5. A *snowballing effect* occurs whereby return migration encourages natives of the former area of destination to migrate to the former area

of origin of the return migrants.
6. The return of *transient* migrants.

In discussing return migration it is perhaps best to distinguish between intentional return and contingent return. By intentional return I mean a stated preference for residence in the area of origin as opposed to all other areas, economic conditions permitting. By contingent return I mean an indifference with regard to residence in area of origin, entry to the area taking place solely on the basis of expansion in employment opportunities. Although one may distinguish between these two categories of return migrants at the level of pure type, and recognize the different orientations attached to each, in practice there is considerable overlap in that shifting perceptions of the situation justify movement from one position to the other.

There are conceptual problems inherent in defining return migration given the potential for rapid shifts in the perception of the situation to take place. Thus, while the responses of Rees's return migrants suggest intentional return, since they would give up better paid jobs to be closer to family in area of origin (Rees 1976), my own sample of return migrants are principally contingent returnees. Though their return itself is primarily a consequence of their affective ties into the area, for it is these ties which generated the information which enabled their re-entry, they would, however, have preferred to remain in Corby had redundancies not been imminent:

> We'd thought we'd finish our days there. We'd got the house and garden so nice. Our kids and grandkids were just round the corner. We were all set up for a good old age. We've got family here but it's not the same as our own bairns. We miss them. One son's talking of going off to Canada, and the other will no doubt follow him. Redundancy is not far away now and they'll be gone.
>
> (Peterhead returnee)

Thus my respondents fit primarily into the first of Lee's six categories: a change in the opportunity structure of the two areas occurs at a time when the network is established in both areas. While the out-migration may be chance transformed into system, the reverse migration follows network channels already prepared – back to the area of origin.

I wish to argue, therefore, that the postulated distance constraints on migration found in the conventional literature do not hold in terms of a return path. This is consistent with the notion that it is information and not transportation costs which constrain migration behaviour. I also wish to suggest that the responsiveness of Peterhead–Corby labour to return makes it part of the local labour market and that from the perspective of the individual return migrant there is little difference between movement within an internal labour market and movement over distance accomplished through an entry network at the level of information provision.

Return migration would also seem to be the most appropriate area in which to suggest a refinement of Stouffer's model of the impact of intervening opportunities on the volume of migration between two points (Stouffer 1940). He offers us a simple traversal model of information-gathering where information is general and obtainable by arrival on site. His model is one of competitive opportunity and as such is particularly inappropriate for return migration where the information distances between points are not adequately reflected by geographical distances. Return migration provides us with the extreme case where guaranteed opportunity in the area of origin must be balanced against competitive opportunity in other locations. Intervening opportunities have to be considered in terms of intervening information networks, as these determine opportunities. Intervening opportunities are thus particular and not general in their information base and as such are socially determined.

Return migrants as agents of social change

Much of the literature on return migration examines patterns of return where there has not necessarily been any change in the level of employment opportunities in the home area. Such return migrants are either labelled as 'failures' (e.g. by Davanzo and Morrison 1978), or viewed as conservative in their orientation, their return being explained principally in terms of affective considerations – an attachment of kinfolk and symbolic attachment to the area of origin (Illsley *et al.* 1963). My argument here is that with return migration of the type identified from Corby to Peterhead, which is explained purely in terms of employment expansion in the area of origin at precisely the point in time when contraction was taking place in the area of past reception, then return migrants may prove to be agents of social change rather than conservativeness. Part of the argument is specific to the mechanisms whereby redundancy was anticipated and a move was made in response. However, part of the argument also relates to the position of such migrants in the social networks of the area of origin.

The key characteristic of return migrants with respect to the local network is that they are both insiders and outsiders. Time spent outside the local network provides the space for the accumulation of and experience with new ideas and techniques, while network-based return to area of origin provides precisely the strong tie context in which diffusion of ideas can take place. Weimann has suggested the distinction between marginal and central agents – the importance of marginals is as importers of information precisely because of their contact with the outside, while widescale adoption of the new is attributed to the role of more centrally located agents (Weimann 1982). Return migrants can be both marginal and central in Weimann's sense, and where the individual's motivation for return migration is itself not conservative, we can expect return migrants to be agents of social change. For return migrants cannot be so easily ignored or described as alien by the local community as can the outsider. Hence containing changes introduced by return migration may prove more difficult.

However, while the returning migrants themselves may be potential agents of change, re-entry which is accomplished through the network mode militates against attempts at change, at least in the workplace. The mode of entry – via the existing network – may be the best method of containing the impact of values and ideas developed elsewhere. Thus my sample of return migrants had indeed been unionized in Corby, but they were now in a non-union sector (because that is where the original network was located and was tapped for direct recruitment) although they maintained at least some of their union consciousness. The respondents maintained, for example, that union activity was not necessary in small firms such as the one they were working for; it was a different case for larger establishments:[13] 'There's no need for a union here. You can speak straight to the boss. When there's only a few of you, he has to take more care not to stand on your toes. You can have him over the barrel no bother, if he plays unfair' (Peterhead returnee).

Although it is difficult to draw precise conclusions because of the different, and opposing, forces at work, I would surmise from the above evidence that among the return migrants, union membership and activity appear to be less constrained by general local values than by the scale of the organization within which the men are now working and the mode of introduction by which they entered.

Return migration and boom and bust

The exact nature of return migration is of interest not merely from the point of view of migration theory. The scale of return migration and the motivation of the returning population have important policy implications, over and above those of social change discussed in the previous sub-section. Consultant reports (Economist Intelligence Unit 1975) have so far assumed that oil-related migrants into the area have no previous contact with the area and have thus assumed that the propensity of this labour to re-migrate given conditions of economic adversity is higher on the part of this group than was its propensity to in-migrate in the first instance.

My material suggests that return migration did indeed take place and this is what one would have predicted upon the basis of the arguments concerning employers' recruitment practices presented in earlier chapters. Furthermore, this dynamic has been exacerbated by dramatic negative changes in employment opportunity in the area of destination. Much of the consultants' literature assumes that competitive models of employee search – critiqued earlier in this book – are in fact operating. My own concentration on information networks and their role in employment search leads one to expect that return migrants would be an important initial source of additional labour in the expanded local labour market. My fieldwork evidence indicates that this is indeed the case.

Where return migrants have returned on account of symbolic attachment, the need for replacement employment at the point of oil's rundown must be an important policy issue, for the desire to remain within the north east will push up local unemployment figures if no such policy is devised. As no estimation of the number of return migrants contained within the area has yet been arrived at, and consequently no research into attachment to the area has yet been conducted, assessing the scale of replacement employment necessary in the Grampian region at the point of rundown of North Sea oil is problematic.

Where return migrants to the north are purely involved in following employment opportunity – although note that the local networks which serve to introduce them to opportunities in oil are a special feature, and that they may not possess the necessary contacts to follow oil as it moves elsewhere – then the replacement employment required is likely to be of a lower order; fewer jobs will be needed. Indeed, it is probably the case that sections of the labour force will become attached to the nomadic oil industry. It is improbable, however, that this will be possible for the whole of the labour force – even were the whole of the labour force to be interested in pursuing such a nomadic form of existence.

A further policy problem is generated, however, if these networks prove sufficient for identifying and capturing employment opportunities outside the area, for if oil diverges from its customary practice and carries local labour away with it, levels of out-migration are likely to be high. Whilst high levels of out-migration do indeed reduce levels of local unemployment, they also adversely affect the prospects of attracting new replacement employment, for typically, high levels of out-migration result in the loss of skilled and semi-skilled workers first. These are the very workers whose retention is crucial to the attraction of replacement employment. Within Chapter 7, we saw that even where the rundown in an industry is planned, replacement employment policies are poorly developed. The rundown of oil, if its demise bears any resemblance to its development and to rundowns elsewhere, is likely to be an even more *ad hoc* affair.

The existing literature on migration indicates that where individuals have already migrated, the likelihood of repeat migration increases. On this count, return migrants are likely to possess a greater propensity to migrate on the rundown of oil than the more sedentary indigenous population. The literature however is silent on the probability of return migrants drawing in the previously more sedentary parts of their networks in such a re-migration. Oil was welcomed as reducing the level of out-migration from the area which was occurring in the previous decade. Typically, however, boom and bust industrial developments leave behind them higher rates of out-migration than those pertaining when they entered and contribute to even worse situations of depopulation than those holding pre-development. It is probable that the rundown of oil will exhibit this self-same pattern; furthermore, it is probable that return migrants will accentuate the degree of out-migration, both directly and indirectly, by eliciting migration from amongst their more sedentary networks.

Labour circulation: Glasgow–Corby

Up to now I have considered return migration simply as return to area of origin. However, I would now like to distinguish two categories of return migration: labour circulation and return migration proper. In the case of the latter, return to the home area is viewed as permanent (although circumstances may later operate so as to effectively change the situation). In labour circulation there is a persistent pattern of oscillation by the same individuals between the home and destination area. The Peterhead–Corby stream examined so far was an example of the former. Let us now turn to an example of the latter unearthed by my fieldwork – a pattern of labour circulation between Glasgow and Corby.

There is some historical evidence on labour circulation, for example in the work of Hareven on French Canadian migration to industrial New England (Hareven 1975a), in the work of Handley on nineteenth-century Irish migration to Scotland (Handley 1943), and in the work of Youngson Brown on Scottish migration to the USA (Youngson Brown 1953/4). All show persisting patterns of oscillation between a home base and employment elsewhere on an agricultural/seasonal basis. The contemporary discussion of labour circulation has largely taken place in the literature on migration in Africa. Indeed, the characterization of such movement as circulation is due to Mitchell, in his work on migration in Northern Rhodesia, as it was called at the time (Mitchell 1961). However, as Chapman and Prothero argue, Mitchell's basic assumption was that such circulation was

> a transitory form of population movement linked to particular processes and phases of socio economic change – notably urbanisation, modernisation and industrialisation. For Mitchell, the circulation of labour between village and town ceases once a rising social commitment external to the rural areas converges with the town based pull of ever expanding economic needs, although more recently Mitchell (1976: personal communication) has admitted that this process is occurring far more slowly in sub-Saharan Africa than he might have forecast 15 years ago.
>
> (Chapman and Prothero 1977: 4)

Chapman and Prothero go on to argue that circulation has and will endure in the Third World. Moreover, Wilkinson has pointed to new considerations – such as legal restrictions in South Africa – which further strengthen the role of labour circulation (Wilkinson 1982).

The bulk of the literature on labour circulation is thus either historical or related to the Third World, and in each case the circulation is between an agricultural/rural area of origin and an urban/industrial area of destination.[14] Labour circulation as a feature of modern industrial societies does not seem to have received much attention. Yet in my fieldwork I have identified a pattern of circulation between one urban industrial area, Glasgow, and another urban industrial area, Corby. Thus without legal restrictions, and without agricultural seasonality, we have labour circulation, and it is the object of this section to analyse its network basis.

Where an individual's social network is divided between two or more geographical locations, then the circumstances exist which provide for an oscillatory pattern. I have shown in previous chapters that social networks are important in the process of job search; the presence of parts of an individual's network in different geographical locations enables the individual to switch between jobs in one location to jobs in another more easily. The presence of contacts in more than one location hosts labour oscillation as and when vacancies become available in any of the areas.

My research shows that such a pattern of labour oscillation holds between Glasgow and Corby. In Chapter 7, I argued that the segregation of Corby from its hinterland prevented dissatisfied steel-workers from entering the local labour market. In order to obtain alternative employment they were obliged to migrate. Contacts were best in the Glasgow labour market and it is to this area that the migrants returned. Many went to Glasgow, only to return to Corby subsequently. The members of the McConnell employment net presented in Chapter 4 are involved in such a pattern of labour circulation, though such a pattern of labour circulation by no means characterizes all workers deriving from Glasgow. The Buchanan net, also presented in Chapter 4, demonstrates no such pattern. A number of sources (Champion, Clegg, and Davies 1977; Coopers and Lybrand 1979) confirm that a pattern of return to Glasgow was extensive, although none of these sources investigates the phenomenon of repeat entry to Corby.[15]

My respondents informed me that they experienced no difficulties in repeatedly re-entering the Corby works. Corby's demand for labour until the late 1970s permitted such a casual approach on the part of the less skilled members of the workforce. Within steel itself there is a dual labour market: at one end, length of service is important – the emphasis is on seniority with a clear historical promotion system.[16] At the other end there is a need for large numbers of unskilled labourers. It was in this category that the oscillating network was found:

> There's no skill in what I do. Just general labouring and donkey work. Not like some of the lads – real skilled jobs they have. With the labouring you can come and go as you like, nothing hangs on it. No responsibility, no promotion, no worries about coming and going.
>
> (Corby worker)

The respondent's account tallies with that of the labour management. Turnover is high within the unskilled workforce, and statutory holidays combined with the technological imperative of steel-making – that work carry on continuously – produces a seasonal pattern of labour demand. Thus temporary labour is required to carry the works over the holiday period; as a consequence, recruiting drives were undertaken immediately prior to this period, the expectation being that the labour attracted would remain for the necessary period. As Corby's labour manager said:

> We didn't have shut downs like the car industry. You can't do that with a furnace. So we did two things. We spread summer holidays out across a period from April to October. If you had a high summer holiday this year, it was your turn to have April or October next. And we recruited day labourers for the holiday period. We would start recruiting around May, June. We didn't recruit so much in the winter. In the holidays the day labourers would go up the promotion ladder to shift workers – more money, that means – and when we were back to full complement some of them would move back down again. Less money and they'd move on.

Viewing steel's labour requirements in this light, it becomes clear why patterns of labour circulation between Corby and Glasgow should have developed. Labour oscillation in this context is explained by the secondary character of employment provided to this group, the degree of seal around the local labour market so that individuals cannot find alternative employment without migrating, and the persistence of attachment to a social network elsewhere. This pattern of oscillation clearly depends upon the acceptance of repeat entry to the works by Corby management and the availability of vacancies in Glasgow.

Asked about the consequences of redundancy for their future, the membership of the net intended returning in the first instance to Glasgow. Within this net, redundancy had neither been anticipated nor come as a shock. Redundancy was to a large extent irrelevant – it ended their relationship with Corby and would be replaced by a similar relationship between Glasgow and somewhere else. The main attraction of steel had been that it provided the freedom to oscillate; Corby was a poor second to Glasgow and provided a paying destination when a Glasgow worker was made redundant one more time:

> Corby doesn't have the life that Glasgow does. It's dull; to be honest, every time I go back to Glasgow, I swear I'll never come back here again. But I always do. A good bit of my family's here and the money's good in the summer. That helps as well. I prefer Glasgow though; there's nowhere to beat it really.
>
> (Corby worker)

Conclusion

The analysis of this chapter, although it derives primarily from an interest in the response of Corby Scots to impending redundancy, has implications for network theory, migration theory, and for policy. Return migration is a particularly interesting vehicle for examining the old controversy in network theory on 'kinship versus friendship'. It is found that migrants returning to an area turn in the first instance to kin rather than friends for help – particularly residential help. Return migration also serves to emphasize the particularistic nature of migration and the information networks which provide the channels for this particularism, and return migration in anticipation of redundancy by part of a workforce opens up the question of the role of strong ties in conveying and sealing information within a network.

One type of return migration which I have identified – labour circulation – raises major issues for migration theory as regards the explanation of such a phenomenon in modern industrial societies: I have suggested that the network basis of this circulation may be a useful starting point. Finally, I would argue that it is of crucial importance to policy-makers to discover the extent of return migration to Scotland in the wake of the oil boom – the response of the regional labour markets in the post-oil period will be affected by the extent and nature of return migration. Yet the parameters of this pattern cannot be discovered from official statistics. A special survey is called for, and must clearly form a major area of further research. This, along with other fruitful areas of research, is taken up in the next chapter.

9
Conclusions and further research

During the 1950s and 1960s, there was considerable migration of Scottish workers and their families to the Corby steel works, in the heart of England. This was preceded by a similar migration from Scotland before the war, when the steel works were established. There was nothing random or individualistic about these migration streams. Rather, they represent the operation of systematic forces of network-based recruitment by the steel employers, and of network-based chain migration which followed in its wake. The latter period of migration has been the empirical focus of this book, but the theoretical focus is on the role of interacting information and kinship networks in preserving kin presence in the workplace.

I have demonstrated that simple name-cluster techniques may understate kin presence in the workplace because they do not take into account the role of female bridges between different parts of a network. As is clear from my investigation of the Sheldrake net in Basildon, it is the Sheldrake sisters who are the anchor of the network; yet a name-cluster technique based on their husbands' names would miss the net altogether. To a casual observer, there would appear to be minimal kin presence in the Carreras Rothman plant in Basildon. Indeed, on the basis of the current orthodoxy in industrial sociology and social-network analysis, such an investigation would not be undertaken in the first place.

Yet a number of studies do reveal the presence of kin in the workplace. But either they present themselves as exceptions to the rule or the identification of kin presence in the workplace is only a by-product of the main investigation, and no further analysis of the network basis of this kin presence is conducted. A useful strategy for future research, I would suggest, is to not dismiss any evidence of kin presence in the workplace as an exception, but to be on the lookout for this presence. The evidence collated from disparate literatures in Chapter 1, as well as my own primary evidence, suggests that what has been thought to be an exception need not be so – at least not in the working-class context. Certainly, there is a need for a more thorough and explicit investigation of the role of social networks in the organization of local labour markets and mainstream labour forces.

I have argued that there is indeed considerable evidence of an overlap between employment and kin in industrial societies, but perhaps the migrant context provides the analyst with the easiest trace on this overlap and on the mechanisms which underly it. Chapter 4 presented evidence on this – again from disparate literatures. Historical migration, rural–urban migration in developing countries, and contemporary international migration from developing to developed countries all provide ample evidence of the role of kin in employment-related migration.

This evidence is accepted and largely non-controversial. However, when it comes to contemporary internal employment-related migration in industrial societies, there is a strange disjuncture in the literature. Despite the existence of, albeit fragmented, evidence that such migration is a phenomenon of at least sufficient empirical significance to be worthy of further investigation, the modern sociological literature is strangely silent on it. And this despite the fact that during the post-war period a major plank of employment policy has been to encourage the mobility of labour from areas of high unemployment to areas of low unemployment.

The sociology of this mobility will bear further investigation. This book makes a start, first by indicating that the secondary evidence is of sufficient weight to be taken note of and, second, by investigating internal employment-related migration for a number of particular migration streams. Further research may be usefully concentrated in identifying other such migration streams to areas of employment opportunity within the UK.

Even short-distance migration streams – such as that from the East End of London to Basildon New Town, in which the Sheldrake net was to be found – would be useful to investigate – in order to identify the network basis of this migration and the role of employers and state employment agencies in inducing or hosting this migration.

The mention of the role of employers leads to another major area of further research which is suggested by the findings of this book. Attention has been drawn, by means of my case study, to the practice of direct recruitment by employers of labour over distance. One obvious answer as to why this practice exists is of course labour shortage in the local labour market. However, I have argued that this is too simple a view. Even were it true, it still leaves open the question of why employers concentrate their direct recruitment drives in some areas rather than others.

More generally, we have to allow the possibility that employers wish to shape their workforce to satisfy certain characteristics, and will recruit from areas where these characteristics are believed to be present. But their search procedures are more sophisticated than this. Even within such areas more screening is done, with the local employment exchange doing this screening in order to select workers with desired characteristics. At the empirical level, my case study establishes the existence of such practices in the UK, and the secondary evidence in Chapter 4 also speaks to this point. However, more case-study evidence is clearly needed for sectors other than those covered in Chapter 4, and this is a fruitful area for further research.

At the theoretical level the practice of direct recruitment and labour-force screening also raises some interesting questions. First, if employers so select their workforces, the workforce of any particular employer cannot be taken to be typical of the working class, at least not without a further investigation of the employer's recruitment practices. Second, there are good reasons, in theory and according to evidence, to believe that such screening processes – which specifically exclude generalized information on vacancies – enhance the role of information and kin networks, and increase the probability of kin-connected direct recruitment and hence of kin presence in the new workplace. I will take up each of these two points in turn.

In Chapter 6 I indicated that my fieldwork, although primarily designed to investigate the practice of direct recruitment from Peterhead to Corby, also turned up evidence of similar practices being used by the Vauxhall car works at Luton – the employers of the famous Affluent Workers studied by Goldthorpe *et al.* (1968a, 1968b, 1969). For that part of the Vauxhall workforce recruited in this manner, therefore, the claims of typicality and prototypicality have to be treated with caution. Even for that part of the workforce recruited from London, I have argued that high degrees of screening and selection were in operation. Three state agencies (London housing authority, London employment exchange, and Luton employment exchange) and the employers themselves were involved in selecting labour with particular characteristics. The extent to which the Luton sample was representative of the solidary working class is thus an important question to be answered.

On a methodological level, it is interesting to observe that the perceived mode of operation of labour-market search also determines research strategy. If search is seen as being individualistic and random, with employers broadcasting vacancies as widely as possible and workers searching in a generalized manner, then we might indeed believe that any particular workforce sampled might be approximately representative. However, if search and employment procurement follow particularistic and systematic channels, with employers attempting to fashion a workforce, and this being accompanied by network-related entry, then we cannot claim any particular sampled workforce as being representative of the whole working class, at least not without a detailed investigation of the recruitment mechanism which gave rise to the current composition of the workforce.

The arguments of this book have implications for network analysis, particularly for the notion that it is weak ties which are relevant and important in information transmission and job search. I have questioned this argument on theoretical as well as empirical grounds. As argued in Chapters 1 and 3, one of the reasons employers use the networks of the existing workforce is the efficiency of this procedure; but another reason is that networks carry within them mechanisms of sanction and control. Lads of dads can be controlled better because they have kin sanction operating on them, but the sponsoring worker also faces a control because the ability to sponsor is granted on the basis of past success and past performance – thus dads of lads are equally well controlled.

These mechanisms of sanction and control are predicated on strong ties and not weak ones. Why should a worker use his influence to ensure the employment of another to whom he is weakly tied? For that matter, why should he convey information about a vacancy to someone with whom he does not have strong ties? A critical test would be the difference between help given to friends and help given to kin. But, as we have seen in this book, most of the literature does not make this distinction whilst collecting data.

My fieldwork does indeed make this distinction, and the results are striking. In Chapter 4, I argued that in long-distance migration employment aid is more likely to be given to kin than to friends, and my case-study evidence bears this out. Similarly, in Chapter 5, I documented residential aid – again given primarily to kin. In Chapter 8, I discussed how the return migrants to Peterhead did not feel they could make direct and immediate call upon friends for help in the same way as they could on kin. All these arguments suggest that an important item on the agenda of future research on the role of networks in job search and aid must, at a minimum, distinguish between kin and friends, and not lump these two together into a single friends and relatives category.

My argument in this book also calls into question the frequency of contact measure which is usually employed in measuring the strength of a tie. It is obvious at once that such a measure will certainly be inappropriate in a migrant context, where the essence of the situation is aid given over distance, that is without any necessary physical contact in a recent period.

Particular attention was drawn to the problems posed, for the strength of weak ties accounts, by the adoption of a non-dyadic perspective. It was argued that aid patterns are frequently non-dyadic in character and that analyses of social exchange should be sensitive to the role of third parties and indirect ties in the process. I may render a service to U not because of any particularly close ties to U, but in repayment of a debt to C (C in turn being indebted to U). Once again, my fieldwork revealed such patterns in both employment and residential aid. It should be clear that frequency of contact between the two parties is inappropriate in explaining the transaction. Such an exchange is predicated upon two strong ties, the tie of I to C and the tie of C to U; unless this history of exchange is unearthed, then the role of weak and strong ties in social exchange is likely to be mischaracterized. This is precisely what occurs in the work of Granovetter. The investigation of such non-dyadic patterns of aid, I would suggest, is a fruitful area of research at both the theoretical and the empirical level.

I have argued in this book that the approach of network analysis, if suitably modified and extended, is a useful vehicle of analysis of the operation of labour markets – both local and migrant. It can provide a framework for understanding particularism in labour recruitment, the nature of information flow, and the highly directed nature of employment-related migration. Chapter 5 combined the approach of network analysis with that of vacancy chains in order to understand patterns of chain migration. Given an existing network, vacancy chains will follow particular paths.

The network pattern helps us to understand the sequencing of residential aid, for example, when such resources are restricted. However, one of the major arguments of this book is that while the network pattern provides an explanation of labour-market phenomena, these in turn influence the network pattern itself. Ties in a network are renewed by the exchange of favours. This exchange need not be contemporaneous, nor need it be dyadic, but a tie which forms the basis for such an exchange is further strengthened by the exchange. Moreover, in the case of non-dyadic exchange, new ties are formed where none (or only weak ones) may have existed before.

In Chapters 4 and 8, we have seen how annual holidays, alternating between the two locations, strengthen and renew kin relations within a geographically separated network. The patterns of labour oscillation discussed in Chapter 8 also serve to further strengthen ties and establish new ones. My empirical evidence thus speaks to this issue, while Chapter 5 investigated formal properties of the process in terms of measures of network density. However, more research – with case studies in other contexts – is clearly needed to back up this analysis.

Apart from the importance of networks in understanding employment-related migration, the arguments and findings of this book have further implications for migration theory which in turn suggest some fruitful areas for further research. In the sociological and economic literature on migration there is a debate about the innovative or conservative nature of migration. I have argued that any analysis must distinguish between the initial spearhead of migration and later parts of the migration stream. The chain migration that follows the initial spearhead has available to it a quite different structure of information and opportunities. In fact, the presence of network members in the area of destination reduces the risk element in migration to an extent that would question the characterization of this migration as innovative. Rather, this migration follows well-worn channels along network routes, with job search and residential aid being provided by network members.

I have argued that employers, even in contemporary industrial society, adopt recruitment strategies which serve to fashion migration streams. Where employers engage in direct recruitment to establish the initial spearhead as documented in Chapters 4 and 6, we must take account not only of incomplete information but of misinformation. It is clearly in the interests of the employer, involved in an expensive direct recruitment drive, not to provide information which may discourage migration. Similarly, the imperative for local employment exchanges is to reduce unemployment in their areas by encouraging migration. The question of migration under misinformation has not received much attention in the literature, and I would identify it as an important area for future research.

The above argument is also relevant to the often encountered view in the literature that return migration is failed migration. This view can be questioned whether it is the initial spearhead or the follow-up chain migration that is being considered. If the migration of the initial spearhead takes place on the basis of misinformation, it is not clear how return migration of the spearhead – if it occurs – can be classified as failure on the part of the individual migrants. On the other hand, if the initial migration is successful and the network establishes itself in both the old area and the new area, then different considerations arise. A pattern of labour circulation can arise whereby certain individuals oscillate between the two locations – this is documented in Chapter 8.

Return migration in this case can hardly be described as failure – it is simply the normal course of events. If, however, return migration takes place on the basis of a sudden loss of employment opportunity in the area of destination, again the return is a rational response to new economic circumstances outside the control of the individual. In my case study, return migration occurred in 1978 in anticipation of redundancy. If anything, this was a successful strategy on the part of my respondents and their network.

The network basis of migration thus provides some important insights into traditional debates on the nature of migration, and future research in the sociology of migration should take these into account. However, the role of employment exchanges in promoting migration of unemployed labour out of their area brings us to the arguments and evidence in this book on the role of state agencies in setting the parameters for the operation of labour markets. Further research is certainly called for here, and it is to this that I turn finally in this concluding chapter.

One of the important implications of the findings of the book is the need for further empirical research into job search, even in local labour markets. In the standard classifications of the literature, job information which is acquired via state employment agencies is classified as information acquired through formal channels, along with such things as newspaper advertisements, and in contrast to the friends-and-relatives category. However, I have argued that such a classification tends to overstate the importance of formal channels. While advertisements in Job Centre windows are clearly more akin to advertisements in newspapers (although even here word of mouth may be important in the speed of information transmission), it has been shown that not all jobs need necessarily be so advertised.

Employers are interested in generating not the largest number of applications, but the right number of applications of the right sort. Jobs under the table was the characterization of this process as given by one of my Corby respondents, and the importance of network connectedness in getting on to such lists was documented in Chapter 6. Future research should therefore treat the classification of state employment agencies as a formal channel of recruitment with caution.

The case study here shows the role played by state agencies not only in the process of direct recruitment from Scotland by the steel employers in Corby but also in the process of maintaining the monopsony of the steel employers in Corby. The planning powers which the state takes in designating a New Town, and which are meant to preserve a balanced development of industry and community, were, in the case of Corby, used precisely to maintain Corby as a one-industry town. Steel expansion was continually supported and other employers were kept out, but equally workers were kept in because of poor communication with the surrounding hinterland. In network terms, the population of Corby is weakly network-connected to the surrounding Northamptonshire countryside but strongly connected to its area of origin.

My fieldwork has, in fact, identified labour-market discrimination by the English employers of the surrounding area against Corby Scots, which is most akin to discrimination against ethnic minorities. The Scots accent persists in Corby, and accent is used as the method of identifying Corby labour. The suddenness of closure of the steel works, together with the above network properties, has led to return migration being almost the only available alternative to unemployment. The policy conclusion is clear: it is the imbalanced industrial and social development of Corby which greatly exacerbates the problems at closure. In both, state planning agencies have played their part.

It is, of course, in the interests of an employer to keep from his workforce any possible knowledge of redundancies to the very end. Otherwise skilled labour, and other labour, would start leaving in the run up to closure. However, it is not entirely possible to maintain such complete secrecy. Some members of the workforce read the signs of a rundown and leave in anticipation – these were the Peterhead returnees. But the network properties of information flow mean that such anticipation is highly segmented. These mechanisms were discussed at the theoretical level in Chapter 8, and at the empirical level I did indeed find that while some anticipated redundancy, to others it came as a complete shock. Of course, these mechanisms only come into operation if there is an overall attempt to keep the possibilities of redundancy a secret.

One policy conclusion is that the state should introduce more stringent redundancy disclosure requirements than are at present in operation – perhaps along the lines of the West German Co-determination Act. While inefficient from the point of view of employers, in the longer run it will be more efficient from the state's point of view because it will prevent, to some extent, major adjustment problems such as those in Corby at closure, as discussed in Chapter 7.

The focus in this book has been on the migration of Scots labour to Corby, and back again in anticipation of redundancy and in the wake of the oil boom in the north and north east of Scotland. Let us finally identify as an important area of further research a study of the possible consequences of the end of the oil boom. As was argued in Chapter 8, there has been substantial in-migration to the boom areas. Much of this labour is not indigenous and has migrated specifically in connection with oil – clearly this labour will leave with the rundown of oil. But what of return migrants? Our fieldwork has established significant return migration. This is only case-study evidence, however, and the major problem is that there is no way of discovering the overall extent of return migration from the UK official statistics.

So far as the nature of this return migration is concerned, from my fieldwork I have identified two forces. On the one hand, the migration is to the area of origin and is network based, so that when the oil boom fades there is a chance that some of these returnees might stay. On the other hand, the presence of the returnees might encourage out-migration at rates higher than before when there is once again a reversal of employment opportunities. Given the time and resources at my disposal, I could not delve deeper into these questions. Apart from improvements in official statistics, therefore, I would argue that there is a need for a large-scale survey specially designed to investigate the extent and nature of return migration to the north of Scotland.

Finally, my major conclusion is that there is substantial evidence of the continued role of kin networks in the social organization of employment in the contemporary period. Family relationships are relevant to the employment chances of the individual in a wide spread of geographical and occupational sectors. Kinship networks operate in modern western society as both employment information systems and employment sponsorship systems. Kinship remains of relevance to occupational choice and functioning in modern industrial society.

Appendix
Background information and research methods

2. Two case studies (fish processing and New Town data collection)

The object of the former of these two studies was, following on from the American labour-market studies, to identify the extent to which informal hiring practices were present in the British labour market. Taking Hill's lead, initially it seemed likely that such practices would be confined to those sectors which made extensive use of casual labour and in which workplaces were characteristically small. It was on this basis that the fishing sector of Aberdeen was chosen for study. In the course of this research, it became apparent that informal hiring practices are by no means confined to the small scale nor to the sphere of casual employment alone, rather they are prevalent in British industry. This understanding, an outcome of the fishworker research, leads us into the study of the Basildon New Town net. Within the social group studied, the source of employment shifted easily between the large and the small scale; the nature of contracts varied enormously, moving from fixed to casual conditions of engagement with an apparent ease unpredicated by the existing literature. What caused us to select the particular workplaces and groups studied?

To commence with the fish-processing data, in an initial survey of the fishing sector of Aberdeen 203 fish-processing establishments were identified. These were identified from the Aberdeen telephone and trade directories. One half of these establishments, randomly chosen, were contacted by telephone. The owner, supervisor, or personnel manager of the enterprise was interviewed on the telephone on this first contact about the size of the establishment, workforce composition, workforce stability, and recruitment methods. There were no refusals. Ten of these were subsequently chosen for in-depth interviews. This sample was stratified so as to capture a variety of circumstances.

These in-depth interviews with employers were all conducted at the workplace and took between two to three hours each, with one exception – establishment A – where research stretched over three days. Part of these interviews with employers was conducted on a formal basis whilst the remaining part consisted of accompanying the interviewee around the workplace as he attended to his normal business. Each interviewee was asked to conduct business as normal despite the presence of the researcher and asked to respond to the normal demands of his position as and when they occurred. Indeed, obtaining these rather lengthy interviews was precisely predicated upon adopting such a flexible approach to interruptions. Thus interviews were subject to interruption; however, this was not without its benefits as it permitted the researcher a higher level of integration into the workplace than is conventionally the case.

In establishment A, research was conducted on a participant observation basis for three days, with the researcher performing a range of routine unskilled tasks. Part of the reason for the adoption of this role was to gain better access to the fishworkers themselves. Fifteen fishworkers, ten of whom were randomly chosen in this workplace and five of whom were socially connected to it, were formally interviewed as a consequence of the access provided by the adoption of this role. All of these interviews were conducted outside the workplace. Informal conversation in the workplace was also an important source of research material; each approach was used as a counterbalance to the other.

A further fifteen fish girls drawn from the other establishments in our qualitative sample were interviewed. These interviews also took place outside of the work environment. Each of these formal interviews took approximately one to one-and-a-half hours apiece. Names used are those found in the research setting, but these have been switched around so that they attach to different individuals from their true owners; anonymity and authenticity are thus both preserved. No formal interview schedule was used, as the research was conceived of primarily as a pilot study but the use of an *aide mémoire* ensured a general similarity to the structure of each interview.

The object of the Basildon New Town study was to investigate the quality of repeated or recurrent employment transactions or exchanges within a single kinship group. It was necessary therefore to obtain data for a relatively long span of time. Ease of access to interviewees would clearly be crucial, as the length of time required to be studied was likely to necessitate the checking and rechecking out of a complex set of data with the various respondents. Furthermore, I wanted a sample from a New Town which was sufficiently close to the area of origin of its present inhabitants for workers to remain in contact with the employment networks of the old location.

This was intended as an explicit contrast with Corby, where the population is drawn from far-removed geographical locations. Also, I wanted a sample drawn from a town which contained more than one employer and more than one industry. Ideally, I wanted a sample that was experiencing the threat of imminent redundancy in order to render it truly comparable with Corby.

All these characteristics were found in the Sheldrake family of Basildon New Town. Family membership provided the access. Redundancy was declared early in 1984 in the enterprise which has been at the core of this group's Basildon work experience; final closure date was early in April 1984. I make no attempt to assess the typicality of this net, nor am I arguing that it is representative of the East End migrant family. It is argued, however, that the existence of such a web of employment and kin relations indicates that the conventional tale about economic co-operation by kin in modern industrial society exhibits a number of lacunae.

Personal knowledge and convenience of access determined the choice of this particular kin group for study. No real surnames have been used in this case – except that of Sheldrake, as given to the whole net, which is taken from the maiden name of the matriarch of this family. All interviews have been conducted informally and in the context of participant observation, with a number of individuals being interviewed repeatedly.

Benefiting from Firth's insight on the existence of kin keepers within the British family group, I first located this pivotal individual and obtained information on the outline structure of employment relations within this kinship group over the last forty years. Thereafter I proceeded to fill in the details by interviewing the relevant workers. Personal knowledge of the structure helped when prompts were necessary. It is unlikely that such detail could have been generated in the context of an initial impersonal contact.

Research on this net commenced in November 1977, with the last interview being conducted in February 1984. The research is on-going. No employers were contacted within this substudy, although application has been made for access to that part of the records of Carreras Rothman which covers family employment.

4. Migration, kinship, and recruitment policies

The telephone directory and electoral registers for Corby were scanned for name clusters – the former source, although less complete, providing for readier identification of same-name frequency within the geographical area as a whole. Taken together the electoral register – which is arranged on an address rather than upon an alphabetical basis – and the telephone directory provided for the easy identification of numerous name clusters within Corby. The name clusters were selected at random, although many more are present within these sources – I identified 201 Scottish name clusters within Corby and its immediate vicinity.

Contact letters were sent out to three households bearing each of these names. The research intention was to snowball through these networks of selected individuals. My assumption was that name clustering provided a good first indicator of potential connectedness. Care was taken not to saturate these name clusters with contact letters, as, if indeed connectedness existed, refusal by one party might lead to refusal by a whole network. To the thirty letters sent out there were twenty-five responses. No follow-up letters were sent out, as once again it was felt that such pressure could lead to those who had already consented being persuaded to change their minds.

These twenty-five pilot interviews gave access to fifteen networks – some persons with same surnames belonging to different kinship systems – of which two were chosen for detailed investigation. As my object was to trace out the possibilities of kin presence in the workplace rather than to generate a representative sample, a position which was very much informed by resource constraints, I selected the two networks to which the pilot interviews gave me best access: the Buchan and Buchanan employment nets. Thus for these two networks my pilot sample generated four and five points of entry respectively. Different surnames were contained within the same kinship system. I decided on the jackpot approach. If kin existed in any strength at all in the workplace, then the problems for the orthodox understanding of the relationship between the family and work were many. It was this understanding which dictated the line of research.

In the twenty-five pilot interviews, I asked a highly preliminary set of questions, the two major issues being whether the respondent had any kin in Corby and whether she or he was willing to introduce us to other members of kin so present.

All twenty-five sets of my respondents had at least one member of their kin network in Corby, apart from spouse and offspring, and there is no reason to suppose that there is any difference between the eight name groups, or thirteen networks, discarded and the two selected either in terms of kin presence or employment help. However, my research material is insufficient to any deeper discussion of this issue.

The two networks chosen were subsequently snowballed with fifty persons in all being interviewed. There was no attempt made to control the snowball, and introduction after the four initial interviews in the Buchan net and five initial interviews in the Buchanan net always occurred through the network itself. Although name-cluster material was used on occasion as a prompt, it was never used directively.

Anonymity was promised – as is normal in urban anthropology. Thus the real names of individuals are not used anywhere in the text, though the names within each net have been kept, but have been switched around and attached to different persons within the same net. It is an attempt to retain the authenticity of the structure whilst at the same time meeting the promise of anonymity.

The sample contains both workers and their spouses, the hypothesis lying behind such an approach being that the kinship systems of both parties to a marriage are mobilized in the search for male employment in the manual sector. Thus wives represent an important part of the job search process. My selection of interviewees enabled the investigation of this particular hypothesis.

Access to the McConnell net was obtained by advertising for lodgings. Both formal interview and participant observation research methods were used in studying this particular network. Study of the McConnell net preceded research on the other two kinship groups. Field study commenced in January 1980 coinciding with the national steel strike, which greatly facilitated the interviewing of male steel-workers. By commencing investigation on a participant observation basis, it was hoped that increased sensitivity would result before the formal interviewing schedule began.

Lodging was a most useful anthropological approach, as it not only gave the opportunity for the collection of more detailed information but also permitted the re-asking of questions. Over time the research relationship to the McConnell net became more intimate and as a consequence responses to questions were more complete. Living with the family produced different presentations of self from those experienced in the formal interview format. Twenty interviews were conducted within this kin network, although casual contact was had with a great many more people connected to the McConnells.

5. Vacancy chains and family networks

Information on residential aid in Corby was collected by two methods. First, individuals both male and female were interviewed against a questionnaire which asked specific questions on residential aid.

Second, accommodation was sought as a lodger in a private household and material was collected by participant observation. Lodging itself permitted a discussion of the rules around this event with the host family. Participant observation permitted access to better quality material on the rules applied both to kin and to non-kin than could have been accomplished on the basis of formal interviews alone. Research was conducted on this basis from January to May 1980.

6. Constructing a workforce

An awareness of Pocock's work on Scots migration to Corby led me to identify Peterhead as a major sending area of labour. As I found return migrants from Corby in the context of a Scottish Office study of the impact of North Sea oil on the north of Scotland, it seemed likely that substantial return migration from this area to Peterhead was taking place. This labour when interviewed believed that redundancy was imminent in Corby. There was reason to suppose that the volume of return migration would increase.

In order to establish the parameters of return, an interview was sought and conducted with an officer of the Peterhead employment exchange in March 1978. This officer confirmed that return from Corby was occurring. Asked about the pattern of migration out of the area over the previous twenty years, he was unable to assist personally but arranged for an introduction to the employment-exchange officer responsible for administering the migration arrangements for the twenty to twenty-five years previous. This officer was still a working member of the bureau and arrangements were made to interview the officer on the same day. It was an unexpected bonus.

This officer alerted me to the previous presence of Vauxhall recruitment teams in the area and provided detailed information on the form taken by Vauxhall's recruitment drives. This material was somewhat at divergence with the account of migratory behaviour provided by the Affluent Worker studies. I therefore attempted to locate Vauxhall's labour manager of the period. This I was unable to do. In August 1979, however, I interviewed a personnel officer from Vauxhall's Luton plant and he confirmed the information provided by the Peterhead employment-exchange officer.

Subsequently to interviewing the Vauxhall personnel officer, I interviewed a Corby labour manager involved in the recruitment of labour from Peterhead to Corby, and he also confirmed the presence of Vauxhall recruiting teams in the area. Corby's labour manager was interviewed twice – the first interview was essentially a contact interview only and lasted but for one hour; the second interview was more detailed in character and lasted for three hours. It was conducted in two parts, a formal taped interview and an off-the-record discussion over lunch. The second interview took place in June 1983.

In March 1980 an employment-exchange officer in Corby was interviewed on the recruitment practices of companies then advertising for labour in the areas. My coverage of direct recruitment to Corby and Luton, of labour migration and direct recruitment from Corby to Luton, of forward migration elsewhere, and of return migration to Peterhead is founded in the interviews reported in Chapter 4 and the interviews with five officials and personnel managers responsible for administering state and employer migration schemes.

Unfortunately I did not have the necessary resources to trace and interview the Glasgow and Luton employment-exchange personnel for the period studied.

7. Corby

Corby labour reported difficulty in obtaining employment in the local hinterland – a position which was supported by the official statistics. The 1961 census workplace table shows that of 11,600 economically active male residents of Corby, only thirty were employed in Wellingborough and 350 in the municipal borough of Kettering. In order to ascertain the accuracy of this perception, it was decided to sample employers in the two nearest market towns, Kettering and Wellingbor-ough.

Eight companies in Wellingborough and eight companies in Ketter-ing were selected for interview from the telephone directory. From each location one enterprise was chosen in each of the following sectors: packaging, injection moulding, electrical components, warehousing, transport, construction, plastics, and engineering. These sectors were chosen on the basis of the jobs that my informants said they had unsuccessfully applied for. Within the sectors the companies were chosen at random. Initial contact was made by telephone rather than letter, in the belief that this was more likely to generate a positive response to the request for an interview. There were no refusals.

The telephone contact was subsequently followed up by a short interview in each case. The firms all employed between thirty and seventy employees. Recruitment was primarily by word of mouth, though all of these companies had advertised at some time in the past for labour. Half of them made use of an external vacancies board. These interviews confirmed the perceptions of Corby labour as to the existence of direct, as well as indirect, labour-market discrimination. Similar results were obtained by Coopers and Lybrand in their commissioned study of the region.

These interviews all took place in April 1980.

8. Return migration from Corby

The twenty Corby return migrants to Peterhead, and five of their spouses, were identified by snowballing through a network of contacts. Marsden used a similar technique in his study of the workless. Peterhead friends and acquaintances were asked by the researcher to supply an introduction to any return migrants from Corby who were known to them. This generated three independent contacts into the one return network studied. Arrangements were made through these contacts for introduction to the rest of the network, the initial contact always taking place on the basis of having a drink together and proceeding upon a highly informal basis.

Subsequent interviews took place in a variety of venues; hotels, homes, and even the harbour. The first set of interviews took place in March 1978 and were followed up by a second set in July, August, and September of the same year. No participant observation was used.

No formal interviews were conducted either with the employers of this labour or with the workplace contacts who had guided their return into local employment.

The twenty workers interviewed worked across five enterprises and were interconnected by kin linkages – although many of these were indirect. These five enterprises were all in the small engineering sector, a sector whose volume of business has been dramatically increased by oil.

These twenty-five individuals provided the names and addresses of ten relatives still living in Corby. These relatives were interviewed in January/February 1980 during the period of the national steel strike and after redundancy had been announced.

Notes

1. Kinship and economic life

1. Christopher provides a statement on and a critique of this position (Christopher 1965: 183–4).
2. Lupton and Cunnison direct our attention to the need for an anthropology of the workplace which considers such factors (Lupton and Cunnison 1964: 127).
3. See, for instance, the work of Firth, who argues that there is 'a marked lack of economic co-operation with kin' in western society (Firth 1956: 14), but he also argues, and apparently without recognizing the contradiction, that kin aid one another in the procurement of work (p. 61).
4. Brody, coming from the new American labour history, pulls together evidence from a number of sources to demonstrate the continuing importance of the family in social organization of work in industrial society. He critiques the 'old' labour history, which focused solely upon the formal and aggregate aspects of labour's activities (see Brody 1979: 111–26).
5. See, for instance, Hechter for a discussion of the role of employment information networks in the preservation of ethnic community in the USA (Hechter 1978: 293–318).
6. Scott et al.'s research into the steel industry demonstrated the strength of kin ties not only in local employment search but also in search over distance. Talking of a shearer who had been recruited over distance by his present employer, Scott reports: 'He accepted the offer and from that time until 1912, he frequently returned to his native district to recruit other skilled sheet metal workers for the growing number of "Staffordshire mills" in the plant' (Scott et al. 1956: 46).
7. Another supporting study is that of Mackay et al. (1971). Mackay found that 53 per cent of all hires in Glasgow and 66 per cent of all hires in Birmingham occurred on the basis of informal information processes – friends, relatives, and casual applications.
8. Note that this finding is in conflict with Granovetter's argument that smaller establishments are most likely to make use of personal contacts as a

recruitment channel (Granovetter 1974: 128). Granovetter's sample was, however, composed of professional, technical, and managerial employees. Other evidence – Jenkins *et al.* (1983), Manwaring (1982), Hareven (1975a; 1975b) and Handley (1943) – does support Brown *et al.*'s 1981 finding that large establishments make extensive use of personal contacts in recruiting labour.

9. Yet another, more recent example of the strength of connections between the existing workforce and direct applicants is to be found in the steel industry itself. Some 700 men applied for thirty jobs, none of which had been externally advertised at British Steel's Roundwood Bar Mill Works, Rotherham in early 1984. Details of the jobs were only advertised on internal notice boards. Reported in the *Sun*, 7 February 1984: 4.

10. Hill was aware of but did not attempt to trace out the network of distant and secondary kin linked by shared occupation and workplace. This is precisely the exercise I attempt on Corby steel-works labour in Chapter 4.

2. Two case studies

1. Marion Miller assisted in the collection of data. A preliminary report of the survey findings was published in Grieco and Miller (1978). The in-depth interviews presented here were conducted alone and subsequent to the general survey.

2. By porterage I mean lifting and carrying internal to the workplace, not harbour porterage, which is a different matter altogether.

3. Torry is an area of Aberdeen which neighbours the harbour area, where most of the fish houses are to be found.

4. Lee and Wrench noted a similar reluctance to employ labour living outside the area amongst Birmingham employers. The same rationale – bad time-keeping – was advanced (Hill and Wrench 1981).

5. Where there is an employer dependence on casual labour, we should also expect – as Hill (1976) points out – a heavy use of social networks in employment search. The existence of such networks serves to stabilize a situation of uncertainty. Preferential hiring, in such circumstances, guarantees employment to a core of workers and provides employers with screening and control capabilities that could not be achieved if selection was random.

6. See Thompson, Wailey, and Lummis (1983) for evidence on the social organization of fish processing in the area historically.

7. Nevertheless, they have good working relationships with the rest of the workforce.

8. An individual who is not connected by kinship, friendship, or employment aid to any other member of the workforce.

9. See Kahn (1964), Wedderburn (1965), and Mann (1973).

10. For an overview of social-network membership on choice of romantic partner, see Milardo (1983). This review, however, does not tackle the special relationship between social network and romantic choice within occupational communities.

11. Twenty-seven members of this partial network of thirty-nine were interviewed. Information on the composition of the net was obtained from at least three sources independently.

12. Shared workplace may act to strengthen the kinship definitions holding

between generations. As one of Allan's respondents indicated of his relationship to his brother who was seventeen years older: 'I never knew I had a brother till I was fifteen and started to work with him' (Allan 1979: 106).

13. Knowing that father and son have the same occupation does not of itself tell us how the situation came to be, yet there is a tendency in the literature to assume that answer is obvious – direct occupational inheritance (Hill 1976).

14. Young and Wilmott argue that kinship relations in job procurement are less important in the contemporary period than they were historically. They have, however, focused solely upon father–son occupational inheritance as a measure; as my data shows, the relationship between family and work is more complex. Expanding the analysis to include other kin relationships reveals a more vigorous role for the family in job procurement (Young and Wilmott 1957: 94–103).

15. Barnes (1979) discussing Kapferer's (1969) analysis of network ties in his famous cell-room study indicates the problems occasioned by Kapferer's failure to take account of the relationships external to the cell room which nevertheless link its members and affect their behaviour. It is precisely this relationship which I have attempted to capture here.

16. See Whipp (1983). See also Mann (1973), who identifies sixteen husband–wife pairings in one workforce but makes no further remark on the phenomenon.

17. For a discussion of female workers in the tobacco industry, see Pollert (1981).

3. Social networks

1. Surveying the US labour-market literature, Granovetter calculated that, depending on the exact question asked, between one-sixth and one-half of all persons entering a new employment contract do so upon the basis of a personal contact in the new workplace (Granovetter 1983). Given the mounting evidence of the extensive use of the existing workforce as a recruitment channel in the UK, it can reasonably be assumed that such figures also hold for the UK. The use of personal contacts as a recruitment and information channel, far from being anachronistic, is an extensive modern practice.

2. Tacit skills approximate to, although they are not fully identical with, the concept of anticipatory socialization developed in an earlier period. Ammasari, writing on blue-collar workers in the modern industrial sector, discusses the role of the family in anticipatory socialization to work: 'Recently, J.H. Goldthorpe has called attention to the importance of "the orientations which mediate between the objective features of the work situation and workers' actual experience of and reaction to this situation". However, he fails to see the inter-play between family occupational tradition, personal experience and, before being a car assembler, industrial sector satisfaction' (Ammasari 1969: 12).

3. See Allan for an analysis of kinship and friendship which greatly underestimates workers' role in the employee selection process (Allan 1979: 2). Critiquing the occupational community literature, in the new idiom of the 'privatized' worker derived largely from his reading of Hill and Goldthorpe, Allan argues that working-class patterns of sociability are

accidental not purposeful; dense networks are an accident of residence not an indication of preference. Job assistance is unconsidered in this analysis, yet a multitude of studies speak to its role in such communities. A thorough consideration of this factor causes me to reject Allan's theorizing (Allan 1979: 71–5). Note that Allan's own study was of a small commuter village and not of an industrial urban area.

4. As we have already seen, the volume of employment applications generated through public advertising in a period of recession may encourage companies to recruit solely through their internal notice boards.

5. The anthropologist Wolf, discussing the relationship between the family and reputation, has this to say: 'It is notable that a relationship continues to exist between the way in which a family carries out these multi-purpose tasks and the ways in which it is evaluated in the eyes of the larger community. The family not only performs all the tasks we have just described; it remains also, even where ties of kinship are highly diffuse, the bearer of virtue, and of its public reflection, reputation' (Wolf 1966: 2). Although Wolf does not directly examine employment relations in modern industrial society through this perspective, it is clearly appropriate to do so.

6. Granovetter fails to appreciate the difference between those to whom one is weakly tied having better access to job information and those to whom one is weakly tied providing better access to job information; possession does not guarantee transmission. Furthermore, it is not at all clear that the possession of information of itself without the accompanying exercise of influence is sufficient to secure opportunity. Granovetter's assumption is that the transmission of information is costless, but the same argument cannot be applied to the exercise of influence.

7. Brinley Thomas, the economic historian, has also something to say on the topic: 'When net advantages are considered from the point of view of the family as a unit, there can be little doubt that the costs of movement for the average household in Lancashire are much higher than in a coal mining area. It is also well known that short-time and under-employment are regarded as in the nature of things in the cotton districts: even in a most severe depression it is not very often that all members of a Lancashire family are out of work at the same time. Conditions are, therefore, materially different from those found in the depressed coalfields' (Thomas 1938: 417).

8. In their account of the mining occupational community, Dennis *et al.* provide us with a number of examples of the customary segregation of information within situations conventionally characterized as of the strong tie variety – husband–wife. Of particular interest is his material on male concealment of wage size (Dennis *et al.* 1956: 186–9).

9. Laumann's Detroit study provides an example of one study in which data was collected from both parties to the 'dyadic' friendship relationship (Laumann 1973: 33). 54.2 per cent of choices were not reciprocated, that is to say, one party understood a strong tie to exist where the other party perceived it as weak. This finding has important consequences for Granovetter's approach, which only permits of a symmetric strong- or weak-tie relationship.

10. Note, however, that Granovetter's categories are too wide to provide sufficient discriminatory power. For example, a contact of the frequency of once a week, which is open to being viewed as very high, on Granovetter's

interval scale counts as occasional and, by association, weak. Furthermore, such contacts are pooled with relations which have a frequency as low as once a year. See also Allan (1979: 10–12) for a critique of frequency of contact as the sole measure of quality or relationship and Bell (1968: 85–6).

11. In Granovetter's sample 68.7 per cent found their present job through past work contacts.

12. For instance, within the Affluent Worker study it is established that even in a 'new unsettled' migrant community high rates of sibling presence may be found (overall 35 per cent of husbands' siblings and 40 per cent of wives'), with low rates of sibling contact, whereas high rates of contact with parents were found. This was assumed to indicate weak ties between siblings; this however fails to take account of the actors' awareness of the efficiency of their network for purposes of remaining in contact. See also Piddington (1965: 161) for an empirical demonstration of indirect links in maintaining communications within a kinship system. My focus on the role of indirect communication and support in the maintenance and establishment of community parallels Firth's identification and analysis of the role of "pivotal kin" on whom other members depend for much of their kin knowledge and communication' (Firth 1956: 62). For a similar analysis see also Allan (1979: 104).

13. Firth noted that there is a contingent aspect to many kin ties which 'implies also that if the third party is no longer there, the kin tie may lapse'. Put in different terms, characterizing the exchange between B and C as purely dyadic when it is dependent upon the relationships between A and B and A and C persisting is problematic. Indirect qualities of any exchange may be as important as 'direct', that is observed, factors. See Firth *et al.* (1969).

4. Migration, kinship, and recruitment policies

1. 'America money' paid for at least three-quarters of all Irish emigration to the United States between 1848 and 1900. See Kennedy (1973: 22). Christopher makes the important point that a money economy permits the extended family greater geographical flexibility. Ties can be maintained through remittances and over greater distances, money can be converted into aid in situations of physical absence. See Christopher (1965).

2. See also Adams (1932: 405) for evidence on employer funding of migration. Berthoff provides extensive evidence on the involvement of US employers in inducing labour migration (Berthoff 1953). He cites many instances of systematic linkages between a specific UK origin and a specific US destination. A particularly graphic example is labour migration from Macclesfield to the US industrial town of Paterson; between 1870 and 1893 15,000 Macclesfielders arrived in the new destination. He provides us with further information on labour contracting: 'The American mills, some of which were established by British manufacturers, imported English hands until Congress in 1885 forbade labour contracts: even thereafter their agents advertised for men in Yorkshire newspapers and came to tacit wage agreements, unenforceable and often unhonoured, with emigrating opera- tives' (Berthoff 1953: 39).

3. For information on organized labour's resistance to employers' use of immigrant labour, in this case Chinese labour (the Chinese Exclusion Act 1882), see Masson and Guimary (1981). See also Ehrlich (1974) for a

discussion of the resistance of organized labour to the use of contract labour and for information on the use of direct recruitment by US employers in order to change the character of their workforce and make it less militant. The manipulation of different labour sources and ethnic groups by employers in order to obtain cheaper and more pliable workforces is well recognized in the New American Labor History.

4. Mormino explicitly presents his analysis as a contrast to the conventional literature which characterizes migration as an uprooting process, challenging the dominant stereotype of Handlin and followers. See Handlin (1951) and Mormino (1982).

5. Lest it be thought that Hareven's evidence relates to the small scale and is thus of limited consequence for the modern enterprise, note that Hareven stresses that the enterprise involved was large scale with an annual workforce of between 12,000 and 14,000 workers (Hareven 1975).

6. Note that Hareven's American evidence (Hareven 1975) is also for the textile industry.

7. The British literature on job search in the context of geographic mobility is highly fragmented – indeed the labour-market economist, P.B. Beaumont, has this to say on the topic: 'In Britain, there has been little or no empirical investigation of the job finding process involved in geographical mobility' (1977b: 62–3).

8. The Affluent Worker team devoted but the barest of attention to labour recruitment practices in a situation where the bulk of the labour force (71 per cent) was drawn from outside the local labour market boundaries. The most detailed statement we are offered on the topic is the following: 'The growth of Luton's industry has produced a situation of chronic labour shortage to which the continuous influx of migrants has been the response. Even so, several Luton firms have at various times had to organize national recruiting campaigns' (Goldthorpe *et al.* 1969: 45).

9. Kahn explicitly recognizes the importance of networks over distance in employment search, when she argues that national ties were important in the composition of the workforce. In establishing this argument she quotes an Irish worker at the plant: 'Well, a chap from home in Ireland was working at . . . and when he was home on holidays, he told me I should come over and try' (in Kahn 1964: 49). 'This kind of thing', Kahn argues, 'no doubt helps to explain some interesting differences in the proportion of various nationals found in different companies' (Kahn 1964: 49).

10. Lupton provides some further evidence in his discussion of the Manchester garment industry. 'Levine's lot', a group of female garment workers, had moved en masse from one factory to another – last employer was a shared employer – and formed a cohesive group within the new workplace (Lupton and Cunnison 1964).

11. Mann provides evidence on husband–wife teams working in Bird's as well as parent–offspring teams. The propensity to relocate was related to having another family member working within the firm (Mann 1973: 156, 181, 199).

12. Put differently, 'the current spatial allocation of migrants is a function of the spatial allocation of migrants during the previous time period. This hypothesis has been tested and substantiated in a number of American studies' (Beaumont 1977b: 62).

13. A particularly good example of the relationship between spearhead and subsequent chain migration is furnished by Leonard Moss in a personal

communication to Macdonald and Macdonald: 'The Bagnolese migration (from Abruzzi-Molise) to Detroit is a typical chain effect. . . . The Detroit cluster sprang from a single migrant (and his family) who persuaded others to follow. One family remains the central focus around which the local Bagnolese revolve' (Macdonald and Macdonald 1969).

14. This is comparable to the 'rate and incidence' of migration discussion opened by Mitchell – with the reservation that instead of focusing on the characteristics of individuals, our attention is focused on the characteristics of groups. See Mitchell (1970).

15. See Petersen (1970).

16. A clear and eloquent recognition of this point occurs in the work of Wood and Cohen. They argue that limiting the focus of redundancy studies to situations in which official notices have been given out is a serious theoretical error. For rumours and instability may be such that workers even leave in anticipation of redundancy. They argue that unofficial notice – the rumours circulating amongst the workforce – must be regarded as part of the process. It is an argument which exactly parallels our own and is borne out by the research results presented on anticipation of redundancy in Chapter 8 (Wood and Cohen 1977/8).

17. Docherty reports of Shotton, a steel town in many ways similar to Corby: 'It was not uncommon in the Shotton area for entire families on both sides to be employed at the works with steel traditions going back three generations' (Docherty 1983: 136).

18. Note that this is a different measure from that provided in Tables 4.1b, 4.2b, 4.3b, as it is anchored on the current workforce.

19. C.R. Walker, *Steel Town*, New York: Harper, 1950, p. 264.

20. Unfortunately, Walker does not provide a figure for past and present employees taken together, so we are unable to compare on this score.

21. Note that Granovetter takes a highly simplistic approach to influence (Granovetter 1974). Individuals are regarded as either possessing it or not; processes of contestation, shifting boundaries of control, and timing factors are disregarded.

22. Scott *et al.* also identify the difficulties inherent in separating out actually being spoken for and the implicit reference contained in the employer's knowledge of the family (Scott *et al.* 1956). They pass over the matter quickly, without registering the implications of this situation for a discussion of power relations within the family.

23. Personal communication from Dian Hosking, October 1982.

24. Family control can be viewed as a substitute for close supervision in the workplace. Close supervision has a number of deleterious effects that make the former arrangement preferable. See Kahn and Katz (1958).

25. See Pahl for the treatment of a similar point (Pahl 1980: 7).

6. Constructing a workforce

1. The three books which form the study are Goldthorpe *et al.* 1968a, 1968b, and 1969. Note that 71 per cent of the Affluent Worker sample were not natives of Luton or the Luton area (Goldthorpe *et al.* 1968b: 9).

2. Information supplied by Peterhead labour-exchange officer who administered the recruitment arrangements; March 1978.

3. The availability of such standing arrangements to employers was widely advertised in the pages of the *Ministry of Labour Gazette* throughout the

1950s. Appearing as a standard item was the following: 'Placing work of the employment exchanges: ... employers who do use the Employment Exchange system may, in certain circumstances (e.g. when they require large numbers of additional work people, or where labour of the kind required is scarce), have a 'Standing Order' with the Employment exchange to submit all suitable applicants to them without 'notifying' any specific number of vacancies, and the vacancies remaining unfilled in such cases will not be included in the figures' (taken from the *Ministry of Labour Gazette*, January 1954, p. 21). One consequence of such an arrangement, as the official source indicates, is that the external visibility of vacancies is radically diminished.

4. Interviews with Corby workers reported in Chapter 4 and information provided by Corby manager, June 1983.

5. Beaumont in his study of geographic mobility (Beaumont 1977a; sample size: 222) under the auspices of the Employment Transfer Scheme – a study which covers migration between Scotland and the 'one plane dominated labour market centres of Corby, Dagenham, Luton and Rugby' – notes that the use of formal channels (60 per cent formal to 40 per cent informal) is greater than that found in local labour-market studies. He does not discuss employer direct recruitment strategies, nor does he consider the extent to which informal contacts may be important even within formal channels. Thus he finds that 33 per cent of Corby respondents claimed that they had found their jobs as a consequence of information generated by relatives and friends but the prospect that these respondents found their jobs both through relatives and friends and through the employment exchange is not considered. Beaumont regards job finding as a one-channel outcome, but our evidence suggests that this is not necessarily the case.

6. However, contract labour from less economically developed areas is still harnessed by modern industrial society. The extensive use of such labour represents a largely unrecognized challenge to those characterizations of advanced industrial society which focus purely upon free wage-labour. Contract labour clearly represents the construction of a form of unfree labour within advanced capitalism. Direct recruitment shares a number of features with contract-labour arrangements and can be viewed as somewhere between the two poles of free wage-labour and indentured labour. For a pertinent discussion of the use of contract labour in industrial society in the modern historical period see Masson and Guimary (1981), who report that of a total cannery workforce of 13,800 in 1902, 5,300 were Chinese contract labour. See also Lyon and Grieco (1981) for a theoretical analysis of the significance of contract labour for western European society.

7. This understanding is consistent with Beaumont's data which indicates that migrants making use of the Employment Transfer Scheme principally (60 per cent) find their new place of employment through formal channels, that is direct recruitment (see Beaumont 1977b).

8. Here it is important to note that entitlement to migratory aid was dependent upon first obtaining a job outside the local labour market.

9. Note that Corby is the only New Town where arrangements have been made for rents to be deducted from the wage packet at the works and forwarded to the Corporation (see Cullingworth and Karn 1968: 78). My evidence on employer administration of the scheme is for Corby only. It may be that Corby is unusual in this respect, given its uniqueness with

regard to rent payment arrangements.

10. Vauxhall were involved in direct recruitment in Corby in 1980, as were British Aerospace of Stevenage and the Steel Company of Canada. Vauxhall's 1980 direct recruitment drive in Corby elicited 550 applications for fifty jobs (*Daily Telegraph*, 4 July 1980).

11. Note that 36 per cent of the couples interviewed had a majority of their closer kin (parents, siblings, and in-laws) living in the town. Goldthorpe *et al.* regard this figure as low, but for a migrant community it is high. Furthermore, these analysts pay no attention to the issue of chain migration. A 'snapshot' taken in the early stages of a migration stream may provide an image of disrupted and attenuated kin and community ties, whereas a later snapshot may very well portray substantial regrouping of kin. Relying solely on an early snapshot of a migration stream may be seriously misleading; for organizing the follow-on migration, so frequently identified in the literature, takes time. See also Goldthorpe *et al.* (1969: 104).

12. During the period 1966/7–1973/4, and thus during the same decade as the Affluent Worker study, on a regional basis, 'the largest single group of assisted labour migrants have come from Scotland'. For the years in question, 'approximately 30 per cent of the total movement under the labour transference programme originated in this region'. Luton, along with Corby, Dagenham, and Rugby, was a major destination for Scottish migrants under this scheme (Beaumont 1977a: 56).

13. This perception is further supported by Beaumont's data, which shows that Corby, Luton, Rugby, and Dagenham were major destinations for Scottish migrants (Scots constitute 30 per cent of all users of the Employment Transfer Scheme) (Beaumont 1975; 1976a).

14. Although we have no systematic direct evidence on the issue, it is highly probable that Ford's made direct use of direct recruitment strategies in obtaining labour for their Dagenham plant as Dagenham was a major recipient of Scottish labour under the Transfer Resettlement Scheme and the Employment Transfer Scheme (see Beaumont 1975).

15. Wood and Cohen provide a useful summary of labour-market economists' perceptions of geographic mobility as the rational solution to redundancy, an ethos which carries through to the policy recommendations which in turn affect employment-exchange practices (Wood and Cohen 1977/8: 22). Martin and Fryer also identify the institutional expectation that adjustment should be accomplished by labour mobility (Martin and Fryer 1973: 21).

16. See Breitenbach (1982: 30) on the difficulties of gaining access to the official statistics.

17. Rees in her major study of migration patterns in South Wales argues that it is appropriate to regard migration as coerced where the prospect of employment is dependent upon geographical movement. She reports that certain of her respondents experienced migration in search of work as coerced. She also reports high rates of return to the area of origin (50 per cent of immigrants are returners) with individuals being materially disadvantaged by such return moves. This she takes as evidence of the strength of attachment to the home region and as evidence that migration was not 'voluntary' in the first instance (Rees 1976: 47). Jansen, writing in the previous decade, and in a period contemporaneous with the Affluent Worker team, took a different view. He argued, 'Since modern migrations are no longer functions of circumstances forcing one to move they should be

studied from other points of view'. It is an over-simplistic perception and one which my evidence, both primary and secondary, challenges. It was, however, a prevalent sociological assumption of the period (Jansen 1968).

18. As my own evidence taken together with that of Beaumont shows, the practice of recruiting from areas of high unemployment persisted from the 1950s, through the 1960s and 1970s, until the 1980s.

19. Support for this understanding can be found in the work of Klassen and Drewe, who briefly discuss the movement of labour into Luton under the auspices of the Transfer Resettlement Scheme, research which is approximately contemporary with the Affluent Worker study. They estimated that around 75 per cent of migrants returned from Luton to their home areas within a year of arrival and that 55 per cent actually returned within the first month. These high rates of return were accompanied by the unavailability of satisfactory housing. Incomers to Luton had to spend two years in Luton before they could be placed on the local authority housing list and could then expect to wait for another eighteen months before obtaining a house. Incomers to Luton who had no friends or relatives in the area were thus forced into poor-quality hostel accommodation (Klassen and Drewe 1973: 81; also Goldthorpe *et al.* 1969: 39). Note also that the Affluent Worker team assumed that the plants studied were stable with regard to labour turnover – in the absence of the necessary data – a perspective not supported by Klassen and Drewe's evidence (see Goldthorpe *et al.* 1968a: 26, 30, 158).

20. The questionnaire did not ask how workers found out about general employment prospects in Luton nor how workers secured their jobs. There is, however, some anecdotal evidence contained in the 'case studies' presented which strengthens my argument (Goldthorpe *et al.* 1968a: 169). Mr Doyle was an Irish worker: 'Through Irish friends he heard about the "big money" available in Luton and eventually he decided to move there and take a factory job'. Mr Doyle, even at a casual glance, would seem to be a likely candidate for a chain-migration explanation of arrival in Luton. Also compare this with Mogey's evidence on Irish migration to the Cowley car works in Oxford in the 1950s (Mogey 1956). The third of the team's three case studies is of migration from Scotland, the Grants. Mr Grant moved because of employment insecurity in Clydebank. We are not told how they heard about opportunities on offer; we do not know whether direct recruitment, chain migration or independent search is the explanation of the Grants' arrival in Luton. However, Mrs Grant's parents and younger sister have also migrated to Luton from Scotland as has an old school friend of Mr Grant's. There is therefore some evidence to the effect that chain migration into Luton is occurring (Goldthorpe *et al.* 1968a: 172).

21. This is a matter of some importance, for if kin provided the introduction necessary for securing employment, then Goldthorpe *et al.*'s evidence on low frequency of contact rates between siblings has to be balanced against provision of major services as a measure of intimacy. If kin were not involved in introducing their relations into the workplace and locale, then despite attempts to escape previous moral community, the migrants' flight was not successful (see Goldthorpe *et al.* 1968a: 150–4).

7. Corby

1. There have been a number of minor redundancy rounds since this date. As

of September 1983, there were 3,300 workers still in the employ of British Steel Tubes division, although the making has been closed down completely. The steel works in 1984 employed approximately 25 per cent of their 1973 workforce size of 14,000.

2. *Northamptonshire Evening Telegraph,* 24 March 1980; *Times,* 22 September 1982.

3. Although the employment-exchange statistics on out-migration from Peterhead to Corby went back no further than 1956, the practice of direct recruitment did. On 13 May 1955 the Corby *Leader* reported that between September 1954 and March 1955, sixty-six men were recruited from Peterhead to Corby, forty-four from Aberdeen and thirty-five from Fraserburgh.

4. Not only is there a strong Scottish bias in recruitment drives but of those migrants who stay, a very high proportion are Scottish (see Thomas 1969: 858).

5. See Thomas (1969: 863).

6. A similar situation was encountered in Carreras Rothmans, where it was reported that workers had been transferred from Scotland in the last year of the plant's operation. Marsden also reports a similar situation (Marsden 1982: 12).

7. Slowe indicates that imminence of redundancy was often concealed from National Coal Board labour, and from relevant official bodies, 'for fear of the impending closures having to be made prematurely on account of the loss of labour. Experience in the mid-fifties in South Wales had shown that when there was alternative male employment available and closure was known about in advance, a substantial proportion of colliery labour could be lost up to four months before planned closure. Since national coal board officials are not trained to appreciate variation of time and space in job availability, this experience was generalised into an assumption and closure was not announced until the last possible minute, typically less than a month in advance' (Slowe 1978).

8. See Brannen *et al.* (1976: 192–5) for evidence on the extent to which closures in the steel industry are kept secret until the latest possible date, and for evidence on the extent to which organizational loyalty triumphs over collective solidarity. 'Hence the very activities which might have served to strengthen the position of workers fighting closure – the breaching of confidentiality, the public statements of opposition, etc. – these worker directors rejected. Similarly, they felt bound by the decisions made, despite the fact that there was no collective responsibility and that they had not been actively involved in the decisions' (Brannen *et al.* 1976: 204).

9. See for instance Corby Development Corporation's 21st Annual Report, p. 110: 'Due, however, to the refusal of applications for Industrial Development Certificates, or to the time taken to announce a decision on applications for these certificates, no large firm has moved to Corby, and there is now a serious risk that the properly balanced development of the town may be jeopardised.' A prophetic statement indeed! Retrospectively, the consequences were obvious. 'Efforts were further inhibited by the difficulties encountered in obtaining IDC's. As a result of its publicity campaign, the Development Corporation was receiving a great many enquiries from industrialists (up to 500 a year) many of which led to serious negotiations. But the refusal of, or delay in considering, applications for

IDC's seriously affected the Corporation's efforts' (Coopers and Lybrand 1979: 5).

10. As Thomas notes: 'the original function of Corby was anti-pathetic to the New Town idea, and it will be many years before the employment structure is as balanced as that of most other towns' (Thomas 1969: 87).

11. A proposal in 1962 to increase the designated area of Corby from 2,700 to 4,926 acres was opposed by the Parish Council and by the Urban District Council. An inquiry was held; the Inspector took the view that the objections both to size and to the siting of the designated area should be overruled. The minister approved the proposal and the designation order was made in 1963.

12. Clark Kerr applied the term 'manorial labour market' to internal labour markets in order to draw attention to the feudal aspect of the employment arrangement – that of lifetime service. I make use of the term to draw attention to yet another feudal aspect of modern employment relations – that of monopsony, where housing and employment are tightly linked together and other sources of employment are excluded from the locality (Kerr 1954).

13. Mullen provides an interesting analysis of Stevenage New Town which draws attention to the relationship between residence and employment in the New Towns. The focus is, however, on an employer group (SIEF) for more than one major employer is present (see Mullen 1980).

14. See Scopes (1968) for a fuller account of the arrangements.

15. 'Arduous' because of the poor quality of transport linkages. The substance of the argument was that by retaining poor communications, and ensuring difficult journeys, the female workers presently journeying into the hinterland would switch to local service employment in Corby as it became available. Were the journey to work easier, then labour might not switch to Corby employment.

16. For more detail, see Barber (1974: 12).

17. Discussing high rates of return migration under the state-assisted mobility schemes, Beaumont makes the following comment: 'The E.T.S. mover in Britain is of the same ethnic group as the general population in the receiving areas, he is generally from an urban area and therefore used to working and living in a modern environment' (Beaumont 1976b: 84). The thrust of the argument is that there is no cultural difference between the sending and receiving areas and thus 'alien-ness' cannot constitute the major explanation of return. I have argued the exact opposite: the environment is different as between Corby and the home areas, there is ethnic difference between migrants and the receiving areas and this does constitute both a direct and indirect – through labour market discrimination – basis of motivation for return.

18. Some measure of the strength of this connection can be gained from the planning literature. In 1959 Corby was listed along with twenty-seven Scottish centres as a reception area for Glasgow's overspill population in a scheme to be carried out under the Housing and Town Development Act 1957.

19. Corby achieved its growth 'through migration, mainly from outside the East Midlands region, with a very significant proportion of the migrants coming from as far away as Scotland. In this Corby is again unusual even amongst other New Towns, most of which grew by migration from an

adjacent region with many people retaining social or employment links with their former home area' (Coopers and Lybrand 1979: 8). This lack of contact with the employment structure of the adjacent region is a factor of critical importance when considering the problems generated for employment search with the rundown of steel.

20. Some measure of the presence of discrimination in the local labour market can be gained from the work of Thomas discussing the interest of the steel works *vis-à-vis* the interest of the community: 'Stewarts and Lloyds suffer from a chronic shortage of labour. The work in the steel works is arduous and many employees, and would-be employees, dislike working a shift system. At any point of time, including the time of writing, there are several hundred vacancies. But at the same time there are 600 unemployed men in Corby' (Thomas 1969: 860). Thus in a period of national full employment, 600 men preferred not to work in steel and could not find, if our sample is characteristic, employment in the local labour market. Clearly, this hinterland discrimination was functional for the steel employers.

21. Enterprise Zones have been subject to considerable criticism and have been viewed as 'a method of bringing the 3rd world home. No real development results as the periphery is simply reproduced in the centre and the new international division of labour exacerbates class inequalities' (Walton 1982: 12). The essence of the Enterprise Zone is a non-union, low-wage, regulation-free environment, comparable to Hong Kong, in the highly depressed urban regions of the First World. The idea of applying this strategy to the urban inner city was developed by Peter Hall, the eminent geographer, in 1977, and was subsequently taken up by the first Thatcher government in the UK and then by the Reagan administration in the US. Effectively, the Enterprise Zone concept rests upon the presence of a trapped labour force, as Hall himself recognized. Such labour is unable to argue for better conditions at work and better wages – that is for the re-regulation of the environment. Mass unemployment in Corby provided the necessary condition for a pilot run. In 1980 Corby was declared Britain's first Enterprise Zone. See Bluestone and Harrison (1982: 224–8) for a more detailed discussion of the relationship between capital and labour within the Enterprise Zone. The public-relations view of Enterprise Zones as cutting through the red tape has been broadcast loudly (see *Times*, 22 September 1983, pp. 18, 19, which said: 'Such is the reluctance of the Corby authorities to interfere with the privacy provided by the enterprise zone that the local job centre does not inquire too closely about the type of workers taken on by new companies. There are no reliable statistics on what proportions of a new company's workforce are former steel workers.'

8. Return migration from Corby

1. See Hunter, Reid, and Boddy (1969) for evidence of widespread disbelief as to the permanence of redundancy on the part of the labour force, even where confirmation of the redundancy has been given officially.

2. Statistics on the age composition of the Corby workforce are relevant here: in 1980, roughly 2,300 men of a total workforce of 11,300 were 55 or older, of which 1,200 had twenty years' service at the works (Job Ownership Ltd 1980). The Job Ownership Ltd report does not explicitly discuss the difficulties experienced by this age group in finding new employment and

disposes of the problem by assuming that this category of workers will take early retirement. See also Jeffreys (1954) for confirmation of this point.

3. The manager of the Corby Job Centre was reported as saying that 'there is a problem with the 45 and overs who have great difficulty in finding jobs' (*Times*, 22 September 1983, p. 19).

4. The Steel Company of Canada received 1,500 applications for forty jobs (*Daily Telegraph*, 4 July 1980).

5. Note that Coventry was a major importer of Scottish labour in the 1930s – 12.6 per cent of all migrants to the town coming from Scotland (Thomas 1938).

6. Since this date, the Dagenham car works have themselves fallen under the certain threat of major redundancies (*Times*, 11 January 1984, p. 1; 12 January 1984, p. 26).

7. Whilst the Grampian region experienced a decrease in population of 0.4 per cent between 1961 and 1971, between 1971 and 1981 its population increased by 7.6 per cent. This is to be compared with a 2.1 per cent decrease in population for Scotland as a whole. See Census 1981 *Regional Report*: Grampian Vol. 2.

8. Other evidence also shows the employment of return migrants in larger, multinational companies as well (Hunt, Grieco, and Miller 1977).

9. Marsden also identifies the increased importance of strong ties in the black economy where discovery carries high penalties (Marsden 1982). A number of commentators (Mars 1982; Pahl 1980; Lozano 1983) have stressed the relationship between the rise of unemployment and the growth of the black economy. On Marsden's reasoning, an argument with which I concur, even stronger ties may be involved in this sector than in normal job-search.

10. A recent piece of newspaper reporting demonstrates the case in point: 'A [company director] will be sentenced today for a tax fraud involving more than £300,000. Jeremy Porter, of the Old Vicarage, Chesterton, Oxfordshire, admitted 14 charges. Six related to PAYE frauds in which he conspired with six companies in the Porter group to pay wages without making proper deductions for income tax and insurance' (*Guardian*, 10 January 1984, p. 2).

11. Piddington finds similar results in his study of migrant French Canadians: 'Kinship relations between people who have been separated by migration do not usually atrophy though they may become latent' (Piddington 1965: 161).

12. See Firth for further information on kin holidaying and accommodation exchange practices (Firth 1956: 61–2).

13. Granovetter reaches just such a theoretical conclusion: 'Difficulties and grievances may be a source of separation where no mechanism exists for resolving them, as has been shown in the inhibitory effects of unions on separation probabilities (Richard Freeman 1980). Reservoirs of trust and interpersonal knowledge from prior relationships may serve a similar function, especially in a small non union firm (though I know of no direct evidence on this)' (Granovetter 1983: 37). Personal networks permit labour to organize in ways and to a degree which go unrecognized in the literature.

14. Note that the nineteenth-century Scottish/US mining labour circulation discussed by Youngson Brown is an exception to this tendency.

15. Herron gives information on the ready mobility of Glasgow labour and its propensity to return (Herron 1975: 48, 83).

16. This promotional system is a vestige of the sub-contracting system upon

which steel production was organized until just before the First World War. Under this contracting system – the butty system – the ganger hired and paid his own team. The entrepreneur paid the ganger.

Bibliography

Adams, B.N. (1971) 'The Social Significance of Kinship', in M. Anderson (ed.) *Sociology of the Family*, Baltimore: Penguin.

Adams, W.F. (1932) *Ireland and Irish Migration to the New World*, New Haven, Conn.: Yale University Press.

Alavi, H.A. (1963) *Pakistanis in Britain*, London: London Council of Social Services.

Allan, G.A. (1979) *A Sociology of Friendship and Kinship*, London: Allen & Unwin.

Ammasari, P. (1969) 'The Italian Blue Collar Worker', *International Journal of Comparative Sociology*, 10: 3–21.

Anand, S. (1971) 'Rural–Urban Migration in India: An Econometric Study', mimeo, Harvard University, Cambridge, Mass.

Anderson, B. (1979) 'Cognitive Balance Theory and Social Network Analysis: Remarks on Some Fundamental Theoretical Matters', in P.W. Holland and S. Leinhardt (eds) *Perspectives on Social Network Research*, New York: Academic Press.

Anderson, M. (1971a) *Family Structure in Nineteenth Century Lancashire*, Cambridge and London: Cambridge University Press.

——(1971b) 'Family, Household and the Industrial Revolution', in M. Anderson (ed.) *Sociology of the Family*, Baltimore: Penguin.

Arensberg, C.M. and Kimball, S.T. (1940, reprinted 1968) *Family and Community in Ireland*, Cambridge, Mass.: Harvard University Press.

Bailey, F.G. (1971) *Gifts and Poison: The Politics of Reputation*, Oxford: Blackwell.

Ballard, R. and Ballard, C. (1977) 'The Sikhs: The Development of South Asian Settlements in Britain', in J.L. Watson (ed.) *Between Two Cultures*, Oxford: Blackwell.

Banerjee, B. (1981) 'Rural–Urban Migration and Family Ties: An Analysis of Family Consideration in Migration Behaviour in India', *Oxford Bulletin of Economics and Statistics* 43: 321–56.

——(1982) 'Who Will Move and When? An Analysis of Rural to Urban Migrants in India', *Oxford Bulletin of Economics and Statistics* 44: 339–56.

——and Kanbur, S.M. (1981) 'On the Specification and Estimation of Rural–Urban Migration Functions: With an Application to Indian Data', *Oxford Bulletin of Economics and Statistics* 43: 7–29.

Banfield, E.C. (1959) *The Moral Basis of a Backward Society*, New York: Free Press.

Barber, S. (1974) 'British Steel Corporation's Ten Year Development Strategy', Labour Studies thesis, Ruskin College, Oxford.

Barnes, J.A. (1969) 'Networks and the Political Process', J.C. Mitchell (ed.) *Social Networks in Urban Situations*, Manchester: Manchester University Press.

——(1979) 'Network Analysis: Orienting Notion, Rigorous Technique or Substantive Field of Study', in P.W. Holland and S. Leinhardt (eds) *Perspectives on Social Network Research*, New York: Academic Press.

Barnum, H.N. and Sabot, R.H. (1977) 'Education, Employment Probabilities and Rural–Urban Migration in Tanzania', *Oxford Bulletin of Economics and Statistics* 39: 109–26.

Batstone, E., Boraston, I., and Frenkel, S. (1977) *Shop Stewards in Action: The Organisation of Workplace Conflict and Accommodation*, Oxford: Blackwell.

Beardsworth, A. *et al.* (1981) 'Employers' Strategies in Relation to Their Demand for Labour: Some Sociological Hypotheses', in P. Windolf (ed.) *Allocation and Selection in the Labour Market*, Berlin: Wissenschaftzentrum.

Beaumont, P.B. (1975) 'Employment Transfers: An Inter-regional Problem', *The Planner*, pp. 370–1.

——(1976a) 'Assisted Labour Mobility in Scotland: 1973–74', *Urban Studies* 13: 75–9.

——(1976b) 'The Problem of Return Migration under a Policy of Assisted Labour Mobility: An Examination of Some British Evidence', *British Journal of Industrial Relations* 14: 82–8.

——(1977a) 'Assessing the Performance of Assisted Labour Mobility in Britain', *Scottish Journal of Political Economy* 24 (1): 55–63.

——(1977b) 'The Means of Finding Jobs Beyond Local Labour Market Boundaries', *Industrial Relations Journal* 8 (1): 62–9.

Bell, C. (1968) *Middle Class Families*, New York: Routledge & Kegan Paul.

——and Newby, H. (1971) *Community Studies*, London: Allen & Unwin.

Berthoff, R. (1953) *British Immigrants in Industrial America: 1790–1950*, Cambridge, Mass.: Harvard University Press.

Beveridge, W. (1944) *Full Employment in a Free Society: A Report*, London: Allen & Unwin.

Beynon, H. (1973) *Working for Ford*, London: Allen Lane.

——and Blackburn, R.M. (1972) *Perceptions of Work: Variations within a Factory*, Cambridge and London: Cambridge University Press.

Blau, P. (1964) *Exchange and Power in Social Life*, New York: Wiley.

Bluestone, B. and Harrison B. (1982) *The De-industrialisation of America*, New York: Basic Books.

Boissevain, J. (1974) *Friends of Friends: Networks, Manipulators and Coalitions*, Oxford: Blackwell.

Bott, E. (1964) *Family and Social Network: Roles, Norms and External Relationships in Ordinary Urban Families*, London: Tavistock.

Brannen, P., Batstone, E., Fatchett, D., and White, P. (1976) *The Worker Directors*, London: Hutchinson.

Breitenbach, E. (1982) *Women Workers in Scotland*, Glasgow: Pressgang.

British Steel Corporation (1973) *Ten Year Development Strategy*, London: HMSO, Cmnd. 5226.

Brody, D. (1979) 'The Old Labor History, and the New: In Search of an American Working Class', *Labor History* 20 (1): 111–26.

Brooks, D. (1975) *Race and Labour in London Transport*, London: Oxford University Press.

——and Singh, K. (1979) 'Pivots and Presents: Asian Brokers in British Foundries', in S. Wallman (ed.) *Ethnicity at Work*, London: Macmillan.

Brown, D.C. (1967) *The Mobile Professors*, Washington, DC: American Council of Education.

Brown, R. and Brannen, P. (1980) 'Social Relations and Social Perspectives Amongst Shipbuilding Workers', *Sociology* 14: 71–84, 197–211.

Brown, W. (1981) (ed.) *The Changing Contours of British Industrial Relations: A Survey of Manufacturing Industry*, Oxford: Blackwell.

Bryer, R.A., Brignall, T.J., and Maunders, A.R. (1982) *Accounting for Steel: A Financial Analysis of the Failure of the British Steel Corporation 1967–1980 and Who Was to Blame*, Aldershot: Gower.

Buchan, M. (1978) 'Social Organisation of Fisher Girls', in D. Hunt (ed.) *The Fisheries*, Aberdeen: Robert Gordon's Institute of Technology.

Buchanan, C. & Partners (1975) *Corby New Town: Master Plan Review*, London.

Byington, M.F. (1909) 'The Family in a Typical Mill Town', *American Journal of Sociology* 14: 648–59.

Caldwell, J.G. (1969) *African Rural–Urban Migration*, New York: Columbia University Press.

Caplow, T. and McGee R. (1958) *The Academic Marketplace*, New York: Basic Books.

Carrier, N.H. and Jaffrey, J.R. (1953) *External Migration: A Study of the Available Statistics 1850–1950*, London: HMSO.

Cavendish, R. (1982) *Women on the Line*, London: Routledge & Kegan Paul.

Census 1981 *Regional Report*: Grampian 2.

Champion, A.G., Clegg, K., and Davies, R.L. (1977) *Facts about New Towns: A Socio-economic Digest*, Newcastle: Retailing and Planning Associates.

Chapman, M. and Prothero, M.R. (1977) 'Circulation between Home Places and Towns: A Village Approach to Urbanisation', paper presented to Working Session on Urbanisation in the Pacific, Association for Social Anthropology in Oceania, Monterey, California.

Choldin, H.M. (1973) 'Kinship Networks in the Migration Process', *International Migration Review* 7: 163–75.

Chorley, R.J. and Haggett, P. (1967) *Physical and Information Models in Geography*, London: Methuen.

Christopher, S.C. (1965) 'A Note on Research Relevant to the Extended Family and Geographical Mobility', *International Journal of Comparative Sociology* 6: 183–4.

Collier, P. and Green, J.M. (1978) 'Migration from Rural Areas of Developing Countries: A Socio-economic Approach', *Oxford Bulletin of Economics and Statistics*, 40 (1): 23–35.

Coopers and Lybrand (1979) *Employment and Industrial Development in Corby*, London.

Corby Development Corporation (1951–79) *Annual Reports*, Corby.

——(1965) 'Corby New Town Extension: Master Plan Report', Corby.

Corporation of Glasgow (1959) *Industry on the Move*, Glasgow.

Cotgrove, S. (1978) *The Science of Society*, London: Minerva.

Courtenay, G. and Hedges, B. (1977) *A Survey of Employers' Recruitment Practices*, London: Social and Community Planning Research.

Crozier, D. (1985) 'Kinship and Occupational Succession', *Sociological Review* 13

(1) 15–43.

Cullingworth, J.B. and Karn, V.A. (1968) *The Ownership and Management of Housing in the New Towns*, London: HMSO.

Curran, J. and Stanworth, P. (1979) 'Self-selection and the Small Firm Worker: Critique and an Alternative View', *Sociology* 13: 427–44.

Daniel, W.W. (1970) *Strategies for Displaced Workers*, London: PEP.

Davanzo, J. and Morrison, P.A. (1978) *Dynamics of Return Migration: Descriptive Findings from a Longitudinal Study*, Santa Monica, Calif.: Rand Corporation.

Davison, R.B. (1962) *West Indian Migrants*, Oxford and London: Oxford University Press.

——(1966) *Black British: Immigrants to England*, Oxford and London: Oxford University Press.

Dennis, N., Henriques, F., and Slaughter, C. (1956) *Coal Is Our Life*, London: Eyre & Spottiswoode.

Desai, R.H. (1963) *Indian Immigrants in Britain*, Oxford and London: Oxford University Press.

Dick, B. and Morgan, G. (1987) 'Family Network and Employment in Textiles', *Work, Employment and Society* 1 (2): 225–46.

Docherty, C. (1983) *Steel and Steel Workers: The Sons of Vulcan*, London: Heinemann.

Dunnell, K. and Head, E. (1973) 'Employers and Employment Services', Office of Population Censuses and Surveys, London: HMSO.

Economist Intelligence Unit (1975) 'Buchan Impact Study'. For Scottish Office, Edinburgh.

Ehrlich, R.L. (1974) 'Immigrant Strike Breaking Activity: A Sampling of Opinion Expressed in the National Labour Tribune, 1878–1885', *Labor History* 15 (4): 528–42.

Ekeh, P. (1974) *Social Exchange Theory*, London: Heinemann.

Erikson, C. (1972) *Invisible Immigrants: The Adaptation of English and Scots Immigrants in Nineteenth Century America*, London: Weidenfeld & Nicolson.

Firth, R. (1956) *Two Studies of Kinship in London*, London: Athlone Press.

Firth, R. *et al.* (1969) *Families and Their Relatives*, London: Routledge & Kegan Paul.

Francis, A., Willman, P., Snell, M., and Winch, G. (1982) 'Management, Industrial Relations and New Technology for the British Leyland Metro', mimeo, Imperial College, London.

Friedman, A. (1977) *Industry and Labour: Class Struggle at Work and Monopoly Capitalism*, London: Macmillan.

Gee, F.A. (1972) *Homes and Jobs for Londoners in the New and Expanded Towns*, London: HMSO.

Giddens, A. (1973) *The Class Structure of Advanced Societies*, London: Hutchinson.

Goldthorpe, J.H. and Hope, K. (1974) *The Social Grading of Occupations: A New Approach and Scale*, Oxford: Clarendon.

Goldthorpe, J.H., Lockwood, D., Bechhoffer, F., and Platt, J. (1968a) *The Affluent Worker: Political Attitudes and Behaviour*, London: Cambridge University Press.

——(1968b) *The Affluent Worker: Industrial Attitudes and Behaviour*, London: Cambridge University Press.

——(1969) *The Affluent Worker in the Class Structure*, London: Cambridge University Press.

—, Llewellyn, C., and Payne, C. (1980) *Social Mobility and Class Structure in Modern Britain*, Oxford: Clarendon.

Goodman, J.F.B. and Samuel, P.J. (1966) 'The Motor Car Industry in a Development District', *British Journal of Industrial Relations* 4 (3): 336–65.

Gouldner, A.W. (1960) 'The Norm of Reciprocity: A Preliminary Statement', *American Sociological Review* 25: 161–78.

Granovetter, M.S. (1973) 'The Strength of Weak Ties', *American Journal of Sociology* 78 (6): 1360–80.

—(1974) *Getting a Job: A Study of Contacts and Careers*, Cambridge, Mass.: Harvard University Press.

—(1983) 'Labor Mobility, Internal Labor Markets and Job Matching: A Comparison of Sociological and Economic Approaches', mimeo, Department of Sociology, State University of New York at Stony Brook.

Graves, B. (1958) 'Breaking Out: An Apprenticeship System among Pipeline Construction Workers', *Human Organisation* 17: 9–13.

Greenwood, M. (1975) 'Research in Internal Migration in the United States: A Survey', *Journal of Economic Literature* 13 (2): 397–433.

Grieco, M.S. (1981) 'The Shaping of a Workforce: A Critique of the Affluent Worker Study', *International Journal of Sociology and Social Policy* 1 (1): 62–88.

—(1982) 'Family Structure and Industrial Employment: The Role of Information and Migration', *Journal of Marriage and the Family* 44: 701–7.

—(1985a) 'Corby: New Town Planning and Imbalanced Development', *Regional Studies*, 19 (February): 9–18.

—(1985b) 'Social Networks in Labour Migration', *Industrial Relations Journal*, 16 (December): 53–67.

—and Hosking, D.M. (1987) 'Networking, Skill and Exchange', in B. Johannison (ed.) *Organising: The Network Metaphor*, special volume of *International Studies of Management and Organisation*.

—and Miller, M. (1978) 'The Fishing Structure of Aberdeen: A Preliminary to Study', in D. Hunt (ed.) *The Fisheries*, Aberdeen: Robert Gordon's Institute of Technology.

—and Whipp, R. (1986) 'Women and the Workplace: Gender and Control in the Labour Process', in D. Knights and H. Wilmott (eds) *Studies in Gender and Technology in the Labour Process*, Aldershot: Gower.

Hall, P. (1977) Address to the British Town Planning Institute, London.

Halsey, A.H. (1972) *Trends in British Society since 1900: A Guide to the Changing Social Structure of Britain*, London: Macmillan.

Handley, J.E. (1943) *The Irish in Scotland*, Cork: Cork University Press.

Handlin, O. (1951) *The Uprooted*, Boston: Little, Brown & Co.

Hareven, T.K. (1975a) 'The Laborers of Manchester, New Hampshire, 1912–1922: The Role of Family and Ethnicity in Adjustment to Industrial Life', *Labor History* 16 (2): 249–65.

—(1975b) 'Family Time and Industrial Time: Family and Work in a Planned Corporation Town, 1900–1924', *Journal of Urban History* 1: 365–89.

—(1982) *Family Time and Industrial Time: The Relationship between Family and Work in a New England Industrial Community*, Cambridge: Cambridge University Press.

Heath, A.F. (1976) *Rational Choice and Social Exchange: A Critique of Exchange Theory*, Cambridge and London: Cambridge University Press.

Hechter, M. (1978) 'Group Formation and the Cultural Division of Labour', *American Journal of Sociology* 84 (2): 293–318.

Hedges, N. and Beynon, H. (1982) *Born to Work*, London: Pluto Press.

Heider, F. (1958) *The Psychology of Interpersonal Relations*, New York: Wiley.

Herron, F. (1975) *Labour Market in Crisis: Redundancy at Upper Clyde Shipbuilders*, London: Macmillan.

Hill, S.R. (1976) *The Dockers: Class and Tradition in London*, London: Heinemann.

Hobsbawn, E. (1964) *Labouring Men*, London: Weidenfeld & Nicolson.

Holford, W. and Myles Wright, H. (1952) 'Report to Accompany the Master Plan of the Corby Development Corporation'.

Hollingsworth, T.H. (1970) *Migration: A Study Based on the Scottish Experience between 1939 and 1964*, Edinburgh: Oliver & Boyd.

Homans, G. (1961) *Social Behaviour: Its Elementary Forms*, New York: Routledge & Kegan Paul.

Hunt, D. (1975) 'Aberdeen and the Oil Boom', *Personnel Management* 7 (2): 24–8.

——, Grieco, M.S., and Miller, M. (1977) *The Engineering Infrastructure of Aberdeen: 1977*, Aberdeen: North East of Scotland Development Agency.

Hunt, E. (1981) *British Labour History 1815–1914*, London: Weidenfeld & Nicolson.

Hunt, P. (1980) *Gender and Class Consciousness*, London: Macmillan.

Hunter, L.C. and Reid, G.I. (1968) *Urban Worker Mobility*, Paris: OECD.

Ianni, F.A.J. and Ruess-Ianni, E. (1972) *A Family Business*, London: Routledge & Kegan Paul.

Illsley, R. *et al.* (1963) 'The Motivation and Characteristics of Internal Migrants: A Socio-medical Study of Young Migrants in Scotland', *Millbank Memorial Fund Quarterly* 41 (3): 217–48.

Jackson, J.A. (1969) *Migration*, London: Cambridge University Press.

Jacobson, D. (1978) 'Scale and Social Control', in F. Barth (ed.) *Scale and Social Organisation*, Oslo: Universitetsforlaget.

Jahoda, M., Lazarsfeld, P.F., and Zeisel, H. (1972) *Marienthal: The Sociography of an Unemployed Community*, London: Tavistock.

Jansen, C. (1968) *Social Aspects of Internal Migration*, Bath: Bath University Press.

Jeffreys, M. (1954) *Mobility in the Labour Market*, London: Routledge & Kegan Paul.

Jenkins, R. (1981) 'Work and Unemployment in Industrial Society: An Anthropological Perspective', SSRC research initiative on local labour markets and the informal economy.

——, Bryman, A., Ford, J., Keil, T., and Beardsworth, A. (1983) 'Information in the Labour Market: the Impact of Recession', *Sociology* 17 (2): 260–7.

Job Ownership Ltd (1980) *Possibilities for Worker Owned Enterprise in Corby*.

Johnson, T.J. (1972) *Professions and Power*, London: Macmillan.

Kahn, H. (1964) *The Repercussions of Redundancy*, London: Allen & Unwin.

Kahn, R.L. and Katz, D. (1958) 'Leadership Practices in Relation to Productivity and Morale', in D. Cartwright and A. Zander (eds) *Group Dynamics*, New York: Harper & Row.

Kannapan, S. (1966) 'Economics of Structuring an Industrial Labour Force: Some Reflections on the Commitment Problem', *British Journal of Industrial Relations* 4: 379–404.

Kapferer, B. (1969) 'Norms and the Manipulation of Relationships in a Work Context', in J.C. Mitchell (ed.) *Social Networks in Urban Situations*, Manchester: Manchester University Press.

Kennedy, R.E. (1973) *The Irish*, Berkeley: University of California Press.

Kerr, C. (1954) 'The Balkanisation of Labor Markets', in W. Bakke (ed.) *Labor*

Mobility and Economic Opportunity, New York: Wiley.

Klaasen, L.H. and Drewe, P. (1967) *Migration Policy in Europe: A Comparative Study*, Farnborough: Saxon House.

Lansing, J.B. and Mueller, E. (1967) *The Geographic Mobility of Labor*, Institute for Social Research, Ann Arbor.

Laumann, O.E. (1966) *Prestige and Association in an Urban Community*, Indianapolis: Bobbs-Merrill.

——(1973) *Bonds of Pluralism: The Form and Substance of Urban Social Networks*, New York: Wiley.

Laurie, B. (1975) 'Immigrants and Industry: The Philadelphia Experience 1850–1880', *Journal of Social History* 9: 219–48.

Lee, E.S. (1966) 'A Theory of Migration', *Demography* 3: 47–57.

Lee, G. and Wrench, J. (1981) *In Search of a Skill*, London: Commission for Racial Equality.

Leonard, H.B. (1979) 'Ethnic Cleavage and Industrial Conflict in Late Nineteenth Century America', *Labor History* 20 (4): 524–48.

Lester, R.A. (1954) *Hiring Practices and Labor Competition*, Industrial Relations Section Report No. 88, Princeton, NJ: Princeton University Press.

Lévi-Strauss, C. (1957) 'The Principle of Reciprocity', in L.A. Coser and E. Rosenberg (eds) *Sociological Theory: A Book of Readings*, New York: Macmillan.

——(1969) *The Elementary Structure of Kinship*, Boston: Beacon Press.

Litwak, E. (1970) 'Geographical Mobility and Extended Family Cohesion', in T.R. Ford and G.F. Dejong (eds) *Social Demography*, New York: Prentice-Hall.

Lozano, B. (1983) 'Informal Sector Workers: Walking Out the System's Front Door', *International Journal of Urban and Regional Research* 7 (3): 340–62.

Lupton, T. and Cunnison, S. (1964) 'Workshop Behaviour', in M. Gluckman (ed.) *Closed Systems and Open Minds: The Limits of Naivety in Social Anthropology*, Edinburgh: Oliver & Boyd.

——and Wilson, C.S. (1964) 'The Social Background and Connections of Top Decision Makers', in J. Urry and J. Wakeford (eds) *Power in Britain*, London: Heinemann.

Lyon, M.H. and Grieco, M.S. (1981) 'Migrant Subordination in the Metropolis: An Analysis of Control', *International Journal of Contemporary Sociology* 18 (1, 2): 1–50.

Macdonald, D.F. (1937) *Scotland's Shifting Population*, Glasgow: Jackson.

Macdonald, J.S. and Macdonald, L.D. (1962) 'Urbanisation, Ethnic Groups and Social Segmentation', *Social Research* 29 (4): 433–48.

——(1964) 'Chain Migration, Ethnic Neighbourhood Formation and Social Networks', *Millbank Memorial Fund Quarterly* 42: 82–7.

Mackay, D.I., Boddy, D., Brack, J., Diack, J.A., and Jones, N. (1971) *Labour Markets under Different Employment Conditions*, London: Allen & Unwin.

Mackenzie, G. (1974) 'The Affluent Worker Study: An Evaluation and a Critique', in F. Parkin (ed.) *The Social Analysis of the Class Structure*, London: Tavistock.

Maclennan, D. (1979) 'Information Networks in a Local Housing Market', *Scottish Journal of Political Economy* 26 (1): 73–88.

Mann, M. (1973) *Workers on the Move*, Cambridge and London: Cambridge University Press.

Manwaring, T. (1982) *The Extended Internal Labour Market*, Berlin: IIM.

——(1984) 'The Extended Labour Market'. *Cambridge Journal of Economics* 8:

161–87.

Mars, G. (1982) *Cheats at Work: An Anthropology of Workplace Crime*, London: Allen & Unwin.

Marsden, D. (1982) *Workless: An Exploration of the Social Contract between Society and the Worker*, London: Croom Helm.

Martin, R. and Fryer, R.H. (1973) *Redundancy and Paternalist Capitalism*, London: Allen & Unwin.

Masson, J. and Guimary, D. (1981) 'Asian Labor Contractors in the Alaskan Canned Salmon Industry: 1880–1937', *Labor History* 22 (3): 377–97.

Mauss, M. (1954) *The Gift*, New York: Free Press.

Milardo, R.M. (1983) 'Social Networks and Pair Relationships: A Review of Substantive and Measurement Issues', *Sociology and Social Research* 68 (1): 1–18.

Milroy, L. (1980) *Language and Social Networks*, Oxford: Blackwell.

Ministry of Labour Gazette (1954).

Mitchell, J.C. (1961) 'Wage Labour and African Population Movements in Central Africa', in K.M. Barbour and R.M. Prothero (eds) *Essays on African Population*, London: Routledge & Kegan Paul.

——(1969) 'The Concept and Use of Social Networks', in J.C. Mitchell (ed.) *Social Networks in Urban Situations*, Manchester: Manchester University Press.

——(1970) 'The Causes of Labour Migration', in J. Middleton (ed.) *Black Africa*, London: Macmillan.

Mogey, J. (1956) *Family and Neighbourhood: Two Studies in Oxford*, London: Oxford University Press.

Moore, R.A. (1982) *The Social Impact of Oil: The Case of Peterhead*, London: Routledge & Kegan Paul.

Mormino, G. (1982) 'We Worked Hard and Took Care of Our Own: Oral History and Italians in Tampa', *Labor History* 23 (3): 395–415.

Moss, P. and Fonda, N. (1980) (eds) *Work and the Family*, London: Temple-Smith.

Mullen, R. (1980) *Stevenage Ltd*, London: Routledge & Kegan Paul.

Myers, C.A. and Shultz, G. (1951) *The Dynamics of Labor Markets*, New York: Prentice-Hall.

NEDC (1963) *Conditions Favourable to Faster Growth*, London: HMSO.

Newcomb, T.M. (1961) *The Acquaintance Process*, New York: Holt, Rinehart & Winston.

Newman, G. (1976) 'Economics of Information and Information for Economists: An Institutional Perspective on Information', *International Social Sciences Journal* 28 (3): 466–92.

Norris, G.M. (1978) 'Industrial Paternalist Capitalism and Local Labour Markets', *Sociology* 12: 469–89.

Oakley, R. (1979) 'Family, Kinship and Patronage: The Cypriot Migration to Britain', in V. Saifullah Khan (ed.) *Minority Families in Britain*, London: Macmillan.

Pahl, R.E. (1968) 'A Perspective on Urban Sociology', in R.E. Pahl (ed.) *Readings in Urban Sociology*, Oxford: Pergamon.

——(1980) 'Employment, Work and the Domestic Division of Labour', *International Journal of Urban and Regional Research* 4 (1): 1–20.

Palmer, G. (1954) 'Interpreting Patterns of Labor Mobility', in E. Bakke (ed.) *Labor Mobility and Economic Opportunity*, New York: Wiley.

Palmer, R. (1977) 'The Italians: Patterns of Migration to London', in J.L. Watson (ed.) *Between Two Cultures*, Oxford: Blackwell.

Park, R.E., Burgess, E.W., and MacKenzie, R.D. (1925, reprinted 1967) *The City*. Chicago: Chicago University Press.

Parnes, H.S. (1954) *Research on Labor Mobility*, New York: Social Science Research Council.

Parsons, T. (1960) *Structure and Process in Modern Societies*, New York: Glencoe.

——(1964) *Social Structure and Personality*, New York: Glencoe.

——and Bales, R.F. (1956) *Family, Socialisation and Interaction Process*, New York: Glencoe.

Payne, P.L. (1979) *Colvilles and the Scottish Steel Industry*, Oxford: Clarendon.

Peach, C. (1968) *West Indian Migration to Britain*, London: Oxford University Press.

Petersen, W. (1970) 'A General Typology of Migration', in C. Jansen (ed.) *Readings in the Sociology of Migration*, Oxford: Pergamon.

Piddington, R. (1965) 'The Kinship Network among French Canadians', *International Journal of Comparative Sociology* 6: 145–65.

Pitt, M. (1979) *The World on Our Backs*, London: Lawrence & Wishart.

Pocock, D.C.D. (1959) 'Corby New Town', unpublished MA thesis, University of Nottingham.

——(1960) 'The Migration of Scottish Labour to Corby New Town', *Scottish Geographical Magazine* 76: 169–71.

——(1967) 'An Urban Geography of Steel Towns', unpublished PhD thesis, University of Nottingham.

Pollert, A. (1981) *Girls, Wives and Factory Lives*, London: Macmillan.

Poster, M. (1978) *Critical Theory of the Family*, London: Pluto Press.

Price, F. (1979) 'Analysing Social Networks', paper delivered to the BSA/SSRC Methodology Conference, University of Lancaster.

Ravenstein, E.G. (1885) 'Laws of Migration', *Journal of the Royal Statistical Society* 48 (2): 167–227.

Rees, A. (1966) 'Information Networks in Labor Markets', *American Economic Review* 56 (2): 559–66.

Rees, T. (1976) 'The Origin and Destination of Migrants to and from the South Wales Valleys', UWIST Working Paper No. 17.

Rempel, H. (1970) 'Labour Migration into Urban Centres and Urban Employment in Kenya', unpublished PhD thesis, University of Wisconsin.

Reynolds, L.G. (1951) *The Structure of Labor Markets: Wages and Labor Mobility in Theory and Practice*, New York: Harper & Row.

Richmond, A. (1967) *Post War Immigrants in Canada*, Toronto: University of Toronto Press.

——(1969) 'Migration in Industrial Societies', in J.A. Jackson (ed.) *Migration*, Cambridge and London: Cambridge University Press.

Rieger, J.H. (1972) 'Geographic Mobility and the Occupational Attainment of Rural Youth: A Longitudinal Evaluation', *Rural Sociology* 37: 189–207.

Ritchey, P.N. (1976) 'Explanations of Migration', *Annual Review of Sociology* 2: 363–404.

Sahlins, M.D. (1965) 'On the Sociology of Primitive Exchange', in M. Banton (ed.) *The Relevance of Models for Social Anthropology*, London: Tavistock.

Schaffer, F. (1970) *The New Town Story*, London: MacGibbon & Kee.

Schwartz, B. (1975) *Queueing and Waiting: Studies in the Social Organisation of Access and Delay*, London: Chicago University Press.

Schwarzweller, H.K. (1964) 'Family Ties, Migration and Transitional Adjustment of Young Men from Eastern Kentucky', *University of Kentucky Agricultural Experimental Station Bulletin*, no. 69.

Scopes, F. (1968) *The Development of Corby Works*, Corby: Stewarts & Lloyds.

Scott, W.H., Banks, J.A., Halsey, A.H., and Lupton, T. (1956) *Technical Change and Industrial Relations*, Liverpool: Liverpool University Press.

Sell, R.R. (1983) 'Transferred Jobs: A Neglected Aspect of Migration and Occupational Change', *Work and Occupation* 10 (2): 179–206.

Shapero, A.R., Howell, R., and Tombaugh, J. (1965) *The Structure and Dynamics of the Defense R and D Industry: The Los Angeles and Boston Complexes*, Stanford, Calif.: Stanford Research Institute.

Sheppard, H.L. and Belitsky, A. (1966) *The Job Hunt: Job Seeking Behavior of Unemployed Workers in the Local Economy*, Baltimore: Johns Hopkins.

Slowe, P.M. (1978) 'The Role and Significance of the Advance Factory in Regional Policy', unpublished DPhil thesis, University of Oxford.

Stacey, M., Batstone, E., Bell, C., and Murcott, A. (1975) *Power, Persistence and Change*, London: Routledge & Kegan Paul.

Stanworth, P. and Giddens, A. (1974) *Elites and Power in British Society*, Cambridge and London: Cambridge University Press.

Stewarts & Lloyds (*c.*1953) *Stewarts and Lloyds 1903–1953*, Corby.

Stouffer, S.A. (1940) 'Intervening Opportunities: A Theory Relating Mobility and Distance', *American Sociological Review* 5: 845–67.

——(1960) 'Intervening Opportunities and Competing Migrants', *Journal of Regional Science* 2: 1–26.

Sussman, M.B. and Burchinall, L.G. (1971) 'The Kin Family Network in Urban Industrial America', in M. Anderson (ed.) *Sociology of the Family*, Baltimore: Penguin.

Taylor, R. (1969) 'Migration and Motivation: A Study of Determinants and Types', in J.A. Jackson (ed.) *Migration*, Cambridge and London: Cambridge University Press.

Thomas, B. (1938) 'The Influx of Labour into the Midlands 1920–1937', *Economica* 5: 410–34.

Thomas, R. (1969) *Aycliffe to Cumbernauld*, London: PEP.

Thompson, P., Wailey, T., and Lummis, T. (1983) *Living the Fishing*, London: Routledge & Kegan Paul.

Tilly, C. and Brown, C.H. (1967) 'On Uprooting, Kinship and the Auspices of Migration', *International Journal of Comparative Sociology* 8: 139–64.

Tilly, L. and Scott, J. (1978) *Women, Work and the Family*, New York: Holt, Rinehart & Winston.

Tunstall, J. (1969) *The Fishermen*, London: MacGibbon & Kee.

Turner, C. (1971) 'The Social Significance of Kinship', in M. Anderson (ed.) *Sociology of the Family*, Baltimore: Penguin.

Wallman, S. (1979) 'The Scope for Ethnicity', in S. Wallman (ed.) *Ethnicity at Work*, London: Macmillan.

Walton, J. (1982) 'Cities and Jobs and Politics', *Urban Affairs* 18 (2).

Watson, J.L. (1977) 'The Chinese: Hong Kong Villagers in the British Catering Trade', in J.L. Watson (ed.) *Between Two Cultures*, Oxford: Blackwell.

Watson, W. (1964) 'Industrial Communities', in M. Gluckman (ed.) *Closed Systems and Open Minds: The Limits of Naivety in Social Anthropology*, Edinburgh: Oliver & Boyd.

Wedderburn, D. (1964) *White Collar Redundancy: A Case Study*, Cambridge and London: Cambridge University Press.

——(1965) *Redundancy and the Railwaymen*, Cambridge and London: Cambridge University Press.

Weimann, G. (1982) 'On the Importance of Marginality: One More Step in the Two Way Flow of Information', *American Sociological Review* 47: 764–73.

——(1983) 'The Strength of Weak Conversational Ties in the Flow of Information and Influence', *Social Networks* 5: 245–67.

Whipp, R. (1983) 'Potbank and Unions: A Study of Work and Trade Unionism in the British Pottery Industry', unpublished PhD thesis, University of Warwick.

——and Grieco, M.S. (1985) 'Family and the Workplace: The Social Organisation of Work', *Management Monitor*, January, pp. 3–7.

White, H. (1970) *Chains of Opportunity: System Models of Mobility in Organisations*, Cambridge, Mass.: Harvard University Press.

Wilkinson, R.C. (1982) 'Migration in Lesotho: Some Comparative Aspects with Particular Reference to the Role of Women', paper delivered to the Development Studies Association, Trinity College, Dublin.

Wolf, E.R. (1966) 'Kinship, Friendship and Patron–Client Relations in Complex Societies', in M. Banton (ed.) *The Social Anthropology of Complex Societies*, London: Tavistock.

Wood, S. (1982a) (ed.) *The Degradation of Work? Skill, Deskilling and the Labour Process*, London: Hutchinson.

——(1982b) 'Recruitment and the Recession', mimeo, London School of Economics.

——and Cohen, J. (1977/8) 'Approaches to the Study of Redundancy', *Industrial Relations Journal* 8 (4): 19–27.

Wrong, D. (1965) *Population and Society*, New York: Random House.

Yans-McLaughlin, V. (1971) 'Patterns of Work and Family Organisation: Buffalo's Italians', *Journal of Interdisciplinary History* 2: 229–314.

Young, M. and Wilmott, P. (1957) *Family and Kinship in East London*, Harmondsworth: Penguin.

Youngson Brown, A.J. (1953/4) 'Trade Union Policy in the Scots Coalfields 1855–1885', *Economic History Review* 6: 35–50.

Index

Aberdeen, fish-processing 11–25, 181–2; recruitment 11–15; training 13–14; workforce employment nets 15–23

accommodation 198; aid with 103–8, 162–4, 185; in Corby 145–6, 196

Adams, B.N. 50

Adams, W.F. 193

adjacency 70, 98–9

advertising, recruitment 12, 14, 37

Affluent Worker study 60, 125–34, 175, 193–4, 197

Africa, migration in 56–7, 169

aid: residential 103–8, 162–4, 185; vacancies 103

Alavi, H.A. 58

Allan, G.A. 190–3

Ammasari, P. 191

analysis of social networks 41–9, 177

Anand, S. 56

Anderson, B. 41

Anderson, M. 3, 54–5

anticipation of redundancy 68–9, 130, 154–60, 179–80

Arensberg, C.M. 51–2, 65

Asians 58–9

Bailey, F.G. 44, 157–9

Bales, R.F. 2–3

Ballard, R. and C. 51

Banbury 62–3

Banerjee, B. 42, 56–7, 122

Barber, S. 142, 200

Barnes, J.A. 110, 191

Barnum, H.N. 56

Basildon 23–33, 173, 182–3

Beardsworth, A. 6

Beaumont, P.B. 194, 196–8, 200

Belitsky, A. 5, 45

Bell, C. 42

Berthoff, R. 193

Beveridge, W. 129

Beynon, H. 8, 39, 61, 67, 128–9

Bird's 62–3

Blackburn, R.M. 128

Bluestone, B. 69, 155, 201

Boddy, B. 201

Brannen, P. 199

Breitenbach, E. 197

British Leyland 60–1

British Motor Corporation 61–2

British Steel 135, 139–41, 150, 155, 190; see also Stewarts & Lloyds

Brody, D. 51, 189

Brooks, D. 35–6, 58–9, 88, 116, 150

Brown, D.C. 5

Brown, W. 6–7, 190

Buchan, M. 9

Buchan employment net 74, 76–7, 80–1, 84–6, 89–91, 159, 184

Buchanan, C., & Partners 140

Buchanan employment net 72–3, 76–9, 84, 86, 89–90, 159, 170, 184

Burchinall, L.G. 42

Caldwell, J.G. 56–7

Caplow, T. 5

car industry 8, 60–2; see also Vauxhall

Carreras Rothman 24, 30–1, 87, 173, 183, 199